Dynamic Efficiency and Productivity Measurement

Elvira Silva, Spiro E. Stefanou, and
Alfons Oude Lansink

OXFORD
UNIVERSITY PRESS

OXFORD
UNIVERSITY PRESS

Oxford University Press is a department of the University of Oxford. It furthers
the University's objective of excellence in research, scholarship, and education
by publishing worldwide. Oxford is a registered trade mark of Oxford University
Press in the UK and certain other countries.

Published in the United States of America by Oxford University Press
198 Madison Avenue, New York, NY 10016, United States of America.

Library of Congress Cataloging-in-Publication Data
Names: Silva, Elvira, author. | Stefanou, Spiro E., author. | Oude Lansink, Alfons, author.
Title: Dynamic efficiency and productivity measurement / Elvira Silva,
University of Porto, Spiro E. Stefanou, University of Florida and
Wageningen University, Alfons Oude Lansink,
Wageningen University.
Description: New York : Oxford University Press, 2021. |
Includes bibliographical references and index.
Identifiers: LCCN 2020018478 (print) | LCCN 2020018479 (ebook) |
ISBN 9780190919474 (hardback) | ISBN 9780190919481 (updf) |
ISBN 9780197537176 (oso) | ISBN 9780190919498 (epub)
Subjects: LCSH: Industrial productivity—Measurement. | Decision making. |
Costs, Industrial. | Organizational effectiveness.
Classification: LCC HD56.25 .S535 2020 (print) | LCC HD56.25 (ebook) |
DDC 658.5/77—dc23
LC record available at https://lccn.loc.gov/2020018478
LC ebook record available at https://lccn.loc.gov/2020018479

1 3 5 7 9 8 6 4 2

Printed by Sheridan Books, Inc., United States of America

To our parents
Maria Sousa and David Silva
Eleni and Euthimios Stefanou
Tonny and Harrie Oude Lansink

Contents

Preface

This book offers a systematic treatment of dynamic decision making and performance measurement. A significant innovation of this project is the development of the dynamic generalizations of concepts measuring the production structure (e.g., economies of scale, economies of scope, capacity utilization) and performance (e.g., allocative and technical efficiency, productivity) in both primal and dual perspectives. The empirical implementation of these production and performance measures is developed at length for both nonparametric and econometric approaches.

Why do we need a book to address the dynamic case? A dynamic production environment can be characterized as one where current production decisions impact future production possibilities. The preponderance of current approaches maintains the firm as being able to adjust all factors instantaneously. The presence of forces preventing the firm to adjust the stock of quasi-fixed factors (both human and physical capital) to its optimal level in a complete and instantaneous fashion implies capital is of a different nature than the variable inputs. Once we address the structural difference in input types, identifying the sources of inefficiencies must recognize that the remedies for variable factors are different than those for quasi-fixed factors. Inefficiencies related to the structures, machinery, and land are often related to asset management practices. In contrast, inefficiencies related to variable factors (e.g., factors that are typically easily metered) can suggest remedies that involve better record keeping. Consequently, the proper accounting and valuation of factors that are out of equilibrium emerge as important components contributing to efficiency and productivity change. As an important source of productivity growth, production efficiency analysis is the subject of countless studies. Yet, theoretical and empirical studies focusing on production efficiency typically ignore the time interdependence of production decisions and the firm's adjustment path over time.

This book is an experience down a long and winding road. Sometimes this was a lonely road with reviewers needing more than a little bit of convincing of the themes we were introducing. As a team and with other collaborators we have pushed through several fronts to advance the implementation and present the value of the dynamic production perspective.

We are grateful to our collaborators in exploring these approaches and frameworks: Frederic Ang, Beshir Ali, Tomas Baležentis, Ching-Cheng Chang, Onelack Choi, Jorge Fernandez-Cornejo, Hervé Dakpo, Grigorios Emvalomatis, Bobby Gempesaw, Maria del Carmen Martinez Victoria, Panos Fousekis, Magdalena Kapelko, Yir-Hueih Luh, Supawat Rungsuriyawiboon, Maman Setiawan, and Teresa Serra.

This book has benefited also from the interaction with many students over time. The Wageningen University Summer School on the Theory and Practice of Efficiency and Productivity started in 2003. We introduced the intensive dynamic week in 2008, which has been offered 10 times since, including at the University of Sao Tomas (Santiago, Chile), Padjadjaran University (Bandung, Indonesia), and the University of Florida (Gainesville, Florida). Early parts of this book were piloted in this course as well as the course inspiring several directions that students found useful. We are obliged to several who read parts of the book including Daniela Puggioni and Haoying Wang.

We also want to thank one another, each bringing something different and valuable to this enterprise, with the result being exceedingly greater than the sum of the parts. We had two joint sessions hosted by the University of Porto. Beyond the scholarly activity and the fellowship, the more memorable events include seeing how many *pingos* Alfons could consume in 14 hours each day (with at least two per sitting), and Alfons and Spiro dodging the infamous Eyjafjallajokull volcano ash cloud to find their way to Porto in 2010.

Elvira Silva is grateful to Kandice Kahl, her master thesis advisor at Clemson University, who was the first one to introduce her to the astounding field of economic research. Her debt to Spiro Stefanou goes back to her days as a PhD student at Pennsylvania State University, and he has been her mentor since then. Spiro is still teaching her about production economics and dynamic analysis. Elvira gratefully acknowledges the generous support of the Center in Economics and Finance at the University of Porto and its former director José Varejão.

Spiro Stefanou is grateful to Dennis Snower, who first introduced him to dynamic economics as an MS student at the University of Maryland, and to Richard Howitt and James Wilen for deepening his enthusiasm for the subject as they addressed bioeconomic dynamic analysis when he was a graduate student at the University of California, Davis. He is also grateful to Quirino Paris, who introduced him to production economics and to mathematical programming theory. A special thanks goes to Marc Mangel, who continues to be an inspiring mentor with the breadth to span applied dynamic analysis across several fields and the philosophy of science. But at the same time, his feet are firmly planted on the ground to bridge the abstract with the reality that individuals and institutions need to use this stuff to advance their understanding of our systems and for the well-being of all.

Alfons's special thanks go to his early mentors Arie Oskam and Geert Thijssen for introducing him to the wonderful world of empirical economics, first as an MS student and later as a PhD student at Wageningen University. Alfons is also grateful to his first colleagues at the Agricultural Economics Group at Wageningen University, including Alison Burrell for her exemplary scientific rigor and Jack Peerlings for making him aware of the power of collaboration. Special thanks also go to Spiro Stefanou, who introduced him to dynamic economics during his sabbatical leave at Wageningen University in 1995. This first encounter was followed by an unforgettable and inspiring four-month visit to his home university, Pennsylvania State University, in the same year and a lifelong collaboration and friendship since then.

We each wish to acknowledge individuals whose encouragement and friendship have energized us over the years we developed and refined the ideas presented in this book. Elvira Silva would like to thank all her family members and, in particular, João, her youngest brother, who is always delighted with even her smallest achievement. Spiro Stefanou would like to thank Candice for her encouragement and patience; children Alexa, Andrew, Joshua, and Zachary; and the inspiration of grandchildren Leo, Reagan, and Ryan. Alfons Oude Lansink would like to thank Ingeborg for her continuous support and Wisse, Jorn, and Fleur for keeping the book project alive by regularly asking the famous "when is the book ready?" question.

Introduction

This book takes a systematic treatment of dynamic decision making and performance measurement. The fundamental starting point is the conceptualization of the production technology that describes the transformation of inputs, or factors of production, into outputs. Quoting Yair Mundlak (2001, p.5):

> There is hardly a subject in economics that can be discussed with production sitting in the balcony rather than playing at center stage.

Production is at the core of any inquiry involving economic exchange. Being clear and precise about how the effort and physical factors of production translate into output realizations is the first element of these inquiries. This foundation postulates how the input-output responses, the input-input and output-output substitution relationships, and input and/or output choices interact with the production environment. Production decision making is driven by choices for both inputs and output: what to produce, how much to produce, and how to produce it. Assumptions regarding the producer's objective drive these choices given the relationship describing how inputs are transformed into outputs.

The notion of a production function has its formal roots in Marshall (1920) and has been the subject of exhaustive and complete exposition by several scholars dating back to Sune Carlson (1939) and later by Ronald Shephard (1953, 1970), Ragnar Frisch (1955 [in Norwegian], 1965 [in English]), and Leif Johansen (1972). Chambers (1988, Chapter 1) presents a succinct history of the production function as a theoretical and empirical framework of economic decision making. This book attempts to stand on the shoulders of a long and distinguished list of contributions in production analysis to include Smith (1961), Nerlove (1963), Fuss and McFadden (1978), Chambers (1988), and Färe and Primont (1995) that are extraordinary foundational

Dynamic Efficiency and Productivity Measurement. Elvira Silva, Spiro E. Stefanou, and Alfons Oude Lansink,
Oxford University Press (2021). © Oxford University Press. DOI: 10.1093/oso/9780190919474.001.0001

contributions that set the stage for moving to the context of production decision making over time.

The characterization of dynamics in production decision making also is a theme of long interest. Samuelson (1947, Chapter IX) provides an overview of the earliest efforts to introduce dynamic notions in economics and identifies the distinction between "dynamic and causal (nonhistorical)" and "dynamic and historical" (Samuelson, 1947, p. 315). The former refers to a subset of variables leading other variables to move, but the parameters of the system remain unchanged. The latter adds the element of allowing for a parameter of the system (such as the state of the art) to lead to changes in the system or in its behavior over time. Frisch (1965, Part V, Chapters 16–19) focuses entirely on the dynamic theory of production by initially commenting on the *time shape* (his italics), or trajectory, of input and output decisions. These early efforts focus on the investment decisions and focus particular attention on the depreciation and replacement of equipment and structures. Frisch and others of this era take on an engineering economics framework to the intertemporal case, with the focus on a replacement theory approach where maintenance investment is the emphasis. The focus on replacement and maintenance motivates consideration of how the investment dynamics influence the installation of additional capital, which can lead to overcapacity (Chenery, 1952).

The nature of factors of production is a driving force of dynamic production decision making. Viner's (1931) distinction between some factors being "freely adjusted" and others being "necessarily fixed" necessitates the distinction between the short-run and long-run production technology. Capital inputs are characterized as having productive value beyond the current period and, at the same time, present a degree of inflexibility that freely adjusted (variable) inputs do not present. Alchian (1959), Smith (1961), and De Alessi (1967) advanced the stock-flow notion of the production function that formalizes the intertemporal investment and production decision making within the long-run cost minimization framework.

Three major components of production decisions have the potential to drive a dynamic decision process. The first is driven by the time scale of decisions and the economic forces related to the adjustment processes arising from the dichotomy between the short and long runs. Morrison (1999) refers to the subequilibrium as the point where decisions are taken when the firm is not in long-run equilibrium. The distinction between the short and long run becomes a prime consideration in determining the appropriate time scale of economic decision-making strategies. These strategies focus on the choice of production factors assumed to be fixed when factor allocation decisions are to be made. All economic activity occurs in the short run to the extent a factor (or factors) of production is taken as fixed (Viner, 1931; Smith, 1961; Ferguson, 1969, p. 198). Fundamentally, economic analysis in a static (or timeless) context entails addressing how a change in an economic variable of interest (e.g., price, tax, level of capital stock) impacts the firm's decision (e.g., how much to invest). This change is assumed to happen instantaneously or, more appropriately, over a time period that happens to be so long that the full impact of the stimulus for change has taken full effect. In fact, this time period may span several years. This is akin to asking the question: how long is the long run? For firms manufacturing automobiles, the answer can vary from 12 hours to 12 weeks, but for politicians, the answer is quite simple: the long run is until the next election. Understanding the decision time path associated with a policy stimulus is as important as understanding the final impact of that stimulus.

The second direction is to introduce the range of concepts we use to measure economic performance. There are several concepts that we can draw upon. In broad terms, this entails asking the difference between firms *being effective* versus *being efficient*. Being effective is choosing to do the "right thing," which relates to the economic performance concepts of productivity, economic capacity, and technological innovation. All of these concepts speak to the notion of growth, which is important to a firm's shareholders and to policymakers as it is the engine that propels economic activity forward and, consequently, the fortunes of individuals and communities. Being efficient is doing the "right thing well," which relates to minimizing waste or extracting the full potential of a prior technology choice. At its core, the optimizing decision maker allocates the mix of resources to achieve the minimal cost for a given production target or the maximum profit when the search is for the optimal output as well. Implicit in this assumption is the concept of efficiency, where a given technology extracts its maximal potential output. The absence of waste in the abstract is maintained, but ultimately this is an empirical question. Thus, it is of interest to distinguish between the level of technical efficiency (realizing the maximum output from a given bundle of inputs applied) and allocative efficiency (assigning input levels to realize the minimum cost to achieve a production target).

The third direction builds on the first two by focusing on the cognitive capacity of the decision maker to manage change and is viewed as a reflection of managerial ability, which is a source of human capital. Being able to measure efficiency allows us to engage in benchmarking a firm against its peers to assess relative performance and get an objective reading to the core questions many decision makers and planners implicitly ask: (a) What is not working well? (b) What is working well? Or, taken together, how can we improve?

Under a dynamic decision environment, managing variable inputs—which tend to be those that are easily metered—and assets (also referred to as quasi-fixed or dynamic factors) is more challenging in a given decision period and across periods. Assets play an important role in characterizing the production potential, which contributes to economic growth. There can be friction or inertia in the adjustment of asset magnitudes, and the management of this adjustment process is a key feature of economic decision making over time. One challenge of measuring economic performance is to have a metric that can be unique to the firm and can serve as the basis of comparison to peers. Being able to self-assess effectively requires the ability to take data, transform these data into information, and then construct key performance indicators that can serve as a mosaic of one's benchmark performance against peers (Bogetoft and Otto, 2011, Chapter 1). Knowing what one does well and where improvements are needed then lies in the domain of the decision maker to act.

There are several approaches to measuring productivity changes and efficiency as indicators of economic performance. The literature presents focuses on econometric and nonparametric approaches that are grounded in the theory of production. In this book, the focus will be on the production technology being represented by distance functions and how this technology characterization is connected to the economic objectives of the decision maker. This structural perspective allows for a transparent connection between what is possible (the technology, or opportunity set of feasible decisions) and what is optimal. There are other modeling perspectives as well.

Färe and Grosskopf (1996) present the network data envelopment analysis (DEA) framework as an appropriate direction to modeling dynamic economic decision making. It is particularly well suited to multistage production systems when an output in one stage feeds into the next stage as an input. Thus, we have time-specific input decisions and the production of time-specific (intermediate) outputs. Färe et al. (2018) provide an overview of efficiency and productivity in the dynamic context.

There are also econometric approaches that seek to capture the sluggish movement of quasi-fixed factors by proposing that the dynamic stochastic frontier models tend to estimate firms' long-run technical inefficiency levels. Tsionas (2006) specifies the persistence of technical inefficiency in an econometric framework. He asks, how can technical inefficiency be present and persist while at the same time this inefficiency is the consequence of factors that are under the firm's control? The answer is that these factors cannot be adjusted without entailing costs; the efficiency improvement will necessarily depend on the costs of adjustment. If such costs are high, we expect to find persistent technical inefficiency. This is a reduced-form perspective in that observed relations lead to the revelation of behavior underlying the choices.

With this brief introduction, we step back and take a broader view of when dynamic decision environments are present. Identifying the sources of inefficiencies to provide implications for remedies must recognize that the remedies for variable factors are different from those for quasi-fixed factors. Inefficiencies related to the quasi-fixed factors (e.g., structures, machinery, land) are often related to asset management practices. In contrast, inefficiencies related to variable factors (e.g., factors that are typically easily metered) can suggest remedies involving better recordkeeping or collecting additional information to provide greater precision in input application. Consequently, the proper accounting and valuation of factors that are out of equilibrium emerge as important components contributing to efficiency and productivity change.

As an important source of productivity growth, production efficiency analysis has been the subject of countless studies. Yet, theoretical and empirical studies focusing on production efficiency have ignored typically the time interdependence of production decisions and the adjustment paths of the firm over time.

Chapter 1 presents a motivation in how we start to characterize production in a dynamic decision-making environment. The classic characterization of firm decision making focuses on the optimal determination of two types of factors of production: those that can be freely adjusted (perfectly variable) and those that are necessarily fixed (imperfectly variable) within a given period of time. Clearly, some movement toward incorporating new capital takes place nearly every decision period (say, annually). The characterization that not all inputs are freely determined within a period of time is motivated by the conjecture that transaction costs are associated with adjusting the capital stock at a rapid rate per unit of time and these costs increase rapidly with the absolute rate of investment. In fact, these costs increase so rapidly that the firm never attempts to achieve a jump in its capital stock at any given moment. Such transaction (or adjustment) costs have implications for the nature of the technology. This interplay is introduced in this chapter and serves as a foundation for the dynamic structure that follows throughout the book.

Chapter 2 develops dynamic production analysis within the context of the adjustment cost model of the firm, where adjustment costs are associated with changes in the level of the quasi-fixed factors, also known as internal adjustment costs. This chapter characterizes axiomatically several primal representations of the adjustment cost production technology (i.e., production technology with internal adjustment costs). The axiomatic approach is a cornerstone to model production technology in both theoretical and empirical work. The existence of several representations of the adjustment cost production technology is essential in the analysis of the firm's decisions and its adjustment path that are conditioned by the technology. Three set representations of the adjustment cost production technology are discussed and characterized axiomatically. Two functional representations of the technology are also analyzed using an axiomatic approach.

Chapter 3 presents the economic model of behavior that exploits the dynamic technology presented in Chapter 2. Dynamic optimization for economic decision making in the context of both dynamic cost minimization and dynamic profit maximization are developed fully given different primal representations of the dynamic technology. The focus is on the Bellman equation of dynamic programming, which serves as the analytical foundation for the duality between the production technology and the economic objective (dynamic cost minimization and dynamic profit maximization). We start with the two-period exposition that illustrates the optimality relations dealing with iso-cost curves under dynamic adjustment and then move to the continuous time case. The dynamic duality relationships in the form of intertemporal versions of Hotelling's and Shephard's lemmas are presented. The chapter concludes with the data envelopment perspective of the dynamic decision-making framework. The data can reveal the nature of the production technology, and both the input and output quantities can be used to reveal the innermost bound of the technology. Alternatively, the technological information can be recovered by exploiting the dynamic cost minimization behaviors using input prices as well as the input and output quantities to reveal the outer bound of the input requirement set.

Chapter 4 addresses three concepts of directional distance functions in the presence of internal adjustment costs, designated as adjustment cost directional distance functions. These functions are the building blocks of technical inefficiency measures. Duality between an adjustment cost directional distance function and an indirect optimal value function allows construction of economic measures of inefficiency. Duality is established between the adjustment cost directional input distance function and the optimal current value function of the intertemporal cost minimization problem. From this dual relation, a dynamic cost inefficiency measure is derived and decomposed into technical inefficiency and allocative inefficiency. Similarly, dynamic input-output measures of inefficiency are derived from the adjustment cost directional technology distance function and duality between this function and the current profit function.

Chapter 5 addresses the intertemporal measurement of economic growth and performance at the firm level. The structure of production is addressed, which involves understanding how outputs respond to input changes, how firms can substitute inputs for given output targets, and how these responses relate to changes in productive capacity (through asset changes) and productive capabilities (through technological innovations). The dynamic generalizations of the economies of scale and scope are developed in the context of the directional distance technology, in addition to the concept of capacity utilization under dynamic adjustment. These concepts serve as the foundation to characterizing the Luenberger productivity indicator and its change at the firm level. We can exploit the decomposition of the Luenberger productivity change indicator into the contribution of inefficiency change, scale inefficiency change, and technical change. Each of these components is impacted by different policy remedies. Inefficiency reductions (or efficiency gains) are associated with improved managerial performance and skills. Scale changes that promote productivity gains are larger firm management strategies that seek to exploit existing technologies for greater scale efficiencies. These gains may arise from the ability to adjust production capacity, which may be supply-side driven by better-functioning capital markets or demand-side driven by enhanced market opportunities. Technical change can be influenced by public policy promoting research and development (R&D) as well as publicly supported programs promoting the conversion of basic R&D into commercialized innovations.

The last two chapters focus on empirical implementation. Chapter 6 addresses both structural and reduced-form econometric approaches to estimating the dynamic directional distance technology directly as well as estimating the cost function that accommodates technical inefficiency. An application to farm-level panel data is presented that estimates the decomposition of dynamic cost inefficiency into technical and allocative inefficiency presented in Chapter 4 and then determines the components of primal and dual Luenberger total factor productivity growth based on the elaboration of these concepts in Chapter 5.

Chapter 7 focuses on the nonparametric DEA framework of structural linear programming models underlying the estimation of efficiency. Chapter 3 introduced the notions of inner- and outer-bound technologies. While the inner-bound technology representation has dominated the nonparametric empirical applications in the literature on measuring efficiency and productivity, the outer-bound representation of the technology presents a viable alternative to measuring technical and cost efficiency as well. An application to farm-level panel data is developed.

This book takes clear aim on the specification of a technology that accommodates factors that can adjust either rapidly or slowly in a given time scale. Focusing on production analysis in the dynamic setting leads us to emphasize the technology specification permitting the theoretical construction that can be translated and amenable to empirical implementation.

This book focuses on understanding the core structure of the technology supporting dynamic decision making and the economic performance measures of scale, scope, productivity, and inefficiency. It is assumed the decision maker knows the current state of nature better than future states. This is a tolerable abstraction. Grasping this starting point firmly provides us with some structure to venture out to address future states of nature where real prices and other forces influencing decisions have elements of randomness.

As this introduction concludes, we turn to two directions that are worthy of attention and discussion but outside the scope of this book. Both directions implicitly admit a degree of uncertainty as a key component to developing a more complete characterization. While the preoccupation in motivating application is with physical quasi-fixed factors of production, quasi-fixed-factor stocks can also be forms of human and knowledge capital (Bernstein and Mamuneas, 2006). This direction connotes a link to activities actively encouraging infusion (or investment) that can arise from activities starting with R&D and going beyond to the commercialization of such infusions to innovations. Hall et al. (2010) provide a review of this direction to include the dynamic factors. There is a rich literature and interest in this direction, and these explorations by their nature imply a degree of uncertainty in the dynamic setting. Aw et al. (2011), Doraszelski and Jaumandreu (2013), and Peters et al. (2017) model the firm's endogenous decisions to engage in R&D investment. These models explicitly address the concept of productivity in the context of knowledge capital while allowing for stochastic shocks to the current productivity. These considerations include addressing the role of R&D in promoting productivity growth and eventually addressing the demand for R&D.

The second is to pull ourselves out of the weeds of a particular technology and how the decision interacts in that setting to a broader view that the nodes composing the system embody several behavioral forces. The system dynamics paradigm has its roots in Jay Forrester's (1961) pioneering work with Vaneman and Triantis (2003) offering a contribution on how to embed system dynamic elements in the network DEA framework. However, it is important to emphasize the role of managing a system that involves manufacturing activities, service delivery, human oversight, and policy decisions regarding the performance of this system.

1
Overview

1.1 What Is a Production Technology?

The production function has its formal roots in Marshall (1920) and has been the subject of exhaustive and complete exposition by several scholars dating back to Sune Carlson (1939) and later by Ragnar Frisch (1955 [in Norwegian], 1965 [in English]), Vernon L. Smith (1961), and Leif Johansen (1972).

The common point of departure is the notion of production: in the technical sense it refers to a transformation process that is directed by decision-making units. As such, the arguments of this transformation function are those that impact and are of interest to the decision-making unit. In Frisch's world, certain goods and services enter the transformation process, lose their identity, and emerge from the process as other constructions (goods and services). In this sense, we can differentiate between factors of production and the resulting products. References to a production function are invariably associated with the notion of a technology. This technology is "summarizing the relevant technical knowledge at a point in time" (Johansen, 1972, p. 6) and can be viewed as a relative concept.

Dynamic production relationships are characterized as ones where current input decisions impact future production possibilities. This perspective necessarily involves the close interplay between stock and flow elements in the transformation process, and how current decisions impact the changes in the stocks. What are these stock elements in a production function? Stock elements in the production transformation process can involve physical elements (such as the volume of capital [buildings, machinery, soil nutrient endowment, etc.] that can be effectively employed in the transformation process) as well as the stock of technical knowledge and expertise available to the decision maker during the decision period.

A common characteristic of transformation/production processes is that there is a production cycle where the beginning and the conclusion are

Dynamic Efficiency and Productivity Measurement. Elvira Silva, Spiro E. Stefanou, and Alfons Oude Lansink, Oxford University Press (2021). © Oxford University Press. DOI: 10.1093/oso/9780190919474.001.0001

well defined. This production cycle can be as short as part of a day (e.g., a baker's activities), 10 weeks (for the assembly of a Rolls Royce Phantom), 16 weeks (in the production of a soybean crop), or 104 weeks (2 years; before harvesting aquaculture-cultivated clams). The production function measures the amount of output that clears the production cycle, which can be alternatively measured in terms of time. In this context, the production function is defined as a flow or rate.

The level of production attained is strongly influenced by the amount of information available to the decision maker. Not all resources are homogeneous, and not all decision makers develop the same information set. While a certain proportion of the information set is theoretically available to all managers, individual managers have unique ways of processing information and unique problems in adapting information to their resource situation. The stock of entrepreneurial ability, the range of resources available to the firm, and the firm's objective function influences how effectively and efficiently the collected information is employed in production decision making.

1.2 Production in the Context of Time

1.2.1 Short Run versus Long Run and Being in Disequilibrium

The distinction between the short run and the long run becomes a prime consideration in determining the appropriate time scale of economic decision-making strategies. In Viner's (1931) characterization, the classical approach characterizes both short-run and long-run cost functions as flows. The long run is merely the case where the fixed factor is now variable—presumably, given the time span, the decision-making consideration is now long enough to allow factors to have sufficient time to adjust fully. Essentially, the long run remains a timeless decision problem. The idea of some factors being "freely adjusted" while others are "necessarily fixed" (Viner's terminology) is sufficiently vague to allow long-run costs to be considered a flow. This characterization of freely adjusted implies that altering the input levels of these factors does not impose a penalty on the firm other than a constant acquisition cost.

When an infinite number of short-run situations are possible, the long-run average cost curve is smooth, without corners. The problem with the classical description of the short run and long run is that the story of the envelope curve is not entirely consistent with the story motivating the distinction between the short run and long run. The long run consists of a range of possible short-run situations available to the firm. As such, the firm always operates in the short run but plans for the long run (Ferguson, 1969, p. 198).

The long run refers to the firm planning ahead to select a future short-run production situation. The classical view of the long run (the case presented in intermediate microeconomic theory texts) is presented as the envelope of all possible short-run situations. In considering the time scale of economic decisions, all economic activity occurs in the short run to the extent that a factor (or factors) of production is inflexible. While it is rare that an input is fully constrained to the point its level cannot be changed, an input can present a limited degree of flexibility in adjustment, which leads to the alternative characterization of the quasi-fixed factor. Oftentimes, a firm cannot readily accommodate large changes in factor use within a decision period. This inability to absorb easily the large changes can be related to forces that are driven internally (e.g., the firm's processes and organization) or externally (e.g., due to market forces, transaction costs associated with expansion). The application of the non–freely adjusted inputs implicitly occurs because some additional costs must be absorbed by the firm beyond the acquisition cost. The consequence of this inflexibility is the economic environment, which places a high cost on adjusting the factor level.

The dichotomy between the short run and long run constrains the conceptualization of the intertemporal production decision problem. In economic analysis, the long run typically refers to the steady-state equilibrium once all factors have adjusted. A more appropriate view may be the trichotomy of (a) the current period decision (or short run), (b) the steady-state equilibrium (or the long run), and (c) the adjustment phase between the current decision and the steady-state equilibrium. This adjustment phase has been alternatively characterized as temporary equilibrium (Berndt and Fuss, 1986), which occurs when the implicit marginal value (known as the shadow value) of any input and/or output differs from its market price. In long-run equilibrium or static situations, the shadow values equal market prices for all inputs and outputs. That is, the firm is making all the right moves in moving toward the steady-state equilibrium, but it is not there yet.[1]

---

[1] The steady-state equilibrium is defined ultimately by the parameters of the optimization problem to be solved, such as intertemporal profit maximization or intertemporal cost

As we move toward an intertemporal production decision environment, we no longer have a short run and a long run, but rather a continuum of runs. Alchian (1959) and Smith (1961) are two early efforts offering a more complete description of dynamic producer behavior by focusing on the minimization of the discounted stream of costs. Such a characterization focuses on intertemporal costs as a stock concept, while the nested current period decision problem involves a flow.

From a modeling building perspective, Hamermesh and Pfann (1996) note that there is rarely a match between the time scale of the decision-making environment and the time intervals between firms' decisions about whether or not to alter factor use. Nearly every applied study ignores the issue of temporal aggregation and assumes that the unit of time in the firm's decision making coincides with the time interval between the recorded observations.

Production relationships changing over time suggest changes in the stock of technical knowledge, or technical change. What drives these changes and how does the decision maker manage when production relationships change over time are two distinct questions. Technical change can be defined in many ways to encompass improvements in the products, product processes, physical inputs, and management methods (Stoneman, 1983). The Schumpeter taxonomy represents the technical change process hierarchically with the invention process, followed by the innovation process, which encompasses the development of the new concepts as marketable products and processes, and finally the diffusion of the new products and processes across the market. Hicks (1965) contributed to this stream by focusing on market forces (namely, prices) inducing changes in production relationships.

1.2.2 Changing Capacity

The problem of economic capacity utilization arises due to the short-run fixity of certain production inputs. A fixed input is under- (over-)utilized if

---

minimization. When prices, the initial capital stock, or the state of the technology is fixed (i.e., taken parametrically), a steady state can exist. However, some of these parameters may shift over time with no predetermined pattern specified. This may occur when the prices are revised without anticipating the revision. This is the case with open-loop dynamic optimization referred to in Chapter 3. In such cases, the steady state is a moving target.

the currently employed stock, K, is less (greater) than the full equilibrium stock, K^*. When all production inputs are at their full equilibrium (steady state) levels, the rate of capacity utilization is unity. The dynamic production problem necessarily involves the management of capacity utilization and its marginal valuation to the firm.

Capacity utilization measures are cyclical economic indicators of longstanding use in public policy formation and the analysis of business decisions. These measures have been employed to explain investment demand, productivity growth, international trade, inventory behavior, and cost-push inflation (Adams et al., 1969; Tatom, 1982; Conrad and Unger, 1989). A number of capacity utilization measures have been generated from the economic theory of production and cost (Berndt and Morrison, 1981; Morrison, 1985a, 1985b, 1986; Hulten, 1986; Berndt and Fuss, 1989). Some of these measures have been applied to assess capacity utilization in several sectors and countries (Morrison, 1985a; Berndt and Hesse, 1986; Hauver et al., 1991) and used to characterize strategic protection of market share by individual firms (Conrad and Veall, 1991).

A common feature of the economic measures of capacity utilization is that they have been derived under the assumption of cost minimization. Berndt and Fuss (1989) offer an initial attempt to obtain a primal (output-metric) index from the static profit maximization perspective by measuring deviations between *ex ante* price expectations and *ex post* realizations. They offer a primal ratio definition, $CU_p = Y''/Y'$, where Y'' and Y' are profit-maximizing supplies *ex ante* and *ex post*, respectively. Y'' is a retrospective characterization since current productive capacity is a result of past planning decisions. Therefore, empirical implementation of this measure requires recovering price expectations from the historical data at the time of the *ex ante* decisions. It has been suggested that analysts should abandon measures of optimal capacity utilization based on profit maximization.

1.3 Characterizing Adjustment

1.3.1 Adjustment Cost Hypothesis

Given the observed fact of economic life that some factors do adjust more slowly than others, the challenge is to articulate a mechanism that reflects the forces leading to this phenomenon. Implicitly, the assumption is that adjustment costs can be linked to the costs of altering a particular input and that the slow adjustment of some input demands is due to these costs. Hamermesh and Pfann (1996) offer an excellent overview of the development of economists' rationalization and modeling of factor adjustment.

The classic characterization of firm decision making focuses on the optimal determination of two types of factors of production: those that can be freely adjusted (perfectly variable) and those that are necessarily fixed (imperfectly variable) within a given period of time. The models are a response to the characterization that not all inputs are freely determined within a period of time typically allowed for decisions to be made and are motivated from the following propositions:

a. There are costs associated with adjusting the capital stock at a rapid rate per unit of time.
b. These costs increase rapidly with the absolute rate of investment—presumably, so rapid that the firm never attempts to achieve a jump in its capital stock at any given moment.

The factors that are not instantaneously adjusted are referred to as quasi-fixed. The stock of quasi-fixed factors is gradually accumulated since it costs more to adjust the stock rapidly rather than slowly. Holt et al. (1960) and Eisner and Strotz (1963) present an intertemporal approach describing optimal investment by allowing for gradual adjustment of quasi-fixed factors of production. Adjustment is gradual rather than instantaneous because it is assumed that the more rapidly quasi-fixed factors are adjusted, the greater the cost. This relationship is captured by the cost of adjustment function that is assumed to capture all of the unobserved forces slowing down the adjustment of some factors of production. In some cases, there may be physical limitations in how quickly adjustment can occur. For example, in agriculture, biological limitations may forestall complete and immediate adjustment of a herd; in high-technology industries, the shortage of qualified personnel can limit expansion. The cost of adjustment function defines the relationship between the cost (in either physical output or value terms) and the size of the adjustment (either net or gross). Consequently, the relative speed can be used to characterize the degree to which a factor is variable or quasi-fixed.

The existence of adjustment costs can lead to lags in the response of some endogenous variables to exogenous changes. The lagged response occurs only when the adjustment costs take on a particular curvature. Define the adjustment cost function as the relationship between the cost and size of adjustment, $\Psi(I)$, where I is the level of gross investment and $\dot{K} = dK/dt = I - \delta K$ is the level of net investment, with δ denoting the rate of depreciation of factor K. The first proposition implies that $\Psi(I) > 0$ for $I \lessgtr 0$. Negative gross investment (or disinvestment) is the active removal of assets from the production plan. A classic example is viewing labor (as human capital) that can incur layoffs. The point remains that large changes in investment (positive or negative) incur adjustment costs (Hamermesh and Pfann, 1996).

Drawing on Brechling (1975), Figures 1.1 present three possible forms for $\Psi(I)$. For illustrative purposes, consider a two-period problem where I^* is the net investment required to achieve the long-run optimal capital stock. Adjustment costs of the concave form $A'\text{-}A$ in Figure 1.1 decline at the margin with increases in the absolute size of the adjustment (i.e., a declining marginal cost of adjustment). A gradual adjustment of $\frac{1}{2}I^*$ in each of the two periods leads to greater total cost of changing the capital stock than an immediate adjustment to I^* (regardless of discounting).

With a declining marginal cost of adjustment, the firm seeks to adjust its capital stock as quickly as possible if not instantly. With adjustment costs of presenting the linear form $B'\text{-}B$ in Figure 1.1, a gradual adjustment strategy of, say, $\frac{1}{2}I^*$ in each of the two periods leads to the same total cost of adjustment as making an immediate adjustment to I^* in the absence of discounting.

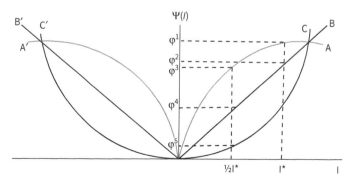

Figure 1.1. Concave, Linear and Convex adjustment cost function.

With discounting, gradual adjustment entails a greater total cost of adjustment over immediate and full adjustment!

Thus, linear adjustment costs cannot lead to gradual adjustment. Adjustment costs of the convex form C'-C in Figure 1.1 increase at the margin with increases in the absolute size of the adjustment (i.e., an increasing marginal cost of adjustment). With a gradual adjustment strategy of $\frac{1}{2}I^*$ in each period, the total cost of changing the capital stock is *less than* with immediate adjustment.

The principal difference between C-C' and the other forms of adjustment costs is that the others are characterized by constant or decreasing marginal adjustment costs, implying there are diseconomies of investment from the outset arising from transaction (or adjustment) costs associated with larger changes in the quasi-fixed-factor stock such as high startup costs, costs of licensing, research and development, and other forces outlined in the introduction. The convexity of the adjustment cost function implies that the average cost of adjustment is increasing in the size of the adjustment. This leads to the presence of diseconomies of greater changes in the quasi-fixed-factor stocks. The economies of investment (i.e., decreasing $\Psi(I)/I$) is what drives the full and immediate adjustment.

The introduction of adjustment costs into a model of firm behavior leads to gradual adjustment of quasi-fixed factors only if the marginal cost of adjustment is increasing with the absolute size of the adjustment. Let the adjustment cost function be denoted as $\Psi(I)$, where

$$\Psi_I(I) \lessgtr 0 \quad for \quad I \lessgtr 0$$

$$\Psi_{II} > 0 \quad for\ all \quad I. \tag{1.1}$$

Internal costs of adjustment suggest a production function specification at time t of the general form

$$y(t) = F(x(t), K(t), I(t)), \tag{1.2}$$

where y is output, and x is a perfectly variable input. In this case the marginal products of variable inputs and capital are influenced by the level of

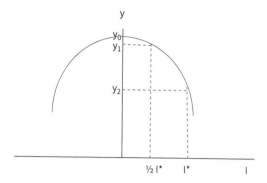

Figure 1.2. Adjustment cost function in terms of physical yield.

adjustment. The adjustment cost in terms of a reduction of physical output has the characteristics

$$F_I(I) \lessgtr 0 \quad for \quad I \lessgtr 0$$

$$F_{II} < 0 \quad for\ all \quad I. \tag{1.3}$$

Figure 1.2 illustrates how a gradual adjustment to the desired level yields a smaller reduction in output than immediate adjustment given x and K. Again, if I^* is the optimal level of investment to place the firm in long-run equilibrium, the output loss of an instantaneous adjustment is $y^0 - y''$. Comparing this loss to the cost of investing $I' = \frac{1}{2} I^*$ in two successive periods yields a cost of $2(y^0 - y') < (y^0 - y'')$ (even in the absence of discounting).

1.3.2 Isoquants

Consider the production function where gross investment leads to adjustment costs as specified in (1.2). In the current period, increasing the variable input levels and starting capital stock lead to increased output, while

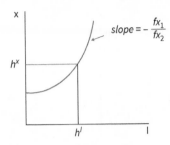

Figure 1.3. Isoquant map (I, x).

increasing investment lowers output. An isoquant mapping of (I, x) is illustrated in Figure 1.3. The tradeoff is illustrated as h^x units of the beneficial factor, x, requires taking h^I units of the (currently) detrimental factor, I. The slope of the isoquant is $-f_I/f_x > 0$ for $I > 0$. However, it remains to be seen how costs relate to this isoquant map.

1.3.3 Nonconvex Production Relationships

An alternative theory of gradual investment behavior focuses on the loan market in obtaining external capital. When financing investment from retained profits and equity, Figure 1.4 illustrates the case of the decision maker who finds that his firm is eligible to acquire a maximum of I^o at the competitive market rate and the loan is not collateralized beyond I^o. However, unsecured financing is possible but at a premium, indicated by the change in the slope of the adjustment cost function to A^1A^2, which is consistent with an increasing additional cost of investment.

The smooth, convex adjustment cost formulation in section 1.3.1 is one mechanism that can lead to the gradual adjustment of stock variables. Is smooth, convex adjustment the rule or the exception? The discussion surrounding Figure 1.1 suggests that nonconvex adjustment costs can lead to investment bursts and the jumps in productive capacity that follow. Davidson and Harris (1981) consider nonconvexity in (a) the adjustment cost function (flow nonconvexity) and (b) the production function with respect to the sluggishly adjusting factor (or a stock nonconvexity). At the micro-level decision-making unit, Cooper and Haltiwanger (2006) review the empirical literature and find that nonconvexity is likely the rule rather than the

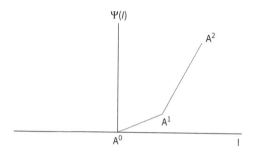

Figure 1.4. Piecewise linear adjustment.

exception. Once we aggregate the data beyond the micro decision units, convexity is likely to be a tolerable abstraction. In the end, the adjustment cost function is a mechanism created by the analyst to rationalize the behavior that generates the observed data. As such, it is a black box that summarizes all the forces that can lead to the gradual adjustment of some factors. From an empirical perspective, it is desirable to specify models that can test for the degree of inflexibility in adjusting a given factor.

Even still, there are a number of factor adjustment structures. Returning to the linear adjust costs such as A'-A in Figure 1.1, Rothschild (1971) and Nickel (1978) addressed this form, noting that there is a value for waiting to adjust to the optimal level, and once that decision to adjust is made, the adjustment is instantaneous. Chang and Hsu (1990) demonstrate that it is the discontinuity of this piecewise linear adjustment structure at the origin that leads to the period of inaction that has been referred to as the asset fixity trap in the agricultural economics literature. Figure 1.5 presents an alternative to the symmetric convex adjustment cost structure found in C'-C in Figure 1.1. The asymmetric convex structure reflects the observation that an expansion can occur at different rates than a contraction. One rationale may be that as a firm grows, it bears a learning cost associated with assimilating additional capital equipment and structures into its operations. But as this firm contracts, it is easier to jettison these factors, and the firm knows how to manage an operation with the smaller capital stock. Alternatively, a rationale for more costly divestment may be environmental reclamation costs associated with a contraction that is not present for an expansion. Chang and Stefanou (1988), Oude Lansink and Stefanou (1997), and Pietola and Myers (2000) empirically address asymmetric adjustment situations with micro-level data.

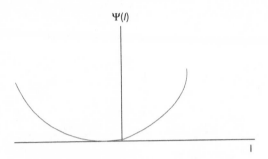

Figure 1.5. Asymmetric adjustment.

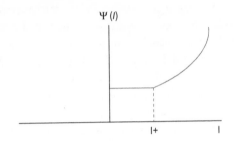

Figure 1.6. Adjustment with Fixed Cost

Yet another factor adjustment structure exhibits a fixed cost component as illustrated in Figure 1.6. This case leads to the minimum investment being zero or $I+$, suggesting that some of the costs of increased factor use to the point of $I+$ are independent of the level of factor expansion (up to a point). In this case, lumpy investment patterns emerge. This is a micro decision unit phenomenon. If we allow for each firm to have a different fixed adjustment cost component, different minimum positive investment, and even different marginal cost of adjustment beyond the firm-specific $I+$, aggregating up to the industry (or higher) level will lead to the appearance of a smooth adjustment function.

1.4 Implications of Adjustment for Measuring Performance

The theory of production addresses rational producers seeking to minimize production costs given their target outputs, maximize revenue given an input bundle, or maximize profit. However, an extensive literature has emerged over the last several decades that addresses how to measure deviations from optimal behavior from both a technical perspective (i.e., not reaching the maximal technical production potential) and an allocation perspective (i.e., factor allocations that are not satisfying first-order conditions). The literature has its roots in Farrell (1957) and Debreu (1959) and is summarized more recently by Kumbhakar and Lovell (2000) and Fried et al. (2008). With a convex production technology and in the absence of technical inefficiency, achieving allocative efficiency is guaranteed once the first-order conditions of cost minimization or profit maximization are satisfied. Achieving allocative efficiency requires input reallocation, and the neoclassical theory assumes no transition costs are associated with this reallocation. Input reallocation focuses on the decision maker moving along an isoquant to find the cost-minimizing input combination. In the context of inefficiency, the decision maker may not even be on the isoquant (i.e., technically inefficient), leaving the reallocation decision to involve moving toward the frontier of the input requirement set and finding the optimal point on that frontier simultaneously. With each point on an isoquant being a technique of a production process (or technology), the smooth isoquant results in the presence of an infinite number of techniques to achieve a given output level. Changing the input bundle as the firm reorients the techniques of production to enhance efficiencies can cause the firm to incur monitoring (or related) costs associated with reorganizing the production process. These reorganization costs and the related inertia in making change are revealed by the presence of adjustment associated with reallocating inputs. Thus, the assumption of costless adjustment (or reallocation) is relaxed and the standard optimization framework (cost minimization, profit maximization) is modified accordingly.

Plans to reduce a firm's inefficiencies require reorganizing production processes. This is a starting point for the dynamic capabilities literature, which addresses how learning, the transformation of existing assets, and the introduction of new assets are managed to address the changing market environments that decision makers face (Teece et al., 1997). In this case, the changes in the variable input combinations toward the fully efficient input bundle is not instantaneous, and the control variable is defined as the change in input levels, while the stock variable is defined as the input level upon entering the decision period. In this context, static approaches to production efficiency analysis are expected to be incomplete in addressing how firms become efficient. The notion of optimality in neoclassical economics is based on a frictionless world absent of transaction costs, which can include the learning costs of reorganizing input combinations. Zero transaction costs arise when all relevant information is available costlessly, and the decision maker exhibits perfect rationality with instantaneous access to all available information. However, positive transaction costs are inevitable in actual production processes, and a human decision maker has bounded rationality and an imperfect ability to promptly adjust (Williamson, 1985). That is, the decision maker's ability to recognize all available options and compare each option to others at a given point in time is limited. In the presence of positive transaction costs and bounded rationality, transition costs can arise whenever input reallocation decisions are made. For example, a decision maker may want to explore and imitate "best practice" firms in the industry to improve the inefficiencies of his or her firm. Each exploratory and imitating activity can be costly and require associated costs in the form of search, learning, and reorganization costs. The sources of inefficiencies are related to managerial ability, factor fixities, regulations, characteristics of capital, and quality or environmental attributes that can prevent a firm from attaining full efficiency in a given time period. There may be residual sources of inefficiencies as well. For example, Peters and Waterman (1982) note that successful learning activity within a firm can reduce the possibility of disagreement and serve as a positive attribute of a successful organization.

The economic consequences of inefficiencies vary with the environment in which firms are operating. If the market is competitive and if there is no government intervention to support inefficient firms, competition will eventually expel an inefficient firm from the market. Productivity growth can be decomposed into a scale effect, an allocative efficiency gain/loss effect measured as the impact of the difference between the observed input cost share and the efficiency input cost share, a technical efficiency gain/loss effect measured by the shifting in the cost function, and a classical exogenously driven technical change effect (Bauer, 1990; Lovell, 1996). A firm's survival over time does not depend on its current efficiency, but on its ability to make efficient decisions over time, which necessarily involves growth. Clearly, faster improvement toward an efficient input allocation will result in greater productivity growth. However, efficiency changes have been treated as exogenous in the literature. An attempt to endogenize efficiency changes can also contribute to the theory and methods for analyzing growth and its causes.

Transition costs are the key factors leading to the dynamic specification of the cost minimization framework since these costs contribute to the flow of costs over time, which inevitably involve dynamic relationships. A firm seeking to improve its efficiencies will incur transition costs as long as the benefits from these transitions are greater than the associated costs.

The policy analysis of growth in industries depends on understanding the cost structure and how it evolves in the face of quasi-fixed-factor adjustment and technical change. As a market-driven economy imposes greater competitive pressure on firms' decision makers, decision making necessarily involves balancing the tradeoff between (a) scale and technical efficiency change by exploiting the full productive potential of implemented technologies and (b) technical change by adopting innovations. Sustaining competitiveness over the long run involves attention to productivity growth prospects in both levels; innovations are needed to keep pushing the competitive envelope, and efficiency gains are needed to ensure that implemented technologies can succeed. Accurate analysis of the factors explaining changes in productivity is important to understanding the future competitiveness of an industry. Oftentimes, discussion of firm growth typically refers to thinking about a steady state for a very long time.

2
Primal Analytical Foundations of Dynamic Production Analysis

2.1 Introduction

Primal analytical foundations of production theory are well established in the context of static decision making. Alternative primal representations of the production technology are defined and characterized axiomatically within the static model of the firm (e.g., Shephard, 1953, 1970; Koopmans, 1957; Debreu, 1959; Fuss and McFadden, 1978; Färe and Primont, 1995). Dynamic models of the firm have been widely used (e.g., Luh and Stefanou, 1993, 1996; Fousekis and Stefanou, 1996; Palm and Pfann, 1998; Nilsen and Schiantarelli, 2003; Letterie et al., 2004; Polder and Verick, 2004), yet the primal analytical foundations of dynamic production theory have not yet been developed and formalized as in the static production analysis.

The adjustment cost model of the firm is a dynamic approach to the theory of the firm where adjustment costs associated with changes in the level of quasi-fixed factors are the source of the time interdependence of production decisions. As introduced in Chapter 1, adjustment costs are usually characterized as either internal or external. Internal adjustment costs may be conceived as output-reducing costs resulting from diverting resources from production to investment support activities (e.g., installing the new capital goods, training personnel), implying a tradeoff between current production and current growth and future production (e.g., Lucas, 1967b; Treadway, 1969, 1970). External adjustment costs arise from market forces, such as monopsony in the market for investment goods (e.g., Eisner and Strotz, 1963; Lucas, 1967a; Gould, 1968). External adjustment costs are typically added to the other costs of the firm, while internal costs are incorporated in the production technology specification.

Silva and Stefanou (2003) show that a well-behaved adjustment cost technology can be represented by a family of input requirement sets satisfying

Dynamic Efficiency and Productivity Measurement. Elvira Silva, Spiro E. Stefanou, and Alfons Oude Lansink, Oxford University Press (2021). © Oxford University Press. DOI: 10.1093/oso/9780190919474.001.0001

some regularity conditions where the dynamics are explicitly addressed in the production specification as an adjustment cost. Capital as a quasi-fixed factor is managed as an asset where rapid expansion or contraction of the stock of capital is accompanied by adjustment costs.

In this chapter, alternative representations of the adjustment cost production technology are analyzed using an axiomatic approach. Capital quasi-fixity is treated as arising from internal adjustment costs. We do not consider the existence of adjustment costs in the dynamics of other production factors (e.g., labor).

This chapter unfolds as follows. In section 2.2, the adjustment cost production technology is investigated using the set theory. Set representations of the adjustment cost production technology are presented. Properties for the technology sets are postulated and the corresponding implications are discussed. In section 2.3, we present the adjustment cost transformation function and the adjustment cost production function.

2.2 Set Representation of the Adjustment Cost Production Technology

The point of departure to characterize completely the adjustment cost production technology is the technology set. A set representation of the production technology allows specifying multiple output, multiple input technologies in a simple way. This section considers three closely related concepts of an adjustment cost production technology: the adjustment cost production possibilities set, the adjustment cost input requirement set (or input correspondence), and the adjustment cost producible output set (or output correspondence). A set of properties (or axioms) is postulated and the corresponding implications are discussed.

2.2.1 Adjustment Cost Production Possibilities Set

Definition 2.1: The adjustment cost production technology at time t is defined by the production possibilities set represented as

$$T(K(t)) \equiv \left\{ (x(t), I(t), y(t)) : (x(t), I(t), y(t)) \text{ is feasible given } K(t) \right\},$$

where $y(t) \in \mathfrak{R}_+^M$ is the vector of outputs, $x(t) \in \mathfrak{R}_+^N$ is the vector of variable inputs, $K(t) \in \mathfrak{R}_+^F$ is the capital stock vector, and $I(t) \in \mathfrak{R}_+^F$ is the vector of dynamic factors (gross investments). If $(x(t), I(t), y(t)) \in T(K(t))$, $(x(t), I(t), y(t))$ is a feasible input-output vector; if $(x(t), I(t), y(t)) \notin T(K(t))$, $(x(t), I(t), y(t))$ is not a feasible combination.

By definition, the adjustment cost production possibilities set at a particular time t, $T(K(t))$, is the set of all technologically feasible combinations of variable and dynamic inputs and outputs, given the capital stock vector. Including gross investment in the definition of $T(K(t))$ implies that maximum output levels depend not only on variable and quasi-fixed factors but also on the magnitude of the dynamic factors (change in the level of the quasi-fixed factors). The adjustment cost production possibilities set, $T(K(t))$, is determined fundamentally by technological restrictions. However, legal constraints or prior contractual commitments may also determine this set.

Properties of $T(K(t))$:

T.1 $T(K(t))$ is a closed, nonempty subset of the $M+N+F$-dimensional space.

T.2 $T(K(t))$ is bounded from above.

T.3 $(x(t), I(t), 0_M) \in T(K(t))$.

T.4 $(0_N, 0_F, y(t)) \notin T(K(t))$, $y(t) \geq 0_M$, $y(t) \neq 0_M$.

T.5 $(x(t), 0_F, y(t)) \in T(K(t))$.

T.6S   If $(x(t), I(t), y(t)) \in T(K(t))$ and $y(t)' \leq y(t)$,
$(x(t), I(t), y(t)') \in T(K(t))$.

T.6W   If $(x(t), I(t), y(t)) \in T(K(t))$ and $0 < \theta \leq 1$,
$(x(t), I(t), \theta y(t)) \in T(K(t))$.

T.7S   If $(x(t), I(t), y(t)) \in T(K(t))$ and $x(t)' \geq x(t)$,
$(x(t)', I(t), y(t)) \in T(K(t))$.

T.7W   If $(x(t), I(t), y(t)) \in T(K(t))$ and $\theta \geq 1$, $(\theta x(t), I(t), y(t)) \in T(K(t))$.

T.8   If $(x(t), I(t), y(t)) \in T(K(t))$ and $I(t)' \leq I(t)$,
$(x(t), I(t)', y(t)) \in T(K(t))$.

T.9   If $(x(t), I(t), y(t)) \in T(K(t))$ and $K(t)' \geq K(t)$,
$(x(t), I(t), y(t)) \in T(K(t)')$ or
$K(t)' \geq K(t) \Rightarrow T(K(t)) \subset T(K(t)')$.

T.10   (a) $T(K(t))$ is a (strictly) convex set.
       (b) $T(K(t))$ is a nonconvex set.

T.11   (a)   If $(x(t), I(t), y(t)) \in T(K(t))$ and $\gamma > 0$,

$(\gamma x(t), \gamma I(t), \gamma y(t)) \in T(K(t))$.

(b)   If $(x(t), I(t), y(t)) \in T(K(t))$ and $0 < \gamma \leq 1$,

$(\gamma x(t), \gamma I(t), \gamma y(t)) \in T(K(t))$.

(c)   If $(x(t), I(t), y(t)) \in T(K(t))$ and $\gamma \geq 1$,

$(\gamma x(t), \gamma I(t), \gamma y(t)) \in T(K(t))$.

The nonemptiness assumption of property T.1 implies feasibility and the closedness of $T(K(t))$ eliminates the possibility that the technology discontinuously changes from being able to produce $y(t)$ to not being able to produce $y(t)$. Property T.2 means that finite quantities of variable and dynamic inputs produce finite quantities of outputs. Properties T.3 and T.4 establish, respectively, the possibility of inactivity and no free lunch. Inactivity means that it is always possible to produce nothing using productive resources, yet the use of some resources is necessary to produce any output quantity (i.e., no free lunch).

As in the static model of the firm, axioms T.1–T.4 are usually postulated when modeling the production technology. Additionally, we also postulate the possibility of investment inaction at time t (T.5). Property T.5 simply asserts that the firm may choose not to invest in a particular time period. This axiom is consistent with infrequent adjustments revealed by microeconomic data (e.g., Ramey, 1991; Bresnahan and Ramey, 1994; Caballero et al., 1997; Caballero, 1999; Nilsen and Schiantarelli, 2003).

Property T.6S (T.6W) asserts that outputs are strongly or freely (weakly) disposable. As in the static production analysis, strong disposability of outputs means that if $(x(t), I(t))$ can produce $y(t)$ given $K(t)$, then $(x(t), I(t))$ can produce any output vector smaller than $y(t)$, implying that additional quantities of outputs can be disposed of without cost. The weak disposability of outputs (T.6W) means that if $(x(t), I(t))$ can produce $y(t)$ given $K(t)$, then $(x(t), I(t))$ can produce any output vector that is a proportional reduction of $y(t)$. The latter property (i.e., T.6W) is necessary in the presence of by-products or bad outputs. If property T.6S is satisfied, then T.6W is satisfied, but the converse does not hold. Thus, T.6S implies T.6W, but the converse is not true. We address these two properties when presenting the output sets in more detail.

Property T.7S (T.7W) imposes strong (weak) disposability of variable inputs. Strong disposability of variable inputs means that additional quantities of variable inputs can be disposed of without reducing the quantities of outputs produced. Weak disposability of variable inputs allows for the presence of variable factors with negative marginal products. We will analyze these two properties in detail when presenting the input sets.

Property T.8 asserts that dynamic factors congest outputs, reflecting the presence of internal adjustment costs associated with gross investment. Internal adjustment costs are conceived as output-reducing costs resulting from diverting resources from production activities to investment support activities (e.g., installing the new capital goods, training personnel). Thus, the marginal product of dynamic factors is negative. In contrast, property T.9 establishes that output levels are increasing in the stock of capital. Axioms T.8 and T.9 together state that a current expansion in the dynamic factors decreases current levels of outputs but increases output levels in the future by increasing the future stocks of capital.

Property T.10(a) postulates that $T(K(t))$ is a (strictly) convex set in $(x(t),I(t),y(t))$. Convexity of $T(K(t))$ implies divisibility of (variable and dynamic) inputs and outputs. Note, however, that divisibility of inputs and outputs does not imply convexity of the adjustment cost production possibilities set. Even if inputs and outputs are perfectly divisible, the presence of scale economies or economies of specialization implies nonconvexity of $T(K(t))$. Convexity (strict convexity) of $T(K(t))$ implies concavity (strict concavity) of the dynamic directional technology distance function, as we will show in Chapter 4. Similarly, it will be shown in this chapter that (strict) convexity of $T(K(t))$ implies (strict) convexity of the transformation function. In the case of a single-output technology, (strict) convexity of $T(K(t))$ is equivalent to (strict) concavity of the production function.

Property T.10(b) allows $T(K(t))$ to be nonconvex. The nonconvexity of the production possibilities set may arise from indivisibilities and other forms of increasing returns to scale in the adjustment cost technology.

Properties T.11(a)–(c) are scale properties. Property T.11(a) imposes constant returns to scale. Properties T.11(b) and (c) impose, respectively, nonincreasing returns to scale and nondecreasing returns to scale.

2.2.2 Adjustment Cost Input Requirement Sets

Definition 2.2: The adjustment cost technology at time t can be defined by a family of input requirement sets. The input requirement set (or input correspondence) is defined as

$$V(y(t):K(t)) \equiv \left\{(x(t),I(t)):(x(t),I(t),y(t)) \in T(K(t))\right\}.$$

The input requirement set, $V(y(t):K(t))$, represents the set of all combinations of variable inputs and dynamic factors capable of producing the output bundle $y(t)$, given capital stock vector $K(t)$. Two input requirement sets can be derived from definition 2.2: the variable input requirement set and the dynamic input requirement set. The variable input requirement set (or variable input correspondence) is represented as

$$V(y(t):K(t),I(t)) = \left\{x(t) \in \Re_+^N : (x(t),I(t)) \in V(y(t):K(t))\right\}$$
$$= \left\{x(t) \in \Re_+^N : (x(t),I(t),y(t)) \in T(K(t))\right\}. \quad (2.1)$$

The dynamic input requirement set (dynamic input correspondence) is defined as

$$V(y(t):K(t),x(t)) = \left\{I(t) \in \Re_+^F : (x(t),I(t)) \in V(y(t):K(t))\right\}$$
$$= \left\{I(t) \in \Re_+^F : (x(t),I(t),y(t)) \in T(K(t))\right\}. \quad (2.2)$$

Properties of $V(y(t):K(t))$:

V.1 $V(y(t):K(t))$ is a closed, nonempty subset of the $N+F$-dimensional space.

V.2 $V(y(t):K(t))$ has a lower bound (or bounded from below).

V.3 $\underset{\substack{y(t)\in\Re_+^M \\ K(t)\in\Re_+^F}}{\cap} V(y(t):K(t)) = \varnothing$.

V.4 $(x(t),I(t)) \in V(0_M:K(t))$.

V.5 $(0_N,0_F) \notin V(y(t):K(t))$, $y(t) \geq 0_M, y(t) \neq 0_M$.

V.6 $(x(t),0_F) \in V(y(t):K(t))$.

V.7S   If $(x(t), I(t)) \in V(y(t) : K(t))$ and $x(t)' \geq x(t)$,
$(x(t)', I(t)) \in V(y(t) : K(t))$.

V.7W   If $(x(t), I(t)) \in V(y(t) : K(t))$ and $\theta \geq 1$,
$(\theta x(t), I(t)) \in V(y(t) : K(t))$.

V.8   If $(x(t), I(t)) \in V(y(t) : K(t))$ and $I(t)' \leq I(t)$,
$(x(t), I(t)') \in V(y(t) : K(t))$.

V.9 $K(t)' \geq K(t) \Rightarrow V(y(t) : K(t)) \subset V(y(t) : K(t)')$.

V.10S $y(t) \geq y(t)' \Rightarrow V(y(t) : K(t)) \subset V(y(t)' : K(t))$.

V.10W   If $(x(t), I(t)) \in V(y(t) : K(t))$ and $0 < \theta \leq 1$,
$(x(t), I(t)) \in V(\theta y(t) : K(t))$.

V.11 $V(y(t):K(t))$ is a (strictly) convex set.

V.12 $V(y(t):K(t))$ is quasi-concave in $y(t)$; that is,
$\forall y(t), y(t)' \in \Re_+^M$, if $0 \leq \lambda \leq 1$, then
$V(y(t) : K(t)) \cap V(y(t)' : K(t)) \subseteq V(\lambda y(t) + (1 - \lambda)y(t)' : K(t))$.

V.13   (a) If $(x(t), I(t)) \in V(y(t) : K(t))$ and $\gamma > 0$,
$(\gamma x(t), \gamma I(t)) \in V(\gamma y(t) : K(t))$.

   (b) If $(x(t), I(t)) \in V(y(t) : K(t))$ and $0 < \gamma \leq 1$,
$(\gamma x(t), \gamma I(t)) \in V(\gamma y(t) : K(t))$.

   (c) If $(x(t), I(t)) \in V(y(t) : K(t))$ and $\gamma \geq 1$,
$(\gamma x(t), \gamma I(t)) \in V(\gamma y(t) : K(t))$.

Considering definition 2.2, some of the properties of $V(y(t):K(t))$ are inherited from the properties of $T(K(t))$ but not all of them. The nonemptiness property of $T(K(t))$ implies that $\exists y(t) \in \Re_+^M, K(t) \in \Re_+^F$ such that $V(y(t):K(t))$ is not an empty set, but it does not imply that $V(y(t):K(t))$ is a nonempty set $\forall y(t) \in \Re_+^M, K(t) \in \Re_+^F$. Closedness of $T(K(t))$ implies that the adjustment cost input requirement set is closed. Closedness of $V(y(t):K(t))$ allows the isoquant of the input set to be defined as a subset of the boundary of $V(y(t):K(t))$. The definition of the isoquant is presented and discussed later.

Property V.3 asserts that finite quantities of (variable and dynamic) inputs cannot generate infinite quantities of outputs. This property results from property T.2. Properties V.4 (inactivity) and V.5 (no free lunch) are implied by axioms T.3 and T.4, respectively. Axiom V.6 allows the firm to decide not to invest in a particular time period. This axiom results from property T.5.

Properties T.7S and T.7W imply properties V.7S and V.7W, respectively. Property V.7S establishes that variable inputs are strongly disposable, implying that additional units of any variable input do not decrease $y(t)$. As a consequence, the marginal product of each variable input factor is nonnegative, excluding upward-sloping isoquants of $V(y(t):K(t),I(t))$. In contrast, property V.7W allows for some variable inputs to congest outputs. According to this property, outputs do not decrease if all inputs increase proportionally; thus, the marginal product of some factors of production is negative. Given V.2, V.7S implies that the slope of the isoquant of $V(y(t):K(t),I(t))$ is nonpositive; in the case of V.7W, the variable input set $V(y(t):K(t),I(t))$ may have backward-bending isoquants. Figure 2.1 illustrates properties V.7S and V.7W, assuming two variable inputs. $ABCD$ defines the boundary of a variable input set that satisfies V.7S; $EBCD$ represents the boundary of a variable input set that satisfies V.7W.

Property V.8 means that $V(y(t):K(t))$ is negative monotonic in $I(t)$, implying that output levels decrease as investment in quasi-fixed factors takes place; thus, the marginal product of the dynamic factors is negative. This reflects the presence of internal adjustment costs associated with gross investment. Property V.9 establishes that output levels are increasing in the stock of capital, implying that the marginal product of the quasi-fixed factors is positive. Properties V.8 and V.9 together state that current changes in the dynamic factors decrease current levels of outputs but increase output levels in the future by increasing the future stocks of capital.

Figure 2.2 illustrates axiom V.8. Assuming two dynamic factors, the slope of the isoquant of $V(y(t):K(t),x(t))$ is negative and output levels increase as we move toward the origin.

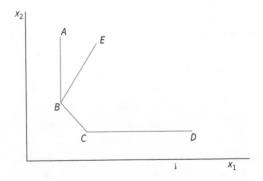

Figure 2.1. Strong and weak disposability of variable inputs.

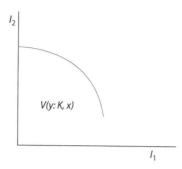

Figure 2.2. Negative monotonicity of *V* in *I*.

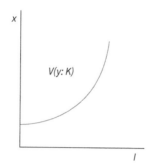

Figure 2.3. *V* in the (x, I) space.

Combining axioms V.7S and V.8, Figure 2.3 illustrates the input sets $V(y(t):K(t))$, assuming one variable input and one dynamic factor. As a consequence of these two axioms, the slope of the isoquant of $V(y(t):K(t))$ is nonnegative and output levels increase as we move northwest in the $(x(t),I(t))$ space.

Property V.10S asserts that outputs can be disposed of freely if necessary, while property V.10W allows for the presence of some bad outputs. We will analyze in detail these two properties when discussing the producible output set.

Axiom V.11 asserts that $V(y(t):K(t))$ is (strict) convex in $(x(t),I(t))$. Convexity of the adjustment cost input requirement set implies divisibility of variable and dynamic inputs. Convexity of $T(K(t))$ is more restrictive than convexity of $V(y(t):K(t))$. Note that convexity of $V(y(t):K(t))$ does not imply divisibility of outputs. Also, convexity of $T(K(t))$ is not compatible with increasing returns to scale, yet convexity of $V(y(t):K(t))$ is consistent with this returns-to-scale hypothesis. Property T.10(a) implies V.11, as shown by proposition 2.1 next, yet the converse is not true.

Proposition 2.1: If $T(K(t))$ is a convex set, $V(y(t):K(t))$ is a convex set in $(x(t), I(t))$.

Proof of proposition 2.1:[1] Assume $T(K)$ is a convex set.
If $(x,I,y), (x',I',y) \in T(K)$, then $[(\alpha x + (1-\alpha)x', \alpha I + (1-\alpha)I', y)] \in T(K)$. Thus, $[\alpha x + (1-\alpha)x', \alpha I + (1-\alpha)I'] \in V(y:K)$.

Property V.12 establishes quasi-concavity of $V(y(t):K(t))$ in $y(t)$. This axiom implies divisibility of outputs. Proposition 2.2 shows that property T.10(a) implies V.12. Yet, quasi-concavity of the input set does not imply convexity of the production possibilities set.

Proposition 2.2: If $T(K(t))$ is a convex set, $V(y(t):K(t))$ is a quasi-concave correspondence in $y(t)$.

Proof of proposition 2.2: Assume $T(K)$ is a convex set. If $(x,I,y), (x,I,y') \in T(K)$, $[(x,I,\lambda y + (1-\lambda)y')] \in T(K)$. This means that if $(x,I) \in V(y:K)$ and $(x,I) \in V(y':K)$, $(x,I) \in V(\lambda y + (1-\lambda)y':K)$. Thus, $V(y:K) \cap V(y':K) \subseteq V(\lambda y + (1-\lambda)y':K)$.

Axioms V.13(a)–(c) postulate several hypotheses on the returns to scale. Each one of these properties is inherited from the corresponding property postulated in T.11.

Next we define subsets of the boundary of $V(y(t):K(t))$: the isoquant set and the efficient set. These subsets are reference sets relative to which efficiency and productivity are measured.

In the static production analysis, the isoquant of the input requirement set is usually a radial concept. In contrast, the isoquant set defined here is a directional concept. Before introducing the concept of the isoquant of the input set, we present the concept of a direction.

Let $z = (x,I) \in \mathfrak{R}_+^N \times \mathfrak{R}_+^F$ and $g = (-g_x, g_I)$, $g_x \in \mathfrak{R}_+^N$, $g_I \in \mathfrak{R}_+^F$, $z + \beta g$ define a line in the direction of g along which the variable input decreases

---

[1] For the sake of a clearer exposition, the time index t is omitted in the proof of this lemma. The time index is also omitted in the other proofs presented later.

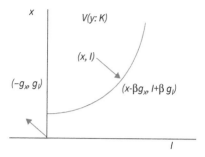

Figure 2.4. The isoquant of V.

and investment increases. Figure 2.4 illustrates the concept of a direction. Notice that this concept is consistent with the strong monotonicity property of $V(y(t){:}K(t))$ in x and the negativity monotonicity property in I.

Definition 2.3: The input isoquant set is a subset of the boundary of $V(y(t){:}K(t))$ defined as

$$Isoq\ V(y(t):K(t)) \equiv \big\{(x(t),I(t)) \in \mathfrak{R}_+^N \times \mathfrak{R}_+^F : (x(t),I(t)) \in V(y(t):K(t)),$$
$$(x(t)-\lambda g_x, I(t)+\lambda g_I) \notin V(y(t):K(t)), \lambda > 0\big\},$$

where $(g_x, g_I) \in \mathfrak{R}_+^N \times \mathfrak{R}_+^F$, $(g_x, g_I) \neq (0_N, 0_F)$ is the direction vector along which the input vector $(x(t), I(t))$ is projected onto the boundary of $V(y(t){:}K(t))$. Note that $IsoqV(0_M : K(t)) = \big\{(0_N, 0_F)\big\}$. The input isoquant is the set of all vectors $(x(t), I(t))$ that can produce $y(t)$, given $K(t)$, yet a contraction of $x(t)$ in the direction of g_x and an expansion of $I(t)$ in the direction of g_I can no longer produce $y(t)$.

Definition 2.4: The efficient input set is a subset of $V(y(t){:}K(t))$ defined as follows:

$$Eff\ V(y(t):K(t)) \equiv \big\{(x(t),I(t)) \in \mathfrak{R}_+^N \times \mathfrak{R}_+^F : (x(t),I(t)) \in V(y(t):K(t)),$$
$$x'(t) \leq x(t),\ I'(t) \geq I(t) \Rightarrow (x'(t),I'(t)) \notin V(y(t):K(t)\big\}.$$

Note that $Eff\ V(0_M : K(t)) = \big\{(0_N, 0_F)\big\}$.

Given definitions 2.3 and 2.4,

$$Eff\,V(y(t):K(t)) \subseteq Isoq\,V(y(t):K(t)) \subset V(y(t):K(t)) \,.$$

Example 2.1: We will illustrate the properties of the production technology using a data set of three firms each producing one output (y) using one variable input (x) and one quasi-fixed factor (K). Investment in the stock of the quasi-fixed factor is denoted by I. The values for y, K, I, and x are presented in Table 2.1.

The data have been constructed such that output and capital are equal for all firms, whereas investment and variable input vary across firms. Keeping output and capital constant allows for illustrating the technology in a two-dimensional figure, where the production technology can be represented by an input requirement set. In this example we will use a piecewise linear technology that is given by

$$V(y:K) = \left\{ (x,I): \; x \geq \sum_{i=1}^{3} \lambda_i x_i; \; I \leq \sum_{i=1}^{3} \lambda_i I_i; \; \sum_{i=1}^{3} \lambda_i = 1; \; \lambda_i \geq 0, \; i = 1,2,3 \right\},$$
$$y \leq 8, \; K \geq 10$$

where λ_i is the weight of the ith firm in constructing the line segments of the technology bounds. Inserting the values of the inputs and outputs, the input requirement set can be rewritten as

$$V(y:K) = \left\{ (x,I): x \geq 2\lambda_1 + 3\lambda_2 + 6\lambda_3; \; I \leq 2\lambda_1 + 4\lambda_2 + 6\lambda_3; \right.$$
$$\left. \lambda_1 + \lambda_2 + \lambda_3 = 1; \; \lambda_i \geq 0 \right\} \tag{2.3}$$
$$y \leq 8, \; K \geq 10\,.$$

Table 2.1 Data of Firms

Firm	Output	Capital	Investment	Variable Input
	(y)	(K)	(I)	(x)
1	8	10	2	2
2	8	10	4	3
3	8	10	6	6

The set $V(y:K)$ is given by the area on and above the isoquant, which consists of the line segments connecting the observations in Figure 2.5.

Some properties of $V(y:K)$ can be illustrated using (2.3) and Figure 2.5. By construction, the input requirement set in (2.3) is closed and bounded from below (V.1 and V.2). The possibility of free lunch (V.5) is excluded as production of the output quantity requires at least two units of variable inputs. Also, investment inactivity (V.6) is allowed for because a value of zero investment (and two units of variable inputs) is part of the technology. Furthermore, strong disposability of the variable input (V.7) and negative monotonicity in investment (V.8) are reflected in the nonnegative slope of the isoquant. The portion of the isoquant with positive slope indicates that the marginal rate of technical substitution between x and I is positive, implying that marginal product of investment is negative (i.e., current investment decreases current production levels). Also, the area above the isoquant represents combinations (x,I) that can produce the same output quantity using more of the variable input and less investment. Convexity of $V(y:K)$ is easily verified from Figure 2.5. Every linear combination of any two pairs of x and I belonging to $V(y:K)$ belongs also to this set.

In addition, the input requirement set specified in (2.3) incorporates properties V.9 and V.10S. Notice that $V(y:K)$ is defined for $K \geq 10$, $y \leq 8$, implying that the output level is nondecreasing in K (V.9) and the output can be disposed of freely (V.10S).

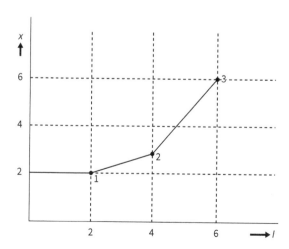

Figure 2.5. Piecewise linear isoquant.

2.2.3 Adjustment Cost Producible Output Sets

Definition 2.5: The adjustment cost technology can be represented by a family of output sets. Each output set (or output correspondence) is defined as

$$P(x(t), I(t) : K(t)) \equiv \left\{ y(t) : (x(t), I(t), y(t)) \in T(K(t)) \right\}.$$

Note that, given definition 2.5, the adjustment cost producible output set can be represented as

$$P(x(t), I(t) : K(t)) = \left\{ y(t) : (x(t), I(t)) \in V(y(t) : K(t)) \right\}. \tag{2.4}$$

In fact, definitions 2.2 and 2.5 yield

$$
\begin{aligned}
(x(t), I(t), y(t)) \in T(K(t)) &\Leftrightarrow (x(t), I(t)) \in V(y(t) : K(t)) \\
&\Leftrightarrow y(t) \in P(x(t), I(t) : K(t)).
\end{aligned} \tag{2.5}
$$

Properties of $P(x(t), I(t):K(t))$:

P.1 $P(x(t), I(t):K(t))$ is a closed, nonempty subset of the M-dimensional space.

P.2 $P(x(t), I(t):K(t))$ is a bounded set.

P.3 $y(t) \notin P(0_N, 0_F : K(t)), y(t) \geq 0, y(t) \neq 0$, or $P(0_N, 0_F : K(t)) = \left\{ 0_M \right\}$.

P.4 $0_M \in P(x(t), I(t) : K(t))$.

P.5 $y(t) \in P(x(t), 0_F : K(t))$.

P.6S If $y(t) \in P(x(t), I(t) : K(t))$ and $y(t)' \leq y(t)$,
$y(t)' \in P(x(t), I(t) : K(t))$.

P.6W If $y(t) \in P(x(t), I(t) : K(t))$ and $0 < \theta \leq 1$ $\theta y(t) \in P(x(t), I(t) : K(t))$.

P.7S If $y(t) \in P(x(t), I(t) : K(t))$ and $x(t)' \geq x(t)$,
$y(t) \in P(x(t)', I(t) : K(t))$, or if $x(t)' \geq x(t)$,
$P(x'(t), I(t) : K(t)) \supseteq P(x(t), I(t) : K(t))$.

P.7W If $y(t) \in P(x(t), I(t) : K(t))$ and $\theta \geq 1$,
then $y(t) \in P(\theta x(t), I(t) : K(t))$ or
$P(x(t), I(t) : K(t)) \subseteq P(\theta x(t), I(t) : K(t)), \theta \geq 1$.

P.8 If $y(t) \in P(x(t), I(t) : K(t))$ and $I(t)' \leq I(t)$, $y(t) \in P(x(t), I(t)' : K(t))$.

P.9 $K(t)' \geq K(t) \Rightarrow P(x(t), I(t) : K(t)) \subset P(x(t), I(t) : K(t)')$.

P.10 $P(x(t), I(t):K(t))$ is a (strictly) convex set; that is,

$$\forall y(t), y'(t) \in P(x(t), I(t):K(t)), \ \forall \alpha \in [0,1], \big[\alpha y(t) + (1-\alpha) y'(t)\big]$$
$$\in P(x(t), I(t):K(t))$$

P.11 $P(x(t), I(t):K(t))$ is quasi-concave in $(x(t), I(t))$;
that is, $\forall (x(t), I(t)), (x'(t), I'(t)) \in \Re_+^N \times \Re_+^F$, if $0 \le \lambda \le 1$,

then $P(x(t), I(t):K(t)) \cap P(x'(t), I'(t):K(t)) \subseteq P(\lambda x(t) +$
$$(1-\lambda) x'(t), \lambda I(t) + (1-\lambda) I'(t))$$

P.12   (a) If $y(t) \in P(x(t), I(t):K(t))$ and $\gamma > 0$,
$\gamma y(t) \in P(\gamma x(t), \gamma I(t):K(t))$.
(b) If $y(t) \in P(x(t), I(t):K(t))$ and $0 < \gamma \le 1$,
$\gamma y(t) \in P(\gamma x(t), \gamma I(t):K(t))$.
(c) If $y(t) \in P(x(t), I(t):K(t))$ and $\gamma \ge 1$, $\gamma y(t) \in P(\gamma x(t), \gamma I(t):K(t))$.

Property P.1 is equivalent to property V.1. Closedness of $P(x(t), I(t):K(t))$ allows the isoquant of the output set to be defined as a subset of the boundary of $P(x(t), I(t):K(t))$. The definition of the isoquant of the adjustment cost output set is presented and discussed later.

Property P.2 is equivalent to axiom V.3, asserting that finite quantities of variable and dynamic factors produce finite quantities of outputs. Axiom P.3 is equivalent to axiom V.5 (no free lunch). Property P.4 can be established using V.4 and axiom P.5 is equivalent to V.6.

Property P.6S is valid if no output is undesirable; that is, all components of vector $y(t)$ have a positive economic or social value (Shephard, 1970). Note that this property is satisfied if and only if V.9S is satisfied. Axiom P.6S implies a nonpositive marginal rate of transformation excluding upward-bending output isoquants.

Property P.6W is equivalent to V.9W; that is, property P.6W is satisfied if and only if property V.9W is satisfied. This property is important in the presence of congestion or in the case of undesirable outputs (e.g., pollution) in the production process and regulation (e.g., environmental regulation) that constrains the capacity of the production units to dispose of those outputs without cost. The weak monotonicity property in $y(t)$ implies that reducing an undesirable output requires decreasing simultaneously a desirable output.

Reduction of an undesirable output utilizes productive resources whose opportunity cost can be expressed in terms of lost production of desirable outputs. Property P.6W allows undesirable outputs to be elements of $y(t)$ with nonpositive shadow prices. In contrast to P.6S, this property allows isoquants of the output set with positive slope.

P.7S (P.7W) is equivalent to V.7S (V.7W). Axioms P.8 and P.9 are equivalent, respectively, to V.8 and V.10. Both axioms assert that current changes in the dynamic factors decrease current levels of outputs but increase output levels in the future by increasing the future stock of capitals.

Axiom P.10 postulates (strict) convexity of $P(x(t), I(t):K(t))$. If $T(K(t))$ is convex (property T.10(a)), then $P(x(t),I(t):K(t))$ is a convex set, as shown in the following proposition.

Proposition 2.3: If $T(K(t))$ is a convex set, then $P(x(t),I(t):K(t))$ is convex.

Proof of proposition 2.3: Assume $T(.)$ is a convex set. If (x,I,y), $(x,I,y') \in T(K)$, $[(x,I,\alpha y + (1-\alpha)y')] \in T(K)$. This is equivalent to stating the following: if $y \in P(x,I:K)$ and $y' \in P(x,I:K)$, then $[\alpha y + (1-\alpha)y'] \in P(x,I:K)$.

Yet, convexity of the adjustment cost output set does not imply convexity of $T(K(t))$. Property P.10 is equivalent to property V.12 (i.e., quasi-concavity of $V(y(t):K(t))$ in $y(t)$). Note that convexity of the adjustment cost output set, $P(x(t), I(t):K(t))$, is not equivalent to convexity of the input set, $V(y(t):K(t))$. The convexity property of $P(x(t), I(t):K(t))$ is equivalent to the assumption of an increasing marginal rate of transformation.

Property P.11 is equivalent to property V.11 (convexity of the input set). Property T.10(a) implies P.11, but the converse is not true.

Proposition 2.4: If $T(K(t))$ is convex, then $P(x(t), I(t):K(t))$ is a quasi-concave set in $(x(t), I(t))$.

Proof of proposition 2.4: Assume $T(K)$ is a convex set. If (x,I,y), $(x',I',y) \in T(K)$, $[(\lambda x + (1-\lambda)x', \lambda I + (1-\lambda)I', y)] \in T(K)$. This means that if $y \in P(x,I:K)$ and $y \in P(x',I':K)$, then $y \in P(\lambda x + (1-\lambda)x', \lambda I + (1-\lambda)I':K)$. Thus, $P(x,I:K) \cap P(x',I':K) \subseteq P(\lambda x + (1-\lambda)x', \lambda I + (1-\lambda)I':K)$.

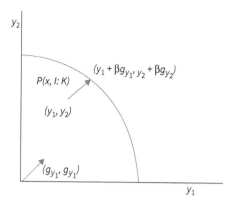

Figure 2.6. The isoquant of $P(x,I{:}K)$.

If $T(K(t))$ is convex, then $P(x(t), I(t){:}K(t))$ is a quasi-concave correspondence in $(x(t),\ I(t))$. Yet, quasi-concavity of $P(x(t),I(t){:}K(t))$ does not imply convexity of the adjustment cost production possibilities set.

We now define two subsets of the boundary of the output correspondence: the isoquant set and the efficient set. We adopt a directional representation of the output isoquant set. The directional representation of the output isoquant set embeds the radial representation, used in the static production analysis, as a special case.

Before introducing the concept of the isoquant of the output set, we present the concept of a direction. Let $y \in \Re_{+}^{M}$ and $g_{y} \in \Re_{+}^{M}$, $y + \beta g_{y}$ define a line in the direction of g_{y}. Figure 2.6 illustrates the concept of a direction in the output space.

Definition 2.6: The output isoquant set is a subset of $P(x(t),I(t){:}K(t))$ defined as follows:

$$Isoq\ P(x(t),I(t):K(t)) \equiv \Big\{ y(t) \in \Re_{+}^{M} : y(t) \in P(x(t),I(t):K(t)),$$
$$y(t) + \lambda g_{y} \notin P(x(t),I(t):K(t)),\ \lambda > 0 \Big\},$$

where $g_{y} \in \Re_{+}^{M}$, $g_{y} \neq 0_{M}$ is the direction vector along which the output vector $y(t)$ is projected onto the boundary of the adjustment cost output set. Note that $Isoq\,P(0_{N},0_{F}:K(t)) = \{0_{M}\}$. The output isoquant is the set of all output vectors that can be produced using the input vector $(x(t),\ I(t))$, given $K(t)$, yet an expansion of $y(t)$ in the direction of g_{y} is no longer feasible with $(x(t), I(t))$.

The radial representation of the output isoquant set is a special case of $Isoq\, P(x(t), I(t) : K(t))$ in definition 2.5. If $g_y = y(t)$, the output isoquant set in definition 2.5 is represented as follows:

$$Isoq\, P(x(t), I(t) : K(t)) = \Big\{ y(t) \in \Re_+^M : y(t) \in P(x(t), I(t) : K(t)),$$
$$y(t)(1 + \lambda) \notin P(x(t), I(t) : K(t)), \lambda > 0 \Big\}; \quad (2.6)$$

that is, the isoquant set is the set of all vectors $y(t)$ that can be produced with the input vector $(x(t),\ I(t))$, given $K(t)$, yet a proportional increase in the output levels is no longer feasible with $(x(t),\ I(t))$.

Definition 2.7: The efficient output set is a subset of the adjustment cost producible output set defined as

$$Eff\, P(x(t), I(t) : K(t)) \equiv \Big\{ y(t) \in \Re_+^M : y(t) \in P(x(t), I(t) : K(t)),$$
$$y(t)' \geq y(t) \Rightarrow y(t)' \notin P(x(t), I(t) : K(t)) \Big\}.$$

Note that $Eff\, P(0_N, 0_F : K(t)) = \{0_M\}$.

Given definitions 2.6 and 2.7, $Isoq\, P(x(t), I(t) : K(t)) \subseteq Eff\, P(x(t), I(t) : K(t))$. Figure 2.7 illustrates these two sets in the case of two outputs, where area abc reflects the $IsoqP(x(t),\ I(t):K(t))$ and area bc is $Eff\, P(x(t),\ I(t):K(t))$.

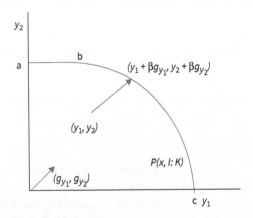

Figure 2.7. The *EFF* P(x,I:K) and *Isoq* P(x,I:K).

2.3 The Adjustment Cost Transformation Function

The term "production function" is typically reserved for the case of a single output. When multiple inputs and multiple outputs characterize a production technology, a transformation function can be defined.

Definition 2.8: The adjustment cost transformation function is a function $F: \mathfrak{R}_+^N \times \mathfrak{R}_+^F \times \mathfrak{R}_+^M \times \mathfrak{R}_+^F \to \mathfrak{R}$ defined as $F(x(t), I(t), y(t), K(t)) \leq 0$.

By allowing the inequality $F(x(t), I(t), y(t), K(t)) \leq 0$, we permit the possibility that a firm is not fully optimizing its technical production potential. We analyze the properties of the adjustment cost transformation function and the relationship between the adjustment cost production possibilities set, $T(K(t))$, and this function.

Properties of $F(x(t), I(t), y(t), K(t))$: If the adjustment cost production possibilities set $T(K(t))$ satisfies properties T.1–T.5, T.6S, T.7S, T.8, T.9, and T.10(a), the adjustment cost transformation function satisfies the following properties:

F.1 $F(0_N, 0_F, y(t), K(t)) > 0$, $y(t) \geq 0_M$, $y(t) \neq 0_M$.

F.2 $F(x(t), I(t), 0_M, K(t)) < 0$.

F.3 $F(x(t), 0_F, y(t), K(t)) \leq 0$.

F.4   If $F(x(t), I(t), y(t), K(t)) \leq 0$ and $y(t)' \leq y(t)$,
then $F(x(t), I(t), y(t)', K(t)) \leq 0$ and
$F(x(t), I(t), y(t)', K(t)) \leq F(x(t), I(t), y(t), K(t))$;
that is, $F(.)$ is nondecreasing in $y(t)$.

F.5   If $F(x(t), I(t), y(t), K(t)) \leq 0$ and $x(t)' \geq x(t)$,
then $F(x(t)', I(t), y(t), K(t)) \leq 0$ and
$F(x(t)', I(t), y(t), K(t)) \leq F(x(t), I(t), y(t), K(t))$;
that is, $F(.)$ is nonincreasing in $x(t)$.

F.6   If $F(x(t), I(t), y(t), K(t)) \leq 0$ and $I(t)' \leq I(t)$,
then $F(x(t), I(t)', y(t), K(t)) \leq 0$ and
$F(x(t), I(t)', y(t), K(t)) \leq F(x(t), I(t), y(t), K(t))$;
that is, $F(.)$ is nondecreasing in $I(t)$.

F.7   If $F(x(t), I(t), y(t), K(t)) \leq 0$ and $K(t)' \geq K(t)$,
then $F(x(t), I(t), y(t), K(t)') \leq 0$ and

$$F(x(t), I(t), y(t), K(t)') \leq F(x(t), I(t), y(t), K(t));$$

that is, $F(.)$ is nonincreasing in $K(t)$.

F.8   If $T(K(t))$ is a (strict) convex set, then $F(x(t), I(t), y(t), K(t))$ is a (strict) convex function in $(x(t), I(t), y(t))$.

F.9 $F(x(t), I(t), y(t), K(t))$ is a continuous function in $(x(t), I(t), y(t))$.

Proof of properties F.1–F.9:

F.1   This property follows from T.4.

F.2   This property follows from T.3.

F.3   This property follows from T.5.

F.4   Property T.6S requires that if $F(x, I, y, K) \leq 0$, then $F(x, I, y', K) \leq 0$ for $y' \leq y$. Suppose that $y \in Isoq\, P(x, I : K)$. Then, $F(x, I, y, K) = 0$. Thus, for the desired inequality to hold, $F(x, I, y, K)$ cannot be decreasing in y.

F.5   Property T.7S requires that if $F(x, I, y, K) \leq 0$, then $F(x', I, y, K) \leq 0$ for $x' \geq x$. Suppose that $(x, I) \in Isoq\, V(y : K)$. Then, $F(x, I, y, K) = 0$. Hence, for the desired inequality to hold, $F(x, I, y, K)$ cannot be increasing in x.

F.6   This property follows from T.8. The proof is similar to the proof of F.5.

F.7   Property T.9 requires that if $F(x, I, y, K) \leq 0$, then $F(x, I, y, K') \leq 0$ for $K' \geq K$. Suppose $F(x, I, y, K) = 0$. For the desired inequality to hold, $F(x, I, y, K)$ cannot be increasing in K.

F.8   We prove that if $T(K)$ is convex, $F(x, I, y, K)$ is a convex function. Strict convexity can be proved in a similar fashion. Assume that $(x, I, y), (x', I', y') \in T(K)$. Then, $F(x, I, y, K) \leq 0$ and $F(x', I', y', K) \leq 0$. By the convexity property of $T(.)$, $F(x'', I'', y'', K) \leq 0$, where $x'' = \alpha x + (1 - \alpha)x'$, $I'' = \alpha I + (1 - \alpha)I'$, and $y'' = \alpha y + (1 - \alpha)y'$ for $\alpha \in [0,1]$. Thus, it must be the case that $F(x'', I'', y'', K) \leq \alpha F(x, I, y, K) + (1 - \alpha)F(x', I', y', K)$.

F.9   This property follows from property F.8.

On the other hand, suppose that we are given the adjustment cost transformation function $F(x(t), I(t), y(t), K(t))$ satisfying conditions F.1–F.9. The production possibilities set $\tilde{T}(K(t))$ corresponding to $F(x(t), I(t), y(t), K(t))$ may be defined as

$$\hat{T}(K(t)) \equiv \left\{ (x(t), I(t), y(t)) : F(x(t), I(t), y(t), K(t)) \leq 0 \right\}. \qquad (2.7)$$

Properties of $\hat{T}(K(t))$:

$\hat{T}.1$ $\hat{T}(K(t))$ is a closed, nonempty subset of $M+N+F$-dimensional space.

$\hat{T}.2$ $\hat{T}(K(t))$ is bounded from above.

$\hat{T}.3$ $(x(t), I(t), 0_M) \in \hat{T}(K(t))$.

$\hat{T}.4$ $(0_N, 0_F, y(t)) \notin \hat{T}(0_F)$.

$\hat{T}.5$ $(x(t), 0_F, y(t)) \in \hat{T}(K(t))$.

$\hat{T}.6$ If $(x(t), I(t), y(t)) \in \hat{T}(K(t))$ and $y(t)' \le y(t)$,
then $(x(t), I(t), y(t)') \in \hat{T}(K(t))$.

$\hat{T}.7$ If $(x(t), I(t), y(t)) \in \hat{T}(K(t))$ and $x(t)' \ge x(t)$,
then $(x(t)', I(t), y(t)) \in \hat{T}(K(t))$.

$\hat{T}.8$ If $(x(t), I(t), y(t)) \in \hat{T}(K(t))$ and $I(t)' \le I(t)$,
then $(x(t), I(t)', y(t)) \in \hat{T}(K(t))$.

$\hat{T}.9$ If $(x(t), I(t), y(t)) \in \hat{T}(K(t))$ and $K(t)' \ge K(t)$, then
$(x(t), I(t), y(t)) \in \hat{T}(K(t)')$ or $K(t)' \ge K(t) \Rightarrow \hat{T}(K(t)) \subset \hat{T}(K(t)')$.

$\hat{T}.10$ $\hat{T}(K(t))$ is a convex set.

Proof of properties $\hat{T}.1$–$\hat{T}.10$:

$\hat{T}.1$ Follows from property F.9 and definition of $\hat{T}(K(t))$ in (2.7).

$\hat{T}.2$ Follows from property F.9 and definition of $\hat{T}(K(t))$ in (2.7).

$\hat{T}.3$ Follows from property F.2 and definition of $\hat{T}(K(t))$ in (2.7),
$(x(t), I(t), 0_M) \in \hat{T}(K(t))$

$\hat{T}.4$ Follows from property F.1 and definition $\hat{T}(K(t))$ in (2.7),
$(0_N, 0_F, y(t)) \notin \hat{T}(0_F)$

$\hat{T}.5$ Follows from property F.3 and definition $\hat{T}(K(t))$ in (2.7),
$(x(t), 0_F, y(t)) \in \hat{T}(K(t))$

$\hat{T}.6$ Follows from property F.3 and definition $\hat{T}(K(t))$ in (2.7)

$\hat{T}.7$ Follows from property F.5 and definition $\hat{T}(K(t))$ in (2.7)

$\hat{T}.8$ Follows from property F.6 and definition $\hat{T}(K(t))$ in (2.7)

$\hat{T}.9$ Follows from property F.7 and definition $\hat{T}(K(t))$ in (2.7)

$\hat{T}.10$ Follows from property F.8 and definition $\hat{T}(K(t))$ in (2.7)

Properties of $\hat{T}(K(t))$ are derived from the properties of $F(x(t), I(t), y(t), K(t))$ and coincide with the properties of $T(K(t))$, used to establish the properties of the adjustment cost transformation function. Hence, $\hat{T}(K(t)) = T(K(t))$. Consequently, we can re-express $V(y(t):K(t))$ and $P(x(t), I(t):K(t))$ in terms of $F(x(t), I(t), y(t), K(t))$:

$$V(y(t):K(t)) = \left\{ x(t) \in \Re_+^N : F(x(t), I(t), y(t), K(t)) \leq 0 \right\}, \qquad (2.8)$$

$$P(x(t), I(t):K(t)) = \left\{ y(t) \in \Re_+^M : F(x(t), I(t), y(t), K(t)) \leq 0 \right\}. \qquad (2.9)$$

Property T.11 of $T(K(t))$ postulates three hypotheses with respect to returns to scale: constant returns to scale (T.11(a)), nonincreasing returns to scale (T.11(b)), and nondecreasing returns to scale (T.11(c)). Each hypothesis corresponds to a global definition of returns to scale. A local measure of returns to scale can be generated using the adjustment cost transformation function $F(x(t), I(t), y(t), K(t))$. The returns to scale emerge from a proportional change in inputs, λ, and a proportional change in outputs, θ:

$$F(\lambda x(t), \lambda I(t), \theta y(t), K(t)) = 0. \qquad (2.10)$$

If $F(x(t), I(t), y(t), K(t))$ is differentiable in $(x(t), I(t), y(t))$, the elasticity of scale at time t can be defined as

$$\varepsilon(x(t), I(t), y(t), K(t)) = \frac{\partial \ln \theta}{\partial \ln \lambda} \bigg|_{\theta = \lambda = 1}. \qquad (2.11)$$

Applying the implicit function rule to (2.10) yields

$$
\begin{aligned}
\varepsilon(x(t), I(t), y(t), K(t)) &= \frac{\partial \ln \theta}{\partial \ln \lambda} \big|_{\theta = \lambda = 1} \\
&= -\frac{\sum_{n=1}^{N} \partial F(.)/\partial x_n \cdot x_n + \sum_{f=1}^{F} \partial F(.)/\partial I_f \cdot I_f}{\sum_{m=1}^{M} \partial F(.)/\partial y_m \cdot y_m} \\
&= \frac{\nabla_x F(.) \cdot x + \nabla_I F(.) \cdot I}{\nabla_y F(.) \cdot y}
\end{aligned} \qquad (2.12)
$$

where ∇ denotes the gradient.

If $\varepsilon(x(t), I(t), y(t), K(t)) = 1$, then the production technology exhibits constantreturnstoscalein $(x(t), I(t), y(t), K(t))$. If $\varepsilon(x(t), I(t), y(t), K(t)) > 1 \, (<1)$, then the technology exhibits increasing (decreasing) returns to scale in $(x(t), I(t), y(t), K(t))$.

The adjustment cost production function is a particular case of the transformation function.

Definition 2.9: The adjustment cost production function is a function $f : \Re_+^N \to \Re_+$ defined as

$$
\begin{aligned}
f(x(t), I(t), K(t)) &= \max\left\{ y(t) \in \Re_+ : (x(t), I(t), y(t)) \in T(K(t)) \right\} \\
&= \max\left\{ y(t) \in \Re_+ : y(t) \in P(x(t), I(t) : K(t)) \right\} \quad . \\
&= \max\left\{ y(t) \in \Re_+ : (x(t), I(t)) \in V(y(t) : K(t)) \right\}
\end{aligned}
$$

Properties of $f(x(t), I(t), K(t))$:

f.1 $f(0_N, 0_F, K(t)) = 0$.

f.2   If $y(t) = f(x(t), I(t), K(t))$ and $y(t) > 0$, then $\exists x_n(t) > 0, K_f(t) > 0$.

f.3 $f(x(t), I(t), K(t))$ is a finite number,
        $\forall (x(t), I(t), K(t)) \in \Re_+^N \times \Re_+^F \times \Re_+^F$.

f.4   If $(x(t), I(t), y(t)) \in T(K(t))$ and $x(t)' \geq x(t)$,
        $f(x'(t), I(t), K(t)) \geq f(x(t), I(t), K(t))$.

f.5   If $(x(t), I(t), y(t)) \in T(K(t))$ and $I(t)' \leq I(t)$,
        $f(x(t), I(t)', K(t)) \geq f(x(t), I(t), K(t))$.

f.6   If $(x(t), I(t), y(t)) \in T(K(t))$ and $K(t)' \geq K(t)$,
        $f(x(t), I(t), K(t)') \geq f(x(t), I(t), K(t))$.

f.7   If $T(K(t))$ is a convex set, $f(x(t), I(t), K(t))$ is a concave function in
        $(x(t), I(t))$.[2]

f.8 $f(x(t), I(t), K(t))$ is a continuous function in $(x(t), I(t))$.

Proof of properties f.1–f.8:

f.1   This property follows from T.3 and T.4.

f.2   This property follows from T.4 and T.5.

f.3   This property follows from T.1 and T.2. Properties T.1 and T.2
        assure the existence of a maximum in definition 2.9. Equivalently,
        this property follows from properties V.1 and V.3 of the adjustment
        cost input requirement sets or properties P.1 and P.2 of the produ-
        cible output sets.

f.4   This property follows from T.7S.

f.5   This property follows from T.8.

---

[2] We can weaken this axiom or property, stating that $f(.)$ is quasi-concave in $(x(t), I(t))$ if, and only if, $V(y(t):K(t))$ is a convex set. In this case, convexity of $T(K(t))$ is not required.

f.6   This property follows from T.9.

f.7   Assume that $f(x,I,K)=y$ and $f(x',I',K)=y'$. By the
       convexity property of $T(.)$, $(x'',I'',y'')\in T(K(t))$, where
       $x''=\alpha x+(1-\alpha)x'$, $I''=\alpha I+(1-\alpha)I'$, and $y''=\alpha y+(1-\alpha)y'$
       for $\alpha\in[0,1]$. By definition 2.7, it must be the case that
       $f(x'',I'',K)\geq y''=\alpha f(x,I,K)+(1-\alpha)f(x',I',K)$.

f.8   This property follows from property f.7.

Note that property f.5 reflects the adjustment costs associated with gross investment. In contrast, property f.6 asserts that output level is nondecreasing in the quasi-fixed factors. These properties imply that current additions to the capital stock are output decreasing in the current period but increase output level in the future by increasing the future stock of capital. Concavity of the production function (property f.7) implies the more rapidly the quasi-fixed factors are adjusted, the greater the cost, leading to sluggish adjustment in the quasi-fixed factors.

Example 2.2: Consider the following data of a sample of three firms.
The data have been constructed such that capital and variable input use are constant and only the values of output and investment vary across firms (Table 2.2). This allows for a graphical illustration of the technology in a two-dimensional figure. The piecewise linear technology of this sample is given by the curve in Figure 2.8.

Figure 2.8 illustrates clearly properties f.5 and f.7. As Figure 2.8 shows, the output level is decreasing in I (i.e., the marginal product of investment is negative), reflecting the presence of adjustment costs associated with gross investment (property f.5). Moreover, Figure 2.8 indicates that the production function is concave in I (property f.7).

Example 2.3: Consider the following information on the adjustment path of three firms, assuming the production technology is the same for all of them and, for the sake of simplification, there is no capital depreciation. Suppose also that there is no technical change.

All three firms produce the same output with the same combination of all factors of production at $t=0$. Furthermore, all three firms end with the same output level and the same capital stock level.

Table 2.2 Data Generated for Three Hypothetical Firms

Firm	Output	Capital	Investment	Variable Input
	(y)	(K)	(I)	(x)
1	8	10	2	2
2	7	10	4	2
3	5	10	6	2

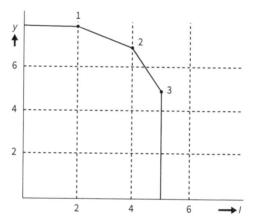

Figure 2.8 Piecewise linear technology in the (y, I) space.

The investment level is constant over time for firm A and it takes six time periods to have a capital stock of 16 units and an output level of 31 units. Firm B chooses to increase substantially the investment level at $t = 1$ and then keeps investment constant and equal to 1 unit. This firm takes three time periods to build to a capital stock of 16 units and an output level equal to 31 units. The increase in the investment level at $t = 1$ depresses substantially the output level to 6 units but firm B reaches an output and capital stock levels at $t = 2$, which takes five time periods for firm A to reach these same levels. For firm C, the investment level increases from 1 unit to 2 units for two periods and then decreases to 1 unit in the next two periods. Firm C takes four time periods to have a capital stock of 16 units and an output level of 31 units.

From Table 2.3 (panel A), for firm A, we can infer that the marginal product of the capital stock, $\Delta Y/\Delta K$, is positive and, in this case, is equal to two. The nonnegativity of the marginal product of the quasi-fixed factors reflects property f.6 of the adjustment cost production function, which states that the

Table 2.3 Production and Investment Trajectories for Three Firms

			Panel A		
Firm A		Y	x	I	K
t = 0	A_0	19	2	1	10
t = 1	A_1	21	2	1	11
t = 2	A_2	23	2	1	12
t = 3	A_3	25	2	1	13
t = 4	A_4	27	2	1	14
t = 5	A_5	29	2	1	15
t = 6	A_6	31	2	1	16
			Panel B		
Firm B		Y	x	I	K
t = 0	B_0	19	2	1	10
t = 1	B_1	6	2	4	11
t = 2	B_2	29	2	1	15
t = 3	B_3	31	2	1	16
			Panel C		
Firm C		Y	x	I	K
t = 0	C_0	19	2	1	10
t = 1	C_1	21	2	1	11
t = 2	C_2	20	2	2	12
t = 3	C_3	24	2	2	14
t = 4	C_4	31	2	1	16

output level is nondecreasing in K (or, alternatively, property V.9 of the input requirement set or property P.9 of the producible output set). Also, production points C_0 and C_1 and C_2 and C_3 in Table 2.3 (panel C) for firm C can be used to compute the marginal product of the quasi-fixed factors. Between points C_0 and C_1 as well as C_2 and C_3, the marginal product of K is equal to two. Given that the production technology is common to all the firms, other points could be used to compute the marginal product of K (e.g., points C_1 and B_2).

Next, we compute the marginal product of investment between some points of the adjustment cost production technology (Table 2.4).

The marginal product of investment is negative, reflecting the property that the output level is nonincreasing in I (i.e., property f.5 of the production function or properties V.8 and P.8, respectively, of the adjustment cost input requirement set and the producible output set). A negative marginal product of investment indicates the existence of internal adjustment costs.

Measuring adjustment costs has been the focus of several studies that include (but are not limited to) Gardebroek and Oude Lansink (2005), Hall (2004), and Groth (2008). The empirical results are diverse. Groth (2008) found evidence of significant adjustment costs in the UK manufacturing and service industry, and results indicate that adjustment costs may have caused half of the deceleration in UK total factor productivity growth during the second half of the 1990s. Gardebroek and Oude Lansink (2005) found that adjustment costs are an important determinant in investment for buildings (and not for machinery) using data on Dutch pig farms. Hall (2004) found evidence of low adjustment costs in both capital and labor in US manufacturing industries over the period 1949–2000, yet the estimates are biased due to specification errors.

Table 2.4 Marginal Product of Investment

	$\Delta Y/\Delta I$
A_1 and B_1	−4
A_4 and B_2	−3
A_2 and C_2	−2
A_4 and C_3	−3
B_1 and C_1	−4

2.4 Remarks

Many economic decisions are intertemporal (e.g., firms' investment decisions) in the sense that current decisions affect not only the firms' current choices but also their choices available in the future. Investment in quasi-fixed factors is the purchasing by firms of newly produced machinery, factories, and the like to increase the output level that can be potentially produced in the future. Thus, this is an intertemporal choice. For this reason, a dynamic or intertemporal analysis distinguishes itself from a multiperiod analysis. A dynamic analysis involves obviously a multiperiod analysis, but the reverse is not true. A multiperiod analysis may not necessarily involve an intertemporal tradeoff. An interesting survey on the intertemporal behavior of the firm using the concept of adjustment costs is presented in Galeotti (1996).

This chapter characterizes the nature of production in the case of adjustment costs. The dynamics of intertemporal production and investment decisions emerge from the presence of internal adjustment costs requiring the balancing between current losses and future gains (i.e., an intertemporal tradeoff). Internal adjustment costs are specified as a negative impact of current investment on the current production level (current loss) and a positive impact in the future production possibilities through investment's enhancement of the future capital stock (future gains). The next chapters build upon this foundation to address how economic decision making adapts to this technological environment and then how to measure decision-making performance when decisions are linked over time.

Several primal representations of the production technology are presented and characterized axiomatically in the presence of internal adjustment costs. For those not familiar with the axiomatic approach to production technology, please see Shephard (1953, 1970) and Debreu (1959), where production axioms are discussed in a static framework.

In the presence of adjustment costs (i.e., internal adjustment costs), the production function has been the most used primal representation of the production technology. Studies using the adjustment cost production function include (but are not limited to) Epstein (1981), Stefanou (1989), Luh and Stefanou (1996), Lasserre and Ouellette (1999), Ouellette and Vigeant (2000, 2001), Hall (2004), Gardebroek (2004), Rungsuriyawiboon and Stefanou (2007, 2008), Wibe (2008), Groth (2008), and Rungsuriyawiboon and Zhang

(2018). Luh and Stefanou (1991, 1993) employ an adjustment cost transformation function and the duality between this function and the optimal value function (long-run profit function) to evaluate total factor productivity growth in the US agricultural sector. Luh and Stefanou (1993) consider additionally the acquisition of learning as a firm-specific capital factor (with other conventional inputs) and evaluate its impact on productivity growth.

Several (theoretical and empirical) studies use other primal representations of the adjustment cost production technology. Nemoto and Goto (1999, 2003), Ouellette and Yan (2008), and Ouellette et al. (2010), for example, employ the adjustment cost production possibilities set to generate measures of productive inefficiency. Silva and Stefanou (2003, 2007) and Silva et al. (2015) employ a family of adjustment cost input requirement sets to characterize the production technology. Silva and Stefanou (2007) construct and characterize a hyperbolic input measure of productive efficiency based on a family of adjustment cost input requirement sets and its properties; Silva et al. (2015) define and characterize the adjustment cost directional input distance function (which is analyzed in Chapter 4) using the definition of the adjustment cost input requirement set and its properties.

3
Dynamic Economic Decision Making

3.1 Introduction

Static optimization models cannot fully account for the balancing of the marginal gains (losses) of current decisions against the marginal losses (gains) to future profitability. The dynamic optimization techniques can be implemented to more fully characterize firm investment behavior. To start, the techniques of the calculus of variations and optimal control are briefly presented. No attempt is made to offer proofs of the optimization conditions. The characterization and interpretation of the dynamic problem are emphasized.[1]

Greater emphasis is placed on the dynamic programming approach. This approach has considerable potential in applying dynamic optimization techniques to address theoretical and empirical measurement of dynamic economic adjustment characteristics in both deterministic and stochastic settings. The dynamic programming approach will be the focus of many of the topics presented in the chapters to follow.

Classical optimization is concerned with the maximization or minimization of a function of several variables, $f(x)$. For the single variable unconstrained case, the procedure is to find one (or more) values of the choice variable x such that $f(x)$ is optimized. For a function with continuous first

---

[1] Many books offer complete presentations of the calculus of variations and optimal control theory, such as those by Intriligator (1971), Fleming and Rishel (1975), Kamien and Schwartz (1981), Takayama (1985), Seierstad and Sydsaeter (1987), Léonard and Van Long (1992), and Caputo (2005). Bellman (1959) introduces the theory of dynamic programming, which is also presented in some of the optimal control theory references. Inequality constraints are considered by Spence and Starrett (1975) and Clark (1976) for the calculus of variations and by Kamien and Schwartz (1971) for optimal control theory. Dorfman (1969) and Clark (1976) offer excellent discussions on the economic interpretations of optimal control theory. Sufficient conditions in optimal control can be found in Kamien and Schwartz (1971) and Seierstad and Sydsaeter (1987) for both the standard control problems and the case of corner solutions for the controls. Benveniste and Scheinkman (1979) identify the sufficient conditions to guarantee that the value function is differentiable.

Dynamic Efficiency and Productivity Measurement. Elvira Silva, Spiro E. Stefanou, and Alfons Oude Lansink,
Oxford University Press (2021). © Oxford University Press. DOI: 10.1093/oso/9780190919474.001.0001

derivatives, these values satisfy $f_x(x) = 0$ with the maxima and minima values distinguished by checking the sign of the second derivative. The calculus of variations is a mathematical theory developed from a solution of a single problem offered as a challenge by Johann Bernoulli in 1696 to the mathematicians of his time (Courant and Robbins, 1941). To easily visualize the famous brachistochrone problem posed, consider a bead sliding down a wire under the influence of gravity alone. The goal is to find the shape of the wire (i.e., the trajectory) to minimize the time it takes the bead to travel from one given point to another given point. Johann Bernoulli particularly directed his challenge at his older brother Jakob, with whom he was locked in a bitter feud. While many prominent mathematicians of that time offered solutions (including Newton, Leibnitz, L'Hospital, and Johann Bernoulli), Jakob's solution surpassed all other solutions. His solution recognized that the selection among an infinity of possible curves to minimize the travel time was a new type of problem requiring the invention of new methods. Years later, Leonard Euler (a student of Johann Bernoulli!) used Jakob's solution to develop the calculus of variations. In the calculus of variations, magnitudes depend on functions rather than the values of variables. Such magnitudes are functions of functions and are known as functionals.

To illustrate, consider the area between the x axis and a curve $y = f(x)$ ranging between $x = a$ and $x = b$. This area is given by

$$A = \int_a^b f(x)dx. \tag{3.1}$$

As Figure 3.1 illustrates, the area depends on the specification of $f(x)$. For example, area A is larger for $f^{(1)}(x)$ than for $f^{(2)}(x)$. Now imagine 100 different curves of the sort illustrated in Figure 3.1 and calculate the areas for each choice of the function $f^{(j)}(x)$, $j = 1, \ldots, 100$, between $x = a$ and $x = b$. Generally, there may be one function for which the area is greater (of course, there may be more than one). Thus, the maximization of the area involves finding the one function that maximizes the integral A from among the 100 different functions.

The calculus of variations requires the differentiability of the functions that enter in the problem, and consequently, only interior solutions can be handled. Optimal control theory can easily deal with nonclassical features such as corner solutions. While the goal of the calculus of variations is to

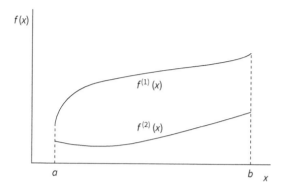

Figure 3.1. Family of potential trajectories.

determine the optimal time path for a state variable, optimal control theory focuses on the choice of the optimal time path for a control variable, $u(t)$, which affects the state variable, $K(t)$, via a state equation (or equation of motion):

$$\dot{K}(t) = f\big(K(t), u(t)\big), \tag{3.2}$$

where $\dot{K}(t) = \dfrac{dK(t)}{dt}$ is the time derivative of the state variable.

The objective is to choose the control variable to optimize (in this case to maximize):

$$\max_{u \in U} \int_t^T G(K(s), u(s))dt, \tag{3.3}$$

subject to the equation of motion (3.2), with the initial value of the state usually known, $K(t) = k$. U is some bounded set of admissible controls, and the terminal value for the state variable, $K(T)$, may be specified or not.

The optimal control approach has several advantages over the calculus of variations. Defining u in terms of $\dot{K}$ allows a broad range of functional relationships between controls and states. By specifying the controls, u, one may explicitly account for control costs in the objective functional. Thus, $G(K(s), u(s))$ automatically optimizes the net effect of control action benefits on K and the control costs. The optimal control approach also introduces a function—known as the costate—which associates a value to the marginal changes in the state variable at each instant.

The maximum principle (or Pontryagin conditions) of optimal control theory requires the formation of an expression reflecting the value of the current decision to the flow of gains known as the Hamiltonian at time t and defined for $K(t) = k$ as

$$H(k,u,\lambda) = \max_{u \in U} \left\{ G(k,u(t)) + \lambda f(k,u(t)) \right\}. \qquad (3.4)$$

In this expression, λ is an additional unknown variable referred to as the costate or adjoint variable. The necessary conditions for optimality are

$$H(k,u,\lambda) = \max_{u \in U} \left\{ G(k,u(t)) + \lambda f(k,u(t)) \right\}, \qquad (3.5)$$

$$H_k = -\dot{\lambda}, \qquad (3.6)$$

$$H_\lambda = \dot{K}, \qquad (3.7)$$

plus transversality conditions if the initial value or the terminal value of the state variable (or both) is not (are not) specified.

These conditions must hold at every point in time along the time horizon. In fact, this approach to solving the dynamic optimization problem allows us to decompose the dynamic problem into a sequence of optimization problems that are executed over the control space rather than over a space of functions of the current state, as is the case with the calculus of variations. Equation (3.5) requires the value of u to maximize the Hamiltonian over all admissible values of u, and with an interior solution this implies $H_u = G_u + \lambda f_u = 0$, supported by an appropriate second-order condition. Equations (3.6) and (3.7), respectively, are the equation of motion for the costate variable and the equation of motion for the state variable.

Taking a historical step back, the calculus of variations seeks a function of K to maximize a functional. The classic statement of the calculus of variations problems is

$$\max_{K} \int_{t_0}^{t_1} G(K,\dot{K}) dt, \qquad (3.8)$$

where the integrand, $G(K,\dot{K})$, is the flow of benefits; $K(t)$ reflects the memory, or state of the system up to time t; $\dot{K}$ reflects the motion over time; and $K(t_0)$ as well as the starting and end points (t_0, t_1) are known. This is a special case of the optimal control problem where the time rate of change in the state is the control variable, $\dot{K}(t) = f\big(K(t), u(t)\big) = u$, rather than a more general function that can include K.

Recognizing that $G(K,u) = G(K,\dot{K})$, the maximum principle in (3.5) is

$$H = G(K,u) + \lambda u, \tag{3.9}$$

and upon optimizing the Hamiltonian and using $\dot{K}(t) = u$,

$$H_u = H_{\dot{K}} = G_u + \lambda = 0, \tag{3.10}$$

implying

$$G_{\dot{K}}(K,\dot{K}) = -\lambda. \tag{3.11}$$

The costate equation in (3.6) becomes

$$H_K = G_K(u,K) = -\dot{\lambda}. \tag{3.12}$$

Upon differentiating (3.11) with respect to time, we have

$$G_{\dot{K}\dot{K}}(K,\dot{K})\ddot{K} + G_{K\dot{K}}(K,\dot{K})\dot{K} = -\dot{\lambda}. \tag{3.13}$$

And using (3.12) in (3.13) results in the fundamental equation of optimization for the calculus of variation approach, known as the Euler-Lagrange equation:

$$G_{\dot{K}\dot{K}}(K,\dot{K})\ddot{K} + G_{K\dot{K}}(K,\dot{K})\dot{K} - G_K(K,\dot{K}) = 0, \tag{3.14}$$

which is a second-order nonlinear differential equation in K. If $G(\cdot) = G(K)$, the Euler condition reduces to the static unconstrained optimization condition $G_K = 0$.

There are a number of practical problems with the calculus of variations approach. The Euler-Lagrange equation often results in a complex set of second-order nonlinear differential equations for which a solution may not exist for all t and the boundary values of K. The calculus of variations requires the integrand to be a function of $(K, \dot{K})$, where the control of the system must be an explicit time rate of change of the state variable, K. In addition, this approach cannot easily handle functions that are linear in $\dot{K}$ and has considerable problems with inequality constraints on $\dot{K}$. However, advantages of the calculus of variations approach tend to center on parametric modeling in the presence of uncertainty. These implications are explored further in Chapter 6.

3.2 Bellman's Dynamic Programming Approach

The heart of dynamic economic decision making is balancing how the gains from the current decisions constrain future production or consumption possibilities. Bellman (1959) offered the definition of an optimal policy as one having the property that whatever the initial state and decision are, the remaining decisions must constitute an optimal policy with regard to the state variables resulting from the first decision; that is, any segment of an optimal path is optimal.

The dynamic programming approach explicitly draws on the principle of optimality to develop the fundamental equation to be optimized, known as the dynamic programming (or Hamilton-Jacobi-Bellman) equation. The dynamic programming equation focuses on choosing the optimal current value of the control. The entire control path can be generated by optimizing the dynamic programming equation over the entire time horizon. The Bellman approach is presented in the context of a two-period model along with the economic interpretations and then more generally. We develop the fundamental optimization equations in dynamic programming by working through the two-period cost minimization model, and then go on to the continuous time case.

A two-period economic optimization model is developed to illustrate the algorithm for the solution of controls over time. The approach will be to follow the principle of optimality by solving the problem via backward recursion. Specifically, we will work backward from the second (or terminal) period to generate a sequence of solutions.

3.2.1 Cost Minimization: Two-Period Framework

Consider the cost minimization objective over the periods t and $t + 1$. While production occurs in both periods, investment occurs only in the first period as it provides the benefit of greater physical capacity in $t + 1$ and a cost in period t due to the presence of adjustment costs. In period $t + 1$, the production decisions involve the allocation of variable inputs, x_{t+1}, using the enhanced capital stock, K_{t+1}. The transformation function presented in section 2.3 is represented as

$$\text{Period } t: \quad F(y(t), x(t), K(t), I(t)) = 0$$

(3.15)

$$\text{Period } t+1: \quad F(y(t+1), x(t+1), K(t+1)) = 0, \qquad (3.16)$$

where y is the output vector, I is the gross investment vector, and K is the capital stock vector.

The optimal decisions are determined using backward recursion. This entails solving the input allocation problem subject to a production target in period $t + 1$ first and then solving the period t problem while being sure to link the two decision problems. Cost minimization for period $t + 1$ has the firm taking its physical capacity as given (i.e., $K(t+1)$ fixed) in determining how much variable input to allocate. The cost minimization problem in period $t + 1$ is defined as follows:

$$
\begin{aligned}
&W(K(t+1), y(t+1), w(t+1), c(t+1)) \\
&\quad = \min_{x(t+1), \lambda(t+1)} \{w(t+1)'x(t+1) + c(t+1)'K(t+1) + \lambda(t+1)F(y(t+1), \\
&\qquad\qquad x(t+1), K(t+1))\},
\end{aligned}
\qquad (3.17)
$$

where $\lambda(t+1)$ is the Lagrangian multiplier associated with the technology and production target constraint at time $t+1$, and is a component of the short-run marginal cost of production in time $t+1$, which equals $\lambda(t+1)F_{y_j}$ for output y_j.[2] The first-order conditions of (3.17) are

$$w(t+1) = -\lambda(t+1)F_x, \tag{3.18}$$

$$F(y(t+1), x(t+1), K(t+1)) = 0, \tag{3.19}$$

which are the classic static necessary conditions of cost minimization. Recalling the property of the transformation function in Chapter 2 related to variable input use (F.5), which states that F is nonincreasing in x, condition (3.18) states that the variable input price is equal to the marginal product of the variable input valued at $\lambda(t+1)$. Condition (3.19) is the technology constraint. Solving (3.18) and (3.19) leads to optimal $x^*(t+1)$ and $\lambda^*(t+1)$ being a function of $(K(t+1), y(t+1))$ in addition to other factors taken parametrically such as prices. The minimum cost in period $t+1$ is

$$
\begin{aligned}
W(K(t+1), & y(t+1), w(t+1), c(t+1)) \\
&= w(t+1)'x^*(t+1) + c(t+1)'K(t+1) + \lambda^*(t+1)F(y(t+1), x^*(t+1), K(t+1)).
\end{aligned}
\tag{3.20}
$$

In the current period, t, the problem is to optimally select x_t and I_t, where the impact of I_t spans both the current and future periods; that is,

$$\min_{x(t), I(t)} \{w(t)'x(t) + c(t)'K(t) + \beta W(K(t), y(t), w(t), c(t))\}, \tag{3.21}$$

subject to (3.15) and

$$K(t+1) = I(t) + (1-\delta)K(t), \tag{3.22}$$

where the specification of the transformation function in (3.15) reflects internal costs of adjustment; (3.22) is the capital accumulation equation

---

[2] Differentiating the optimized version of (3.17) with respect to the jth output in time $t+1$, $y_{j,t+1}$, and applying the static envelope theorem yields $W_{y_{j,t+1}} = \lambda_{t+1}F_{y_{j,t+1}}$.

relating how $K(t)$ grows to $K(t + 1)$ through gross investment, $I(t)$, and allowing for depreciation $\delta K(t)$; $K(t)$ is fixed and known; β is a discount factor converting income in period $t + 1$ to the present; and the output targets, $y(t)$ and $y(t)$, are known.

The optimal level of $K(t + 1)$ is known if the optimal level of I is known (with $K(t)$ given). Knowing the optimal level of $K(t + 1)$, in principle, identifies the optimal investment choices in period $t + 1$ as by (3.22).

The Lagrangian for the current period is

$$
\begin{aligned}
&W(K(t), y(t), y(t+1), w(t), w(t+1), c(t), c(t+1)) \\
&= \min_{x(t), I(t), \lambda(t)} \{w(t)'x(t) + c(t)'K(t) + \beta W(I(t) - (1-\delta)K(t), \\
&\qquad y(t+1), w(t+1), c(t+1)) + \lambda(t)F(y(t), x(t), K(t), I(t))\},
\end{aligned}
$$

$$(3.23)$$

where $\lambda_t \geq 0$ is the Lagrangian multiplier associated with the current period production target and is interpreted similarly to the case of $t + 1$ as related to marginal cost of production in time t.

The first-order conditions are

$$w_t = -\lambda_t F_x,$$

$$(3.24)$$

$$\beta \cdot \frac{\partial W(K_{t+1}, y_{t+1}, w_{t+1}, c_{t+1})}{\partial K_{t+1}} = -\lambda_t F_I,$$

$$(3.25)$$

$$F(y(t), x(t), K(t), I(t) + (1-\delta)K(t)) = 0.$$

$$(3.26)$$

Equation (3.24) is the familiar static first-order condition concerning variable input allocation. Recalling the property of the transformation function in Chapter 2 related to investment use (F.6), which states that F is nondecreasing in I, the dynamic linkages emerge in (3.25) in describing the optimal investment rule where the marginal cost of adjustment is balanced against the marginal value of adding another unit of capital. Equation (3.26) guarantees that production, $y(t)$, is satisfied within the technology available.

When $I(t) \geq 0$, $-\lambda(t)F_{I(t)} \leq 0$ and $\dfrac{\partial W(K(t+1), y(t+1), w(t+1), c(t+1))}{\partial K(t+1)} \leq 0$,

implying that costs are lower in the future as a result of current investment.

We can obtain an expression for the arbitrage equation by differentiating the optimized version of (3.20) with respect to K_{t+1}, which yields how the optimal cost in the future responds to additional capital in $t+1$. Upon applying the envelope theorem, this leads to

$$\frac{\partial W(K(t+1), y(t+1), w(t+1), c(t+1))}{\partial K(t+1)} = c(t+1) + \lambda^*(t+1)F_K, \quad (3.27)$$

where the left-hand side is the future value of an additional unit of capital and the right-hand side is the rental cost of capital plus the value of the marginal product of capital.

Taylor expanding $W(K(t+1), y(t+1), w(t+1), c(t+1))$ around $(K(t+1), y(t+1), w(t+1), c(t+1))$ and assuming the current production target persists into the future (i.e., $y(t) = y(t+1)$) and that prices do not change (i.e., $w(t) = w(t+1)$ and $c(t) = c(t+1)$) leads to

$$W(K(t+1), y(t+1), w(t+1), c(t+1))$$
$$= W(K(t), y(t), w(t), c(t)) + W_K(K(t), y(t), w(t), c(t))'(K(t+1) - K(t)) + o(dt),$$
$$(3.28)$$

where $o(dt)$ refers to higher-order terms of the expansion that are negligible since these terms possess the property that $\lim_{dt \to 0} \frac{o(dt)}{dt} = 0$. Using (3.22) and (3.28) in (3.23) leads to

$$(1 - \beta)W(K(t), y(t), w(t), c(t))$$
$$= \min_{x_t, I_t, \lambda_t} \{w(t)x(t) + c(t)K(t) + \beta W_K(K(t), y(t), w(t),$$
$$c(t))(I - \delta K(t)) + \lambda(t)F(y(t), x(t), K(t), I)\}$$
$$(3.29)$$

with the same first-order conditions as in (3.24)–(3.26). Readers with more extensive experience in dynamic optimization modeling will recognize (3.29) as the Hamilton-Jacobi-Bellman equation, which is the fundamental equation for optimally choosing the current period choice variables. There are a number of advantages to this characterization of the dynamic economic optimization that will be developed further along, but for now, this equation provides a transparent economic interpretation.

$W_K(K(t), y(t), w(t), c(t))$ reflects how the flow of costs into the future period in the firm's optimal production plan changes with an increase in the capital stock, and the discounted flow of costs is βW_K. This reflects an internal marginal valuation and is viewed as the shadow value of capital. This value does change over time with changes in the capital stock through net infusions (investment) or net disinvestment (through depreciation). But at a given point in time, it is a fixed imputed or shadow price; that is, the value to the firm of an additional unit of capital is measured by how much it reduces its discounted flow of costs and, thus, is unique to the firm and not a market valuation. The term $\beta W_K(K(t), y(t), w(t), c(t))(I - \delta K(t))$ imputes the contribution of net investment to total costs. An alternative characterization is seen by totally differentiating the discounted flow of costs, $\beta W_K(K(t), y(t), w(t), c(t))$, with respect to time (and assuming the production targets and market input prices remain constant over the time horizon) to yield

$$\beta \frac{dW_K(K(t), y(t), w(t), c(t))}{dt} = \beta \dot{W}\left(K(t), y(t), w(t), c(t)\right)$$
$$= \beta W_K\left(K(t), y(t), w(t), c(t)\right)\dot{K}, \quad (3.30)$$

which reflects the capital gain (or loss) from adding another unit of capital.

The optimized version of (3.29) states that the opportunity cost of the initial capital stock employed in the optimal production plan, $(1 - \beta)W(K(t), y(t), w(t), c(t))$, equals the current period (or short-run) costs, $w(t)x(t) + c(t)K(t)$, plus the current period capital gain/loss, $\beta \dot{W}(K(t), y(t), w(t), c(t))$.

3.2.2 Isocost Analysis

Consider the case where the firm seeks to choose the long-run cost-minimizing bundle of variable and dynamic factors (x, I). The (input) isoquant set for (x, I) developed in Chapter 2 is illustrated again in Figure 3.2 and reflects higher output associated with isoquants that are to the northwest part of the first quadrant. In the current period, using more of the beneficial factor, x, requires taking more of the (currently) detrimental factor, I. The cost equation (preoptimization for period t) is

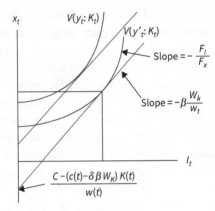

Figure 3.2. Isoquant and isocost map where $y_t > y'_t$.

$$C = w(t)x(t) + c(t)K(t) + \beta W_K\big(K(t), y(t), w(t), c(t)\big)(I - \delta K(t)). \quad (3.31)$$

The isocost curve is

$$x(t) = \frac{C - (c(t) - \delta\beta W_K)K(t)}{w(t)} - \beta\frac{W_K}{w(t)}I, \quad (3.32)$$

where $\dfrac{dx}{dI}\Big|_{dy=0, dw=0, dc=0} = -\beta\dfrac{W_K}{w(t)} > 0$ is the slope of the isocost curve, where higher costs are associated with higher intercepts.

Similar to the static cost minimization problem, the current period cost-minimizing input bundle is a tangency point between the isoquant set with slope as $(-F_I/F_x)$ and an isocost curve with slope equal to $-\beta W_K/w(t)$. Notice that this equality can be obtained by dividing the first-order condition (3.25) by condition (3.24).

3.2.3 Cost Curves in the Short Run and Long Run

Two conceptualizations of the cost function emerge. The optimized discounted flow of total costs in (3.23) is a stock notion. The optimized version of (3.29) is the flow version of long-run and short-run total costs, respectively, denoted as $LRTC$ and $SRTC$, and can be expressed as

$$LRTC = SRTC + \beta W_K (I^* - \delta K(t)), \qquad (3.33)$$

where $\dot{K} > 0, W_K < 0$, implying that $LRTC < SRTC$. In the long-run equilibrium (where $I^* = \delta K(t)$), $LRTC = SRTC$. The result that the short-run and long-run curves coincide at long-run equilibrium reflects the decision structure that all decisions are made in the short run with a view toward moving to a future short-run position. In the current period, t, we can address the long-run average total costs and the long-run marginal costs as

$$LRATC = \frac{LRTC}{y(t)} = SRATC + \beta W_K \frac{I^* - \delta K(t)}{y(t)}, \qquad (3.34)$$

where $SRATC = \dfrac{SRTC}{y(t)}$. Note that, in the two-period model, the long-run and short-run average total costs coincide in period $t + 1$.

When the output targets can vary over the two periods, the marginal cost of changing the production target in $t + 1$ arises from (3.20) as

$$W_{y(t+1)} = \lambda^*(t+1) F_{y(t+1)} (y(t+1), x(t+1), K(t+1)), \qquad (3.35)$$

and the marginal cost in period t arises from (3.29) as

$$(1 - \beta) W_y = \lambda_t^* F_y (y(t), x(t), K(t), I^*) + \beta W_{K,y} (I^* - \delta K(t)). \qquad (3.36)$$

The short-run marginal cost is $\lambda^*(\tau) F_y(\cdot)$ in period $\tau = t, t + 1$. In period $t + 1$, the long-run and short-run marginal costs coincide, not surprisingly, since this decision period is not linked to future ones. In period t, the long-run marginal cost is composed of the current (or short-run) marginal cost plus the discounted value of the change in the long-run marginal cost ($\beta W_{K,y}$). Note that $\frac{dW_y}{dt} = W_{K,y} \cdot (I^* - \delta K)$, assuming $dy(t) = 0, dw(t) = 0$, and $dc(t) = 0$, reflecting the firm being in dynamic disequilibrium since $\dot{K} \neq 0$. Figure 3.3 illustrates the distinction between the static (or short-run) equilibrium

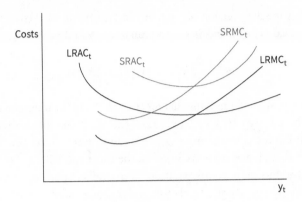

Figure 3.3. Short-run and long-run cost curves in time t for the single output case.

average and marginal cost curves and the dynamic disequilibrium counterparts at a gi. This figure is ven point in time, t.

Unlike the textbook case, note that the short-run and long-run average cost curves are not tangent at period t; in fact, they will be one in the same at the long-run equilibrium. This is consistent with the characterization presented in Ferguson (1969, p. 198) that the long run consists of a range of possible short-run situations available to the firm.

3.2.4 Profit Maximization

The discounted flow of cost in (3.23) reflects the optimal choice of inputs (x, I) conditioned on the output targets. Profit maximization is the problem addressing optimal output choice and, therefore, the optimal, unconditional input demands. In the two-period case, this problem translates to

$$
\begin{aligned}
&J(K(t), p(t), p(t+1), w(t), w(t+1), c(t), c(t+1)) \\
&= \max_{y_t, y_{t+1}} \left\{ \begin{array}{l} p(t)y(t) + \beta p(t+1)y(t+1) - (1-\beta)W(K(t), \\ y(t), y(t+1), w(t), w(t+1), c(t), c(t+1)) \end{array} \right\},
\end{aligned} \qquad (3.37)
$$

where $W(K(t), y(t), y(t+1), w(t), w(t+1), c(t), c(t+1))$ embodies the technology through the constraint in the successive cost minimization problems in (3.20) and (3.23), and how the investment decision drives capital accumulation in (3.22). The first-order conditions for $y(t), y(t+1)$ relate the output price in a given period with the long-run marginal cost in that period and are expressed as

$$p_t = (1 - \beta)W_{y(t)} = (\lambda^*(t)F_y + \beta W_{K,y}(I^* - \delta K(t)))$$
$$= SRMC(t) + \beta \dot{W}_y \qquad [\text{using} (3.36)], \qquad (3.38)$$
$$\beta p(t+1) = (1 - \beta)W_{y(t+1)} = \lambda^*(t+1)F_y = SRMC(t+1)$$

where $\dot{W}_y = \dfrac{dW_y}{dt}$.

3.3 Generalization to the Continuous Time Case

3.3.1 Cost Minimization

In the continuous time case, we move toward exponential discounting with a discount rate, r, and the discount factor at time t, e^{-rt}. Assuming static expectations on prices, discount rate, and depreciation rate, the dynamic cost minimization problem is defined as

$$L(k, t_0, w, c, \underline{y}) = \min_{x, I} \int_{t_0}^{\infty} e^{-rs} [w(s)'x(s) + c(s)'K(s)]ds \qquad (3.39)$$

$$\dot{K} = I - \delta K, K(t_o) = k$$

$$F(y(s), x(s), K(s), I(s)) = 0 \quad s \in [t_0, \infty),$$

where $L(k, t_0, w, c, \underline{y})$ is the long-run cost function in present value terms with $\underline{y}$ indicating the sequence of production targets over the time horizon $s \in [t_0, \infty)$. Again, following the principle of optimality, we can break this optimization problem up into two time periods, $(t_0, t_0 + h)$ and $(t_0 + h, \infty)$, as

$$L(k,t_0,w,c,\underline{y}) = \min_{x,I} \left\{ \begin{array}{l} \int_{t_0}^{t_0+h} e^{-rs} \left[w(s)'x(s) + c(s)'K(s) \right] ds + \\ \\ \int_{t_0+h}^{\infty} e^{-r(s-h)} [w(s)'x(s) + c(s)'K(s)] ds \end{array} \right\}$$

$$= \min_{x,I} \left\{ \int_{t_0}^{t_0+h} e^{-rs} \left[w(s)'x(s) + c(s)'K(s) \right] ds \right\} + $$
$$e^{-rh} L(k + \dot{K}*(h), t_0 + h; w, c, \underline{y}). \qquad (3.40)$$

In the time interval $(t_0, t_0 + h)$, the state variable, capital, moves from k to $k + dK$, where $dK = (I - \delta k)dt$. After some manipulations involving Taylor expanding the expression in (3.40) around the initial points of (k, t),[3] we obtain a fundamental equation of optimization for the current period, t, as

$$0 = L_t(k,t,w,c,\underline{y}) + \min_{x,I,\lambda} \left\{ \begin{array}{l} e^{-rt}[w(t)'x(t) + c(t)'k] + \\ L_k \dot{K} + \lambda F(y(t), x(t), K(t), I(t)) \end{array} \right\}. \qquad (3.41)$$

With L in present value terms, the conversion of L into current value terms is accomplished by setting

$$L(k,t,w,c,\underline{y}) = e^{-rt} W(k,w,c,\underline{y}), \qquad (3.42)$$

implying

$$L_k(k,t,w,c,\underline{y}) = e^{-rt} W_k(k,w,c,\underline{y}) \qquad (3.43)$$

---

[3] Taylor expanding the integral in (3.40) around (k, t) yields $e^{-rt}[w(t)'x(t) + c(t)'k] + o(dt)$, where $o(dt)$ refers to an order of magnitude such that $\lim_{dt \to 0} \frac{o(dt)}{dt} = 0$. Taylor expanding $L(k + \dot{K}*(h), t_0 + h, w, c, \underline{y})$ around (k, t) yields

$$L(k + \dot{K}*(h), t_0 + h; w, c, \underline{y}) = L(k,t) + L_t dt + L_K dk + \frac{1}{2}(L_{kk}(dk)^2 + 2L_{kt}(dk)(dt) + L_{tt}(dt)^2)$$

$+ higher\text{-}order\ terms$ where $(dk)^2 = (I - \delta k)^2 (dt)^2 = o(dt), (dk)(dt) = (I - \delta k)(dt)^2 = o(dt)$ and the higher-order terms are also $o(dt)$. Dividing through by dt and letting $dt \to 0$ yields the expression in (3.41).

and

$$L_t(k,t,w,c,\underline{y}) = -re^{-rt}W(k,w,c,\underline{y}), \tag{3.44}$$

where $W(k,w,c,\underline{y})$ is the current value cost function.

We can now rewrite the fundamental equation in (3.41) into current value terms

$$rW(k,w,c,\underline{y}) = \min_{x_t,l_t}\{w(t)'x(t) + c(t)'k + W_k(I^* - \delta k) + \tilde{\lambda}F(y(t),$$
$$x(t),K(t),I(t))\}, \tag{3.45}$$

where $\tilde{\lambda}$ is the current value of the Lagrangian multiplier; implicitly, $\tilde{\lambda} = e^{-rt}\lambda$. The first-order conditions of cost minimization are

$$w = -\tilde{\lambda}F_x, \tag{3.46}$$

$$W_k = -\tilde{\lambda}F_I \tag{3.47}$$

and have the same interpretation as in the earlier discussion with the two-period model. Equation (3.46) is the static condition on the allocation of variable input factors, and (3.47) is the optimal investment decision balancing the shadow value of capital against the marginal cost of adjustment.

The optimized version of (3.45) indicates that the opportunity cost of the production plan, $rW(\cdot)$, equals the instantaneous flow of cost, $w_t'x_t + c'k$, plus the shadow value of optimal net investment, $W_k\dot{K}^*$. This last term can be alternatively viewed as the capital gain/loss of capital, since $\dfrac{dW(\cdot)}{dt} = W_k\dot{K}$, when prices and production targets are not changing over time.

The arbitrage relationship can be developed by differentiating the optimized version of the Hamilton-Jacobi-Bellman equation in (3.45) with respect to the starting capital level, k, to yield

$$(r+\delta)W_k = c + \tilde{\lambda}F_K + \frac{dW_k}{dt}, \tag{3.48}$$

where $\dfrac{dW_k}{dt} = W_{kk}\dot{K}$. The left-hand side of this expression reflects the opportunity cost of adding another unit of capital, $(r + \delta)W_k$, where this cost depends on the opportunity rate that capital could earn in the next best alternative plus the amount of capital that will erode away from depreciation. This is balanced against the right side, which is the sum of the capital acquisition cost and the marginal value of capital, $c + \tilde{\lambda}F_K$, plus the instantaneous capital gain/loss of an additional unit of capital. The optimized expression in (3.45), which is the flow version of the long-run cost function, will be the foundation for much of our analysis.[4]

The properties of W can be established using (3.45) and some of the properties of the transformation function, discussed in section 2.3.

(3.A.1) The value function W is nonincreasing in K:
This property can be established using the first-order conditions in (3.46) and (3.47). Using the first-order condition (3.46) and the property that F is nonincreasing in x (property F.5, section 2.3), then $\tilde{\lambda} > 0$. Given that F is nondecreasing in I (property F.6, section 2.3) and $\tilde{\lambda} > 0$, $W_k \leq 0$ is established using the first-order condition (3.47).

(3.A.2) W is nondecreasing in (w, c):
Differentiating (3.45) with respect to w and applying the static envelope theorem yields

$$rW_w = x^* + W_{kw}\dot{K}^*. \tag{3.49}$$

Differentiating (3.45) with respect to c and applying the envelope theorem:

$$rW_c = k + W_{kc}\dot{K}^*. \tag{3.50}$$

Equations (3.49) and (3.50) must hold for all possible optimal choices of x and $\dot{K}$. In particular, (3.49) and (3.50) also hold for $\dot{K}^* = 0$. Thus, $W_w \geq 0$ and $W_c \geq 0$.

---

[4] Those familiar with optimal control theory will recognize the bracketed term in (3.45) as the Hamiltonian and W_k is the costate variable. The maximum principle optimization conditions are also present, as the optimization conditions (3.46) and (3.47) are equivalent to (3.5) and the arbitrage relation in (3.48) is equivalent to the equation of motion in (3.6). Condition (3.7) is a restatement of the equation of motion for the state variable, which is already embedded in (3.45).

(3.A.3) W is linear homogenous in (w, c):
The proof of this property uses the objective functional, ignoring constraints:

$$W(w,c,k,y) = \min_{x,I} \int_t^\infty e^{-rs}[w'x_s + c'k_s]ds$$

Multiplying w and c by a factor α yields

$$W(\alpha w, \alpha c, k, y) = \min_{x,I} \int_t^\infty e^{-rs}[\alpha w'x_s + \alpha c'k_s]ds$$

$$= \alpha \min_{x,I} \int_t^\infty e^{-rs}[w'x_s + c'k_s]ds = \alpha W(w,c,k,y)$$

(3.A.4) W is concave in (w, c):
The diagonal elements of the Hessian matrix of W are

$$rW_{w_i w_i} \geq W_{k w_i w_i} \dot{K}^* + W_{k w_i} \frac{\partial \dot{K}^*}{\partial w_i} - \frac{\partial x_i^*}{\partial w_i}, \quad i = 1,...,n, \tag{3.51}$$

$$rW_{c_j c_j} \geq W_{k c_j c_j} \dot{K}^* + W_{k c_j} \frac{\partial \dot{K}^*}{\partial c_j}, \quad j = 1,...,J. \tag{3.52}$$

In particular, W concave in (w, c) is necessary but not sufficient since the second-order and third-order derivatives of W cannot be signed a priori.

(3.A.5) W is nondecreasing in y:
Differentiating (3.45) with respect to y and applying the static envelope theorem yields

$$rW_y = W_{ky}\dot{K}^* + \tilde{\lambda}F_y. \tag{3.53}$$

This equality must hold for all optimal choices of net investment, including $\dot{K}^* = 0$. Using property F.4, in section 2.3 (i.e., F is nondecreasing in y) and given that $\tilde{\lambda} > 0$, $W_y \geq 0$ can be established using (3.53).

These five properties imply that the higher-order derivative properties of the value function are required to obtain a complete characterization of W. The rationale is that the third-order derivatives concern the shadow value of capital, which is an endogenously determined valuation of net investment's contribution to the flow of costs over time. The full characterization of W involves the response of W_k to changes in prices. The full response requires knowing if W_k is increasing or decreasing in prices and if the response of W_k is changing at an increasing or decreasing rate, that is, knowledge of the first-order and second-order derivatives of W_k, which are the third-order derivatives of W.

3.3.2 Profit Maximization

Consider the case of the firm facing competitive input and output markets to the extent that all real prices are taken parametrically and cannot be influenced by the firm. Further, let the firm hold static expectations on the discount and depreciation rates and the set of input prices and rental rates of capital. Starting at time t, the present value form of dynamic profit maximization with multiple output is

$$J(p,w,c,k) = \max_{x,I} \int_t^\infty e^{-rs} \left[p'y_s - w'x_s - c'k_s \right] ds, \qquad (3.54)$$

subject to

$$\dot{K} = I - \delta K, \quad K_t = k,$$

$$F(y_s, x_s, K_s, I_s) = 0 \quad s \in [t, \infty).$$

The current value Hamilton-Jacobi-Bellman equation is

$$rJ = \max_{y_t, x_t, I_t, \mu} \left\{ p'y_t - w'x_t - c'k + J_k'\dot{K} - \mu F(y_t, x_t, k, I_t) \right\}, \qquad (3.55)$$

where J_k is the shadow value of another unit of capital and μ is the Lagrangian multiplier associated with the technology constraint. The first-order conditions are

$$p_i(t) = \mu F_{y_i}(y(t), x(t), k, I(t)) \quad i = 1, \ldots, m \tag{3.56}$$

$$w(t) = -\mu F_x(y(t), x(t), k, I(t)), \tag{3.57}$$

$$J_k = \mu F_I(y(t), x(t), k, I(t)), \tag{3.58}$$

along with the technology constraint $F(y(t), x(t), k, I(t)) = 0$.

The first-order condition in (3.56) sets the ith output price equal to the marginal cost of producing that output. The first-order condition (3.57) states that the input price of a variable input equals the value of its marginal product. Condition (3.58) relates the shadow value of capital to the marginal cost of adjustment. We can also show the arbitrage results for the dynamic profit-maximizing firm by differentiating the optimized version of (3.55) with respect to k to yield

$$(r + \delta)J_k = -\mu F_k - c + \frac{dJ_k}{dt}, \tag{3.59}$$

where $\dfrac{dJ_k}{dt} = J_{kk}\dot{K}$. The left-hand side, again, reflects the opportunity cost of an additional unit of capital that is balanced against the instantaneous short-run profit gain, $-\mu F_k - c$, plus the capital gain/loss of an additional unit of capital.

The properties of the value function, $J(k, \ldots)$, in (3.55) follow from some of the properties of the transformation function presented in section 2.3.

(3.B.1) The value function J is nondecreasing in K:
This property can be established using the first-order conditions in (3.56)–(3.58). Using the first-order condition (3.56) (or (3.57)) and the property that F is nondecreasing in y, property F.4 (or F is nonincreasing in x, property F.5), then $\mu > 0$. Given that F is nondecreasing in I (property F.6, Chapter 2) and $\mu > 0$, $J_k \geq 0$ is established using the first-order condition (3.58).

(3.B.2) J is nonincreasing in (w, c) and nondecreasing in p:
Differentiating (3.55) with respect to w and applying the static envelope theorem yields

$$rJ_w = -x^* + J_{kw}\dot{K}^*. \tag{3.60}$$

Differentiating (3.55) with respect to c and applying the envelope theorem:

$$rJ_c = -k + J_{kc}\dot{K}^*. \tag{3.61}$$

Equations (3.60) and (3.61) must hold for all possible optimal choices of x and $\dot{K}$. Thus, (3.60) and (3.61) also hold for $\dot{K}^* = 0$. Thus, $J_w \leq 0$ and $J_c \leq 0$.

Similarly, differentiating (3.55) with respect to y and applying the envelope theorem:

$$rJ_p = y^* + J_{kp}\dot{K}^*. \tag{3.62}$$

(3.B.3) J is linear homogenous in (p, w, c):

$$J(p,w,c,k) = \max_{y,x,I} \int_t^\infty e^{-rs}\left[p'y_s - w'x_s - c'k_s \right]ds.$$

Multiplying (p, w, c) by a factor α yields

$$J(\alpha p, \alpha w, \alpha c, k) = \max_{y,x,I} \int_t^\infty e^{-rs}\left[\alpha p'y_s - \alpha w'x_s - \alpha c'k_s \right]ds$$

$$= \alpha \max_{x,I} \int_t^\infty e^{-rs}\left[p'y_s - w'x_s - c'k_s \right]ds = \alpha J(p,w,c,k).$$

(3.B.4) Convexity of J in (p, w, c):

The diagonal elements of the Hessian matrix of J are

$$rJ_{ww} \leq J_{kww}\dot{K}^* + J_{kw}\frac{\partial \dot{K}^*}{\partial w} - \frac{\partial x^*}{\partial w}, \tag{3.63}$$

$$rJ_{cc} \leq J_{kcc}\dot{K}^* + J_{kc}\frac{\partial \dot{K}^*}{\partial c}, \tag{3.64}$$

$$rJ_{pp} \leq J_{kpp}\dot{K}^* + J_{kp}\frac{\partial \dot{K}^*}{\partial p} - \frac{\partial y^*}{\partial p}. \tag{3.65}$$

In particular, J convex in (p, w, c) is necessary but not sufficient since the second-order cross and third-order derivatives of J cannot be signed a priori.

As with cost minimization, these four properties imply that the higher-order derivative properties of the value function are required to obtain a complete characterization of J.

3.3.3 Dynamic Duality Implications

The value of the dual approach, in general, is that the input demand and output supply functions can be generated by exploiting the properties of the value functions (e.g., profit functions). Shephard's 1953 monograph developed many of these insights and even then acknowledged the potential of econometric applications. We have now come to know these relationships as Shephard's lemma (for cost minimization) and Hotelling's lemma (for profit maximization), which, respectively, reveal that (a) the conditional input demands can be generated by the price gradient of the cost function and (b) the supply and unconditional input demands can be generated by the price gradient of the profit function.

The dual (or inverse) problem associated with the dynamic cost minimization problem presented in (3.45) is given by

$$F(y_t, x_t, k, I_t) = \max_{w,c}\left\{\frac{rW(k,w,c,\underline{y}) - \left[w'x + c'K + W_K(k;w,c,\underline{y})'\dot{K}\right]}{\tilde{\lambda}}\right\}, \tag{3.66}$$

where $\tilde{\lambda} > 0$, as established in (3.A.1).

The first-order conditions for an interior solution are as follows:

$$\frac{rW_w - x - W_{kw}\dot{K}}{\tilde{\lambda}} = 0,$$

$$\frac{rW_c - k - W_{kc}\dot{K}}{\tilde{\lambda}} = 0,$$

which, given that $\tilde{\lambda} > 0$, can be rewritten as

$$rW_w - x - W_{kw}\dot{K} = 0, \tag{3.67}$$

$$rW_c - k - W_{kc}\dot{K} = 0. \tag{3.68}$$

The dynamic version of Shephard's lemma is already revealed by rewriting the first-order conditions presented in (3.67) and (3.68), leading to

$$\dot{K}^* = W_{kc}^{-1}(rW_c - k), \tag{3.69}$$

$$x^* = rW_w - W_{kw}\dot{K}^* = rW_w - W_{kw}W_{kc}^{-1}(rW_c - k), \tag{3.70}$$

as long as W_{kc}^{-1} exists.

The properties of the transformation function F can be established from the maximization problem in (3.66) and the properties of W established in (3.A.1)–(3.A.5).

(3.C.1) $F(x, I, y, K) \leq 0$:
This property can be established using the maximization problem in (3.66), the definition of cost function, and the fact that $\tilde{\lambda} > 0$.

(3.C.2) F is nondecreasing in y:
Differentiating (3.66) with respect to y and applying the envelope theorem yields

$$F_y = \frac{rW_y - W_{ky}\dot{K}}{\tilde{\lambda}}.$$

This equality holds for all possible vectors of net investment, including $\dot{K} = 0$. Given that $W_y \geq 0$ and $\tilde{\lambda} > 0$, then $F_y \geq 0$.

(3.C.3) F is nonincreasing in K:
This proof is similar to the proof of (3.C.2).

(3.C.4) F is nonincreasing in x:
The proof is similar to the proof of (3.C.2).

(3.C.5) F is nondecreasing in I:
The proof is similar to the proof of (3.C.2).

Note that (3.C.1)–(3.C.5) are precisely the properties of F used to establish the properties of W in (3.A.1)–(3.A.5). This is the essence of duality. The primal minimization problem in (3.45) establishes that the current value of the total cost function can be recovered from the transformation function; the dual maximization problem in (3.66) implies that the transformation function can be recovered from the current value of the total cost function.

For the case of dynamic profit maximization, we focus on the dual to the problem posed in (3.55); that is,

$$F(y(t),x(t),k,I(t)) = \min_{p,w,c}\left\{ \frac{p'y(t)-w'x(t)-c'k+J_k'\dot{K}-rJ}{\mu} \right\}, \qquad (3.71)$$

with first-order conditions for an interior solution given by

$$\frac{-x+J_{kw}\dot{K}-rJ_w}{\mu} = 0,$$

$$\frac{-k+J_{kc}\dot{K}-rJ_c}{\mu} = 0,$$

$$\frac{y+J_{kp}\dot{K}-rJ_p}{\mu} = 0,$$

which, given $\mu > 0$, can be rewritten as

$$-x+J_{kw}\dot{K}-rJ_w = 0, \qquad (3.72)$$

$$-k+J_{kc}\dot{K}-rJ_c = 0, \qquad (3.73)$$

$$y+J_{kp}\dot{K}-rJ_p = 0. \qquad (3.74)$$

The dynamic Hotelling's lemma can also be revealed by rewriting these first-order conditions in (3.72)–(3.74), leading to

$$\dot{K}^* = J_{kc}^{-1}(rJ_c - k),$$ (3.75)

$$x^* = -rJ_w + J_{kw}\dot{K}^*,$$ (3.76)

$$y^* = rJ_p - J_{kp}\dot{K}^*,$$ (3.77)

as long as J_{kc}^{-1} exists.

The empirical implications are similar to the static case. Namely, for a given value function specification, the optimal variable and dynamic factor demands and the output supply can be expressed as derivatives of the specified value function. An extended discussion and operationalization of these dynamic duality implications are presented in Chapter 5.

The properties of the transformation function F can be established from the minimization problem in (3.71) and the properties of J established in (3.B.1)–(3.B.4).

(3.D.1) $F(x,I,y,K) \le 0$:
This property can be established using the minimization problem in (3.71), the definition of profit function, and the fact that $\mu > 0$.

(3.D.2) F is nondecreasing in y:
Differentiating (3.71) with respect to y and applying the envelope theorem yields $F_y = \dfrac{p}{\mu}$. This equality implies $F_y \ge 0$.

(3.D.3) F is nonincreasing in K:
This proof is similar to the proof of (3.D.2).

(3.D.4) F is nonincreasing in x:
The proof is similar to the proof of (3.D.2).

(3.D.5) F is nondecreasing in I:
The proof is similar to the proof of (3.D.2).

The properties (3.D.1)–(3.D.5) of the transformation function are the same properties of F used to establish the properties of the value function J in

(3.B.1)–(3.B.4). The primal maximization problem in (3.55) establishes that the current value of the total profit function can be recovered from the transformation function. Moreover, the dual minimization problem in (3.71) establishes that the transformation function can be recovered from the current value of the total profit function. This is the essence of duality.

An alternative characterization of profit maximization is the difference between the discounted flow of revenue less the discounted flow of cost. The discounted flow of cost has already been addressed in section 3.3.1. Since this dynamic cost function, $W(w,c,y,K)$, already embodies the constraints of the technology and the capital accumulation, we can simply present the dynamic profit function as

$$H(k,p,w,c) = \max_y \int_t^\infty e^{-rs} p' y(s)ds - W(w,c,K(t),\underline{y}). \qquad (3.78)$$

Alternatively, this problem can be presented using the flow version of dynamic cost, $rW(w,c,y,K)$, found in (3.45), as

$$H(k,p,w,c) = \max_y \int_t^\infty e^{-rs}[p' y(s) - rW(w,c,K(s),\underline{y})]ds, \qquad (3.79)$$

where the integrand defines the instantaneous current value net returns, $p' y(s) - rW(w,c,K(s),\underline{y})$, as total revenues less the shadow cost of producing y at a given point in time. In either characterization, the optimization of y reduces to the necessary condition for the current value dynamic programming problem,

$$rJ = \max_{y(t)}\left\{p' y(t) - rW(w,c,K(t),\underline{y})\right\},$$

leading to $rJ_y = 0$, or

$$p = rW_y, \qquad (3.80)$$

where rW_y is the long-run marginal cost of producing output vector in the current period and is defined for the ith output, y_i, by differentiating (3.45) with respect to y_i and applying the envelope theorem to yield

$$rW_{y_i} = \tilde{\lambda}F_y + W_{k,y_i}\dot{K} = SRMC + \dot{W}_y,\qquad(3.81)$$

which is the continuous time version of (3.36).

3.4 Formulating the Cost Minimization Problem in Data Envelopment Analysis

There are a variety of approaches to translate the dynamic decision-making problem into estimable form. Our first excursion into implementation is to notice that the dynamic cost minimization problem in (3.29) can be formulated in the context of a data envelopment analysis (DEA) problem, which is facilitated by expressing the technology as a set of linear inequality constraints. Afriat (1972) and Diewert and Parkan (1983) observe that many families of input requirement sets satisfying properties V.1–V.13 in section 2.2.2 can be derived from a finite number of data points. Varian (1984) formalized this observation, indicating the theoretical foundations to use these finite number of data points to bound the true input requirement set by defining the inner bound (using the set of input quantities for a given output) and the outer bound (using the prices as well as the set of input quantities for a given output). Later, Banker and Maindiratta (1988) calculate technical efficiency scores with reference to the DEA frontier by focusing on the upper bound of the true but unknown input requirement set. Further developments in the use of this approach to characterize the nature of technical change are developed in Chavas et al. (1997) and Hailu and Veeman (2001).

In Chapter 2, the input requirement set defined by properties V.1–V.13 in section 2.2.2 follows Silva and Stefanou (2003). Silva and Stefanou (2003) construct the tightest inner and outer bounds on the adjustment cost input requirement set, generalizing Varian (1984) to the adjustment cost framework.

We can further construct the dynamic version of the input requirement set using physical quantities (x, I, y, K), known as the tightest inner bound for the dynamic input requirement set. Consider we have the following data points, $(x^i(t), I^i(t), y^i(t), K^i(t))$, where the superscript i denotes firm i, $i = 1, \ldots, I$. The tightest inner bound to $T(K(t))$ is the convex monotonic hull of $(x^i(t), I^i(t), y^i(t))$, denoted by $T_I(K(t))$, and can be constructed as follows:

$$T_I(K(t)) = \left\{ (x(t), I(t), y(t)) : x(t) \geq \sum_j \lambda^j(t) x^j(t); \; I(t) \leq \sum_j \lambda^j(t) I^j(t); \right.$$

$$\left. y(t) \leq \sum_j \lambda^j(t) y^j(t); \; K^j(t) \leq K(t); \; \sum_j \lambda^j(t) = 1; \; \lambda^j(t) \in \Re_+, \; \forall j \right\},$$

$$(3.82)$$

where $\lambda(t)$ is the intensity vector at time t. Note that the set in (3.82) is convex (axiom $y(t) \leq \sum_j \lambda^j(t) y^j(t)$ T.10(a)) if $(x^j(t), I^j(t), y^j(t)) \in T_I(K(t))$, $(\sum_j \lambda^j(t) x^j(t), \sum_j \lambda^j(t) I^j(t), \sum_j \lambda^j(t) y^j(t)) \in T_I(K(t))$. $T_I(K(t))$ is positive monotonic in x (T.7S) and negative monotonic in I and y (T.6S and T.8) if $(\sum_j \lambda^j(t) x^j(t), \sum_j \lambda^j(t) I^j(t), \sum_j \lambda^j(t) y^j(t)) \in T_I(K(t))$, $x(t) \geq \sum_j \lambda^j(t) x^j(t)$ $I(t) \leq \sum_j \lambda^j(t) I^j(t)$, and then $(x(t), I(t), y(t)) \in T_I(K(t))$. Also, $T_I(K^j(t)) \subset T_I(K(t))$ for $K(t) \geq K^j(t)$.

Similarly, the tightest inner bounds to the adjustment cost input requirement set, $V(y(t):K(t))$, and the adjustment cost producible output set, $P(x(t), I(t):K(t))$, can be generated as follows:

$$V_I(y(t) : K(t)) = \left\{ (x(t), I(t)) : x(t) \geq \sum_j \lambda^j(t) x^j(t); \; I(t) \leq \sum_j \lambda^j(t) I^j(t); \right.$$

$$y(t) \leq \sum_j \lambda^j(t) y^j(t); \; K^j(t) \leq K(t);$$

$$\left. \sum_j \lambda^j(t) = 1; \; \lambda^j(t) \in \Re_+, \; \forall j \right\},$$

$$(3.83)$$

and

$$P_I(x(t), I(t) : K(t)) = \left\{ y(t) : x(t) \geq \sum_j \lambda^j(t) x^j(t); \; I(t) \leq \sum_j \lambda^j(t) I^j(t); \right.$$

$$y(t) \leq \sum_j \lambda^j(t) y^j(t); \; K^j(t) \leq K(t);$$

$$\left. \sum_j \lambda^j(t) = 1; \; \lambda^j(t) \in \Re_+, \; \forall j \right\}.$$

$$(3.84)$$

The notion is to use firm data to reveal technology sets using the properties of these sets established earlier in Chapter 2. The system of constraints described in (3.82)–(3.84) can be operationally implemented using a linear programming format, which is discussed further in the chapters to follow, namely, Chapter 7.

Technological information can also be recovered by drawing on the theory of dynamic cost minimization and the data points generated by the dynamic cost minimization procedure. This approach involves using the physical quantities (x, I, y, K) along with the input valuation measures (w, c, W_K) and construct input requirements sets consistent with dynamic cost minimization. Again, we emphasize that W_K is a fixed and known value given that it is a function of (w, c, y, K), all of which are known in the current period.

Following Silva and Stefanou (2003, Theorem 3, p. 11), the tightest outer bound to the true input requirement set is

$$V_O(y:K) = \left\{ (x,I) : w^{i\prime}x + W_K^{i\prime}I \geq w^{i\prime}x^i + W_K^{i\prime}I^i ; y \geq y^i ; K \leq K^i \right\}. \quad (3.85)$$

The tightest outer bound is constructed by finding the intersection of closed upper half-spaces, determined by the isocost hyperplanes for observation i that support the input combination (x^i, I^i) given (y^i, K^i). The construction of the tightest outer bound on the input requirement set requires the data to be consistent with dynamic cost minimization. Silva and Stefanou (2003, Theorem 1) establish the conditions for the observed firm data to be consistent with dynamic cost-minimizing behavior. Dynamic cost minimization for the ith firm implies, given $(x, I) \in V(y^i, K^i)$,

$$w^{i\prime}x^i + c^{i\prime}K^i + W_K^{i\prime}(I^i - \delta K^i) \leq w^{i\prime}x + c^{i\prime}K^i + W_K^{i\prime}(I - \delta K^i), \quad (3.86)$$

or, equivalently,

$$w^{i\prime}x^i + W_K^{i\prime}I^i \leq w^{i\prime}x + W_K^{i\prime}I. \quad (3.87)$$

When (3.87) holds for all i given $y \geq y^i$ and $K^i \leq K$, the data are said to be consistent with dynamic cost minimization behavior. This is referred to as the weak axiom of cost minimization and defines the constraints in (3.85).

Building on the example presented in Chapter 2 using Table 2.1, Figure 3.4 illustrates the case of one variable input and one investment

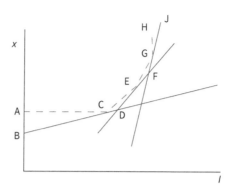

Figure 3.4. The inner and outer bounds of the adjustment cost input requirement set.

input. Recall that C, E, and G are observations. The inner bound in (3.83) is constructed using convex combinations of observed data on firms' input combinations and output levels as long as the current capital stock is less than or equal to K. This set is denoted as $ACEGH$ in Figure 3.4. Similarly, the outer bound in (3.85) is the intersection of closed upper half-spaces determined by the isocost hyperplanes with slope equal to $-\dfrac{W_K^i}{w^i}$. This set is denoted by $BDFGJ$ in Figure 3.4. The result is that $V_I(y;K) \subset V(y;K) \subset V_O(y;K)$ for all y and K, which is established in Silva and Stefanou (2003).

The next point to recognize is that different technologies necessarily imply different cost functions. Focusing on the ith firm, the flow version of the dynamic cost minimization for the inner bound is called the dynamic overcost function and is defined as (Silva and Stefanou, 2003)

$$rW(w^i,c^i,y^i,K^i;V_I)=\min_{x,I}\left\{\begin{matrix}w^{i\prime}x+c^{i\prime}K^i+W_K^{i\,\prime}(I-\delta K^i):\\ (x,I)\in V_I(y^i,K^i)\end{matrix}\right\}. \tag{3.86}$$

Given the tightest inner bound in (3.83), the optimization problem in (3.86) can be restated as

$$rW(w,c,y,k)=\min_{x_s,I_s}\{w\cdot x+c\cdot k+W_k I\}$$

subject to

$$x(t) \geq \sum_j \lambda^j(t)x^j(t)$$
$$I(t) \leq \sum_j \lambda^j(t)I^j(t)$$
$$y(t) \leq \sum_j \lambda^j(t)y^j(t)$$
$$K^j(t) \leq K(t);$$
$$\sum_j \lambda^j(t) = 1;$$
$$\lambda^j(t) \in \Re_+, \forall j. \tag{3.87}$$

We refer to the ith firm's dynamic cost function for the outer bound input requirement set as the dynamic undercost function (Silva and Stefanou, 2003):

$$rW(w^i, c^i, y^i, K^i; V_O) = \min_{x,I} \left\{ \begin{matrix} w^{i\prime}x + c^{i\prime}K^i + W_K^{i\prime}(I - \delta K^i): \\ (x, I) \in V_O(y^i, K^i) \end{matrix} \right\}, \tag{3.88}$$

where V_O is defined in (3.85).

Given the relationship between $V_I(y:K)$, $V(y:K)$, and $V_O(y:K)$, the dynamic cost minimization in (3.86) or (3.87) and the dynamic cost minimization problem in (3.88) bound the true dynamic cost function; that is,

$$rW(w^i, c^i, y^i, K^i; V_O) \leq rW(w^i, c^i, y^i, K^i; V) \leq rW(w^i, c^i, y^i, K^i; V_I) \tag{3.89}$$

for all y and K.

3.5 Remarks

Chapters 6 and 7 offer a fuller presentation of empirical modeling aspects of dynamic production analysis in both nonparametric and parametric formats. The next two sections provide an overview on how the theory presented in this chapter connects to modeling approaches.

The empirical implementation of the dynamic model can take on nonparametric or parametric approaches. The choice of approach depends on the nature of the research question and the level of detail in the data available to address this research question. The nonparametric approach to the dynamic theory of production is paradoxically both a less and a higher structured approach relative to the parametric approach. On the one hand, the nonparametric approach is a free-functional form approach permitting the analysis and measurement of the production structure without imposing explicitly or implicitly a functional form on the production technology. On the other hand, first-order and second-order conditions are incorporated simultaneously in the production analysis. As a result, the weakness of the data is more easily and fully revealed in a nonparametric approach than in the parametric approach that embodies first-order conditions only. The parametric approach embodies first-order and second-order conditions when the set of first-order conditions from a primal specification or the system of equations from a dual specification plus the concavity (convexity) of the cost (profit) function is imposed in the estimation.

3.5.1 Nonparametric Approaches

The revealed preference approach to production analysis is one that focuses on allowing the data to reveal the technology without the constraints of a functional form. The statement of this problem is presented in section 3.4 where the data are used to recover technological information presented by each firm. When prices are available as well, the theoretical foundation of cost minimization can be used to assess if the data rationalize the dynamic cost-minimizing behavior yielding the inner and outer bounds of the production technology. Silva and Stefanou (2003) present a detailed empirical investigation of this approach with firm-level data. At this point we return to the earlier observation that the constrained optimization problems involving the shadow value of capital, W_k (see [3.86] or [3.89]), are a primal optimization problem with the presence of a dual variable; hence, both the primal and dual variables are present simultaneously. We discuss the empirical options to estimate the shadow value of capital in Chapters 6 and 7.

Alternatively, network DEA is a computational decision process framework that is appropriate to model dynamic economic decision making (Färe and Grosskopf, 1996). It is particularly well suited to multistage production systems when an output in one stage feeds into the next stage as an input. Thus, we have time-specific input decisions and the production of time-specific (intermediate) outputs. The constraints from one stage (or decision period) to the next can be input constrained just as capital-like factors can be in the dynamic problems addressed in this chapter. This is a mathematical programming problem where the optimization takes place over all stages (periods) to generate the optimal trajectories for the control variables. There are two clear points of difference between the network DEA and the Hamilton-Jacobi-Bellman equation framework presented in this chapter. The Hamilton-Jacobi-Bellman approach solves for the current period choice variables while looking to the impact of the flow of profits or costs into the future. As such, this approach has the ability to look at the dynamic generalizations of modern production theory, many of which are discussed in the next chapters. In addition, the Hamilton-Jacobi-Bellman approach is more akin to decision-making process where firms make decisions in the short run as they look to the future. Since both approaches are consistent with dynamic optimization theory, they yield the same answers. As the network DEA framework solves for the current period forward, a trajectory is generated for the future periods, thus, clearly, linking current decisions to the future flow of profits or costs.

3.5.2 Parametric Approaches

Econometric approaches to modeling dynamic production decisions have typically taken on primal-based or dual-based formulations. Traditionally, the linear accelerator in univariate or multivariate form was an ad hoc specification decision that is not the explicit result of the producer's optimizing behavior. The accelerator model specifies current investment as a fixed proportion of the gap between the current and desired capital stock. With the advent of the adjustment cost hypothesis, Eisner and Strotz (1963) and Lucas (1967a, 1967b) find that by constraining the specification of the production technology and the adjustment cost function, a closed-form solution to investment is the linear accelerator. The value of the linear accelerator model for capital adjustment remains an attractive feature in applied work.

The primal-based approach develops the consistent system of supply and input demand equations by dealing directly with the primal functions (e.g., the production function, the instantaneous—or restricted—cost or profit function conditioned on investment, the cost of adjustment function) rather than the indirect or value function. By further restricting the model, a closed-form expression for investment can be developed.

The dynamic duality between the value function and the underlying technology permits the derivation of a system of supply and both dynamic and variable input demand equations consistent with dynamic optimizing behavior. This is developed in section 4.3 in Chapter 4. Without relying on closed-form expressions for the endogenous function of input demands and output supplies, the value functional specification is driven by the need (a) to satisfy local and global regularity conditions and (b) to maintain the flexibility of the value function by imposing fewer implied restrictions on the underlying production technology as compared to the primal approach.

4
Dynamic Decision Making, Distance Functions, and Productive Efficiency

4.1 Introduction

Although productive efficiency has been the topic of investigation since the first contributions to economic thought, a rigorous analytical approach to the measurement of productive efficiency originated in the 1950s with the works of Koopmans, Debreu, and Farrell. Koopmans (1957) defined technical efficiency as follows: a producer is technically efficient if and only if an increase in any output or a decrease in any input is possible only by decreasing some other output or increasing some other input. Debreu (1959) introduced a (radial) measure of input technical efficiency, called the coefficient of resource utilization, that is defined as the maximum equiproportionate reduction in all inputs that still allows production of given outputs. An input-output vector can be classified as technically efficient on the basis of Debreu's radial measure and technically inefficient according to Koopmans's definition. This is because an equiproportionate reduction of all inputs at given output levels ignores the possibility of slack in inputs. This divergence occurs whenever the input-output vector belongs to the boundary of the production possibilities set but it does not belong to the efficient subset (Färe et al., 1994).

Farrell (1957) conducts the first empirical study on productive efficiency and introduces the notions of cost efficiency and allocative efficiency. Cost efficiency is decomposed into the product of input technical efficiency and allocative efficiency (Farrell, 1957). The study of Farrell (1957) was crucial for the development of other measures of productive efficiency and the corresponding decompositions, such as output technical efficiency and revenue efficiency (e.g., Färe et al., 1983, 1985, 1994). However, the radial distance functions developed by Shephard (1953, 1970) were also important for the

Dynamic Efficiency and Productivity Measurement. Elvira Silva, Spiro E. Stefanou, and Alfons Oude Lansink, Oxford University Press (2021). © Oxford University Press. DOI: 10.1093/oso/9780190919474.001.0001

development of the literature on the efficiency measurement (Kumbhakar and Lovell, 2000). The Shephard input and output distance functions are the reciprocal of the Debreu-Farrell measure of input and output technical efficiency (Lovell, 1993). The theoretical literature on the efficiency measurement developed mainly on the basis of the (input and output) radial distance functions.

Based on the definition of Koopmans's technical efficiency, Färe and Lovell (1978) and Zieschang (1984) introduced nonradial measures of input technical efficiency, and Deprins and Simar (1983) developed the first nonradial measure of output technical efficiency. The rationale underlying the nonradial measures is the fact that firms may not be able to reduce all inputs or expand all outputs in the same proportion. Nevertheless, the radial measures of technical efficiency have been used by the bulk of empirical studies. The popularity of radial measures of technical efficiency is partly attributable to its linkage with the Shephard distance functions (Shephard, 1953, 1970). Also, radial distance functions allow the measurement of technical efficiency to be combined with the characterization of the production technology. Another advantage of the radial approach is that its technical efficiency measures are easily interpreted and communicated as the maximum percentage reduction of inputs required to produce a given output bundle, or the maximum percentage expansion of outputs allowed for at given inputs.

More recently, Chambers, Chung and Färe (1996) and Chambers et al. (1998) explore the work of Luenberger (1992, 1995) and propose the directional distance functions. The directional distance functions allow the construction of productive efficiency measures that encompass the radial efficiency measures as a particular case.

The previous chapters have introduced primal representations of an adjustment cost production technology and its properties (Chapter 2) and the notion of dynamic optimization with an adjustment cost transformation function (Chapter 3). It was assumed throughout that producers are successful in exploiting the production technology to its full potential and that they make no errors in choosing a mix of inputs and/or outputs that at given prices maximizes profit or minimizes costs. In this chapter we conjecture that firms are not always successful in achieving their objectives. We distinguish situations where the source of underperformance is inefficiency in the technical transformation of inputs into outputs (technical efficiency) or in the choice of the mix of inputs and/or outputs at prevailing prices (allocative efficiency), or both.

In the dynamic framework, technical efficiency would be modified according to Koopmans's definitions as follows: a producer is dynamic technically efficient if (a) an increase in any output requires a reduction of at least one other output or investment or an increase of at least one variable input, or (b) a decrease in any variable input requires a reduction of at least one output or investment or an increase of at least one other variable input, or (c) an increase in any investment requires a reduction of at least one output or other investment or an increase of at least one variable input. Evaluating technical efficiency in an adjustment cost (dynamic) framework requires a nonradial measure. Focusing on, say, input technical efficiency, its measure must allow for a contraction of variable inputs and simultaneously an expansion of investments. Hence, hyperbolic measures of technical efficiency (Silva and Stefanou, 2007) or directional measures of technical efficiency have been employed (Silva et al., 2015).

The determination of efficient behavior discussed here is temporal in nature by describing the degree of efficiency of the firm at a particular point of its adjustment path. The firm's optimal adjustment path over time and the steady state may vary with temporal efficiency. This chapter discusses conceptual issues revolving around the measurement of economic performance when firms make decisions linked over time. The chapter builds on the model of dynamic production decisions presented in Chapters 2 and 3.

In the remainder of this chapter, we will elaborate on the different sources of inefficiency in a dynamic context. In section 4.2, we introduce the adjustment cost directional distance functions as a generic framework for measuring the performance and demonstrate how various measures of technical inefficiency are derived as special cases. This chapter shows that the directional distance functions are capable of representing the adjustment cost production technology that was elaborated in Chapter 2. In section 4.3, we introduce dynamic decision making by assuming that producers either minimize long-term costs or maximize long-term profit. Duality between the dynamic profit (cost) function and the dynamic directional technology (input) distance function is established and the decomposition of overall profit (cost) inefficiency into the contributions of allocative inefficiency and technical inefficiency is demonstrated.

Example 4.1: Dynamic input-oriented technical efficiency
This example illustrates the concept of input technical efficiency in the variable input investment space, using example 2.1 in Chapter 2 and adding a fourth firm.

Table 4.1 Data of Firms

Firm	Output (y)	Capital (k)	Investment (I)	Variable Input (x)
1	8	10	2	2
2	8	10	4	3
3	8	10	6	6
4	8	10	3	5

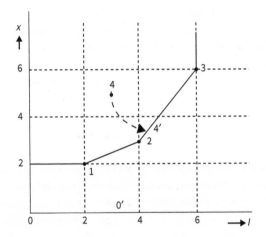

Figure 4.1. A hyperbolic measure of input technical efficiency.

Figure 4.1 depicts the adjustment cost input requirement set $V(y = 8 : K = 8)$, whose boundary is determined by firms 1, 2, and 3 as in example 2.1. Thus, firms 1, 2, and 3 are technically efficient. Firm 4 is in the interior of the input requirement set, implying that it is not technically efficient.

The long-term adjustment plan for firm 4 involves contracting the use of its variable input (x) and, at the same time, expanding the level of investment (I) as investment allows for cost savings over the long run. Figure 4.1 illustrates the hyperbolic measure of input technical efficiency, which we refer to as E. This measure contracts the use of variable inputs and expands the investment level using the same factor. The hyperbolic measure projects firm 4 at point $4'$ on the isoquant. This point is located in the line connecting points 2 and 3; that is,

$$x = -3 + \frac{3}{2}I. \tag{4.1}$$

Furthermore, the values of x and I at point $4'$ are related to the observed values for firm 4 through the hyperbolic technical efficiency measure (E) as

$$x = 5 \cdot E, \tag{4.2}$$

$$I = 3 / E. \tag{4.3}$$

Inserting (4.2) and (4.3) into (4.1) gives a value of 0.7 for E, the hyperbolic dynamic input technical efficiency, which results in the following values at point $4'$: $x \approx 3.6$ and $I \approx 4.3$.

An alternative to the hyperbolic measure is to define the contraction in x and the expansion in I using the notion of a directional vector. The directional representation of the input isoquant was introduced in definition 2.3 in Chapter 2.

Figure 4.2 illustrates the use of a directional vector in evaluating input-oriented technical efficiency for firm 4. The directional vector (g_x, g_I) chosen

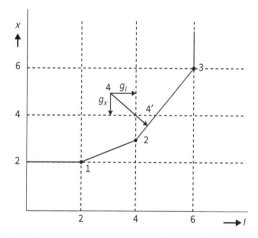

Figure 4.2. A directional measure of input technical efficiency.

in this case is $(-1,1)$, implying a reduction of the variable input and an increase in investment. Point 4 is projected onto the isoquant, in the direction $(-1,1)$, at point $4'$ whose coordinates are $(5 - \beta, 3 + \beta)$, where β is the directional measure of input technical efficiency. Note that point $4'$ is on the line connecting points 2 and 3, defined by (4.1). Substituting the coordinates of point $4'$ in (4.1) yields $\beta = 1.4$, implying that firm 4 should reduce the variable input by 1.4 units and expand investment by 1.4 units. Hence, the coordinates of point $4'$ are $(3.6, 4.4)$.

The directional measure of input technical efficiency is based on the adjustment cost directional input distance function that is presented in more detail in section 4.2.

4.2 Adjustment Cost Directional Distance Functions

The benefit function, developed in the context of the consumer theory, is a directional representation of the consumers' preferences (Luenberger, 1992, 1995). Chambers, Chung, and Färe (1996) extend the benefit function to the static theory of the firm and interpret it as a directional input distance function. Based on the notion of shortage function, Chambers et al. (1998) define the directional technology distance function and demonstrate that this function embeds several known functions representing the production technology, namely, Shephard's distance functions. Furthermore, Chambers et al. (1998) establish the relation between the directional technology distance function and the directional input and output distance functions. The directional distance functions are a directional representation of the production technology. In contrast, Shephard's distance functions are a radial representation of the technology.

We now proceed to generalize the directional distance functions to the adjustment cost theory of the firm allowing a directional representation of the adjustment cost production technology. In section 4.2.1, the directional technology distance function is defined in an adjustment cost framework and is shown to be a complete representation of the production technology. Properties of this function are presented and demonstrated, followed by a discussion of particular cases of the adjustment cost directional technology distance function. The adjustment cost directional input distance and output distance functions are presented, respectively, in sections 4.2.2 and 4.2.3.

The main reasons for invoking the directional distance functions are twofold. First, the directional distance functions allow for flexibility in choosing the direction of the projection of the observed production bundle on the frontier, that is, the direction to measure the distance of the production bundle to the frontier. This flexibility allows the construction of directional measures of technical efficiency as opposed to radial measures. In an adjustment cost framework, measurement of technical efficiency requires a nonradial measure. Measurement of input technical efficiency requires that variable inputs and investment in the quasi-fixed factors (i.e., dynamic factors of production) are treated asymmetrically. The firm's long-term plan involves contracting the variable input quantities and expanding investment in the quasi-fixed factors since investment provides cost savings in the long run. Hence, in the variable input investment space, measurement of technical efficiency requires determining the maximum possible contraction in the use of the variable inputs and expansion of investment in the quasi-fixed factors. Similarly, measurement of technical efficiency in the input-output space requires determining the maximum possible contraction of the variable inputs and expansion of outputs and investment in the quasi-fixed factors.

This flexibility allows for incorporating technological constraints in the directional vector. The operator employing a production technology may be limited to contractions of inputs and expansions of investments only in certain nonradial proportions. These restrictions may be dictated by regulations intended to limit the use of certain inputs (e.g., quantity restrictions on the expanded use of agricultural chemical that can be deemed harmful to the environment) that would be tied to the current use levels.[1] Such technological constraints imposed externally can be reflected in the choice of the directional vector. It should be noted, though, that the flexibility of the choice of

[1] We can even have this case emerge when considering the output choices. When a quota on production of an output is tied to the firm's historical production, the policy constraint will be implicitly limiting the direction. This has been the case in agriculture for the case of milk quotas (Canada and European Community), sugar beets (European Community), and a range of products in the United States (e.g., peanuts, tobacco).

the directional vector asks for a more careful interpretation of the technical inefficiency term. The convenient interpretation of the inefficiency term of the radial distance function as a percentage is only preserved in special cases of the directional distance function.

The second reason for invoking the directional distance function is its duality with long-term cost and profit functions. As we will show in section 4.3, intertemporal duality allows for a computationally very convenient additive decomposition of long-term profit inefficiency and long-term cost inefficiency into allocative and technical inefficiency components.

4.2.1 Directional Technology Distance Function

We introduced the directional concept in the context of the input isoquant set as a subset of the boundary of the adjustment cost input requirement set, $V(y(t):K(t))$, in definition 2.3, and the output isoquant set of the subset of the adjustment cost output set, $P(x(t), I(t):K(t))$, in definition 2.6. In this section, we move on to defining the dynamic directional distance function and demonstrate the duality between this function and the value functions associated with intertemporal cost and profit maximization.

Definition 4.1: The adjustment cost directional technology distance function is a function, $\vec{D}_T : \Re_{++}^N \times \Re_{++}^F \times \Re_+^M \times \Re_+^F \times \Re_{++}^N \times \Re_{++}^F \times \Re_{++}^M \to \Re$, $g = (g_x, g_I, g_y) \in \Re_+^N \times \Re_+^F \times \Re_+^M$, $g \neq 0_{N+F+M}$, defined as

$\vec{D}_T(x(t), I(t), y(t), K(t); g_x, g_I, g_y) \equiv \max\{\beta \in \Re : (x(t) - \beta g_x, I(t) + \beta g_I,$
$y(t) + \beta g_y) \in T(K(t))\}$, if $(x(t) - \beta g_x, I(t) + \beta g_I, y(t) + \beta g_y) \in T(K(t))$ for some β,

$\vec{D}_T(x(t), I(t), y(t), K(t); g_x, g_I, g_y) = \max\{\delta \in \Re : (y(t) + \delta g_y) \in \Re_{++}^M\}$, otherwise.

The vector $g = (g_x, g_I, g_y) \in \Re_+^N \times \Re_+^F \times \Re_+^M$, $g \neq 0_{N+F+M}$ determines the direction in which the directional distance function is defined. The dynamic directional technology distance function involves a contraction of variable inputs and simultaneously an expansion of dynamic factors and outputs. This function projects the input-output vector $(x(t), I(t), y(t))$, in a preassigned direction, onto the adjustment cost production possibilities frontier. If $\vec{D}_T(.) \geq 0$, $(x(t), I(t), y(t)) \in T(K(t))$. If $\vec{D}_T(.) < 0$, $(x(t), I(t), y(t)) \notin T(K(t))$.

Lemma 4.1: Let $g = (g_x, g_I, g_y) \in \mathfrak{R}_+^N \times \mathfrak{R}_+^F \times \mathfrak{R}_+^M$, $g \neq 0_{N+F+M}$. If the production possibilities set satisfies properties T.1–T.5, T.6S, T.7S, and T.8 in Chapter 2, then

$$\vec{D}_T(x(t), I(t), y(t), K(t); g_x, g_I, g_y) \geq 0 \Leftrightarrow (x(t), I(t), y(t)) \in T(K(t)).$$

Lemma 4.1 shows that if $T(K(t))$ is positive monotonic in variable inputs and negative monotonic in dynamic factors and outputs, the directional technology distance function characterizes fully the adjustment cost production technology. Thus, lemma 4.1 establishes that $T(K(t))$ and $\vec{D}_T(x(t), I(t), y(t), K(t); g_x, g_I, g_y)$ are equivalent primal representations of the production technology. The proof of lemma 4.1 is found in appendix 4.1.

Properties of $\vec{D}_T$:
If $T(K(t))$ satisfies properties T.1–T.5, T.6S, T.7S, T.8, T.9, and T.10(a), $\vec{D}_T : \mathfrak{R}_{++}^N \times \mathfrak{R}_{++}^F \times \mathfrak{R}_+^M \times \mathfrak{R}_+^F \times \mathfrak{R}_{++}^N \times \mathfrak{R}_{++}^F \times \mathfrak{R}_{++}^M \to \mathfrak{R}$ satisfies the following properties:

DDT.1 Translation property:
$\vec{D}_T(x(t) - \alpha g_x, I(t) + \alpha g_I, y(t) + \alpha g_y, K(t);$
$g_x, g_I, g_y) = \vec{D}_T(x(t), I(t), y(t), K(t); g_x, g_I, g_y) - \alpha, \forall \alpha \in \mathfrak{R}.$

DDT.2 $\vec{D}_T(x(t), I(t), y(t), K(t); g_x, g_I, g_y)$ is a continuous function in $(x(t), I(t), y(t))$.

DDT.3 $\vec{D}_T(x(t), I(t), y(t), K(t); g_x, g_I, g_y)$ is homogeneous of degree (-1) in $g = (g_x, g_I, g_y)$; that is,
$\vec{D}_T(x(t), I(t), y(t), K(t); \mu g_x, \mu g_I, \mu g_y) = (1/\mu)\vec{D}_T(x(t), I(t), y(t), K(t);$
$g_x, g_I, g_Y), \mu > 0.$

DDT.4 $\vec{D}_T(x(t), I(t), y(t), K(t); g_x, g_I, g_y)$ is nonincreasing in $y(t)$; that is,
$y(t)' \geq y(t) \Rightarrow \vec{D}_T(x(t), I(t), y(t)', K(t); g_x, g_I, g_y) \leq \vec{D}_T(x(t), I(t),$
$\qquad\qquad\qquad\qquad\qquad\qquad\qquad\qquad\qquad\qquad y(t), K(t); g_x, g_I, g_y).$

DDT.5 $\vec{D}_T(x(t), I(t), y(t), K(t); g_x, g_I, g_y)$ is nondecreasing in $x(t)$; that is,
$x(t)' \geq x(t) \Rightarrow \vec{D}_T(x(t)', I(t), y(t), K(t); g_x, g_I, g_y) \geq \vec{D}_T(x(t), I(t),$
$\qquad\qquad\qquad\qquad\qquad\qquad\qquad\qquad\qquad\qquad y(t), K(t); g_x, g_I, g_y).$

DDT.6 $\vec{D}_T(x(t), I(t), y(t), K(t); g_x, g_I, g_y)$ is nonincreasing in $I(t)$; that is,
$$I(t) \cdot \geq I(t) \Rightarrow \vec{D}_T(x(t), I(t)', y(t), K(t); g_x, g_I, g_y) \leq \vec{D}_T(x(t), I(t), y(t),$$
$$K(t); g_x, g_I, g_y).$$

DDT.7 $\vec{D}_T(x(t), I(t), y(t), K(t); g_x, g_I, g_y)$ is nondecreasing in $K(t)$; that is,
$$K(t)' K(t) \Rightarrow \vec{D}_T(x(t), I(t), y(t), K(t); g_x, g_I, g_y)$$
$$\geq \vec{D}_T(x(t), I(t), y(t), K(t); g_x, g_I, g_y)$$

DDT.8 $\vec{D}_T(x(t), I(t), y(t), K(t); g_x, g_I, g_y)$ is (strictly) concave in $(x(t),$ $I(t), y(t))$.

The formal proof of DDT.1–DDT.8 is found in Appendix 4.2. The reader may notice that most of the properties are similar to the properties of the directional technology distance function defined in the context of the static model of the firm. The adjustment cost hypothesis is introduced through properties DDT.6, DDT.7, and DDT.8. Property DDT.6 is equivalent to property T.8 of the adjustment cost production possibilities set $T(K(t))$ discussed in Chapter 2. This property states that dynamic factors congest outputs, reflecting the presence of internal adjustment costs associated with gross investment. Internal adjustment costs can be conceived as output-reducing costs resulting from diverting resources from production activities to investment support activities (e.g., installing the new capital goods, training personnel). Property DDT.7 is equivalent to property T.9, establishing that output levels are increasing in the stock of capital. Properties DDT.6 and DDT.7 together assert that a current expansion in the dynamic factors decreases current levels of outputs but increases output levels in the future by increasing the future stocks of capital. Property DDT.8 results from property T.10(a) of $T(K(t))$.

Several particular directional distance functions can be derived from the adjustment cost directional technology distance function. Those functions are important for efficiency and productivity analysis.

Particular cases of $\vec{D}_T$:

1. If $g_y = y(t), g_x = x(t),$ and $g_I = I(t),$
$$\vec{D}_T(x(t), I(t), y(t), K(t); x(t), I(t), y(t))$$
$$= \max_{\beta} \{\beta \in \Re : (x(t)(1-\beta), I(t)(1+\beta), y(t)(1+\beta)) \in T(K(t))\}.$$

In this case, $\vec{D}_T(.)$ represents a maximum proportional decrease in variable inputs and simultaneously a maximum proportional increase in the dynamic factors and in the outputs.

2. If $g_y = 0_M$, then

$$\vec{D}_T(x(t), I(t), y(t), K(t); g_x, g_I, 0_M)$$
$$= \max_{\beta}\left\{\beta \in \Re : (x(t) - \beta g_x, I(t) + \beta g_I, \ y(t)) \in T(K(t))\right\}$$
$$= \vec{D}_i(x(t), I(t), y(t), K(t); g_x, g_I),$$

where $\vec{D}_i(.)$ is the adjustment cost directional input distance function.

3. If $g_y = 0_M, g_x = x(t)$ and $g_I = I(t)$, then

$$\vec{D}_T(x(t), I(t), y(t), K(t); x(t), I(t), 0_M)$$
$$= \max_{\beta}\left\{\beta \in \Re : (x(t)(1 - \beta), \ I(t)(1 + \beta), \ y(t)) \in T(K(t))\right\}$$
$$= \vec{D}_i(x(t), I(t), y(t), K(t); x(t), I(t)).$$

In this case, $\vec{D}_i(.)$ represents simultaneously a maximum proportional decrease in variable inputs and a maximum proportional increase in the dynamic factors.

4. If $g_y = 0_M$ and $g_I = 0_F$, then

$$\vec{D}_T(x(t), I(t), y(t), K(t); g_x, 0_F, 0_M)$$
$$= \max_{\beta}\left\{\beta \in \Re : (x(t) - \beta g_x), I(t), y(t)) \in T(K(t))\right\}$$
$$= \vec{D}_{vi}(x(t), I(t), y(t), K(t); g_x),$$

where $\vec{D}_{vi}(x(t), I(t), y(t), K(t); g_x)$ is the directional variable input distance function.

5. If $g_y = 0_M, g_I = 0_F$ and $g_x = x(t)$, then

$$\vec{D}_T(x(t), I(t), y(t), K(t); x(t), 0_F, 0_M)$$
$$= \max_{\beta}\left\{\beta \in \Re : (x(t)(1 - \beta), I(t), y(t)) \in T(K(t))\right\}$$
$$= 1 - \max_{\beta}\left\{(1 - \beta) \in \Re_+ : (x(t)(1 - \beta), I(t), y(t)) \in T(K(t))\right\},$$
$$= 1 - \frac{1}{D_{vi}(x(t), I(t), y(t), K(t))}$$

where $D_{vi}(x(t),I(t),y(t),K(t)) = \max_{\lambda}\{\lambda > 0 : (x(t)/\lambda, I(t), y(t)) \in T(K(t))\}$ is the radial variable input distance function. This is a Shephard-type input distance function defined in the variable inputs space.

6. If $g_y = 0_M$ and $g_x = 0_N$, then

$$\vec{D}_T(x(t),I(t),y(t),K(t);0_N,g_I,0_M)$$
$$= \max_{\beta}\{\beta \in \Re : (x(t),I(t)+\beta g_I, y(t)) \in T(K(t))\}$$
$$= \vec{D}_{di}(x(t),I(t),y(t),K(t);g_I),$$

where $\vec{D}_{di}(x(t),I(t),y(t),K(t);g_I)$ is the directional dynamic input distance function.

7. If $g_y = 0_M, g_x = 0_N$ and $g_I = I(t)$, then

$$\vec{D}_T(x(t),I(t),y(t),K(t);0_N,I(t),0_M)$$
$$= \max_{\beta}\{\beta \in \Re : (x(t),I(t)(1+\beta), y(t)) \in T(K(t))\}$$
$$= \max_{\beta}\{(1+\beta) \in \Re_+ : (x(t),I(t)(1+\beta), y(t)) \in T(K(t))\} - 1$$
$$= D_{di}(x(t),I(t),y(t),K(t)) - 1,$$

where $D_{di}(x(t),I(t),y(t),K(t)) = \max_{\theta}\{\theta > 0 : (x(t),\theta I(t), y(t)) \in T(K(t))\}$ is the radial dynamic input distance function. This is a Shephard-type input distance function defined in the dynamic factors (or gross investments) space. Note, however, that $D_{di}(x(t),I(t),y(t),K(t)) \geq 1$.

8. If $g_x = 0_N$ and $g_I = 0_F$, then

$$\vec{D}_T(x(t),I(t),y(t),K(t);0_N,0_F,g_y)$$
$$= \max_{\beta}\{\beta \in \Re : (x(t),I(t), y(t)+\beta g_y) \in T(K(t))\}$$
$$= \vec{D}_O(x(t),I(t),y(t),K(t);g_y),$$

where $\vec{D}_O(.)$ is the adjustment cost directional output distance function.

9. If $g_y = y(t), g_x = 0_N$ and $g_I = 0_F$, then

$$\vec{D}_T(x(t),I(t),y(t),K(t);0_N,0_F,y(t))$$
$$= \max_{\beta}\left\{\beta \in \mathfrak{R}:(x(t),I(t),y(t)(1+\beta)) \in T(K(t))\right\}$$
$$= \max_{\beta}\left\{(1+\beta) \in \mathfrak{R}_+ :(x(t),I(t),y(t)(1+\beta)) \in T(K(t))\right\} - 1$$
$$= \frac{1}{D_O(x(t),I(t),y(t),K(t))} - 1,$$

where $D_O(x(t),I(t),y(t),K(t))$ is the radial output distance function. This is a Shephard-type output distance function defined in the output space.

Cases 1–9 show that the adjustment cost directional technology distance function embeds several distance functions and, in particular, the Shephard-type distance functions. Consequently, the properties of each distance function, derived in cases 1–9, can be established using the properties of the adjustment cost directional technology distance function.

In the next two sections, we analyze the adjustment cost directional input distance function (case 2) and the directional output distance function (case 8). The functions derived in cases 3–7 are obviously particular cases of the adjustment cost directional input distance function; the function derived in case 9 is a particular case of the adjustment cost directional output distance function.

4.2.2 Directional Input Distance Function

The adjustment cost directional distance function (case 2 in previous section) is discussed next. This section draws on Silva et al. (2015), where the directional input distance function is defined in the adjustment cost framework and its properties established.

Definition 4.2: The adjustment cost directional input distance function is a function

$$\vec{D}_i : \mathfrak{R}_{++}^M \times \mathfrak{R}_{++}^F \times \mathfrak{R}_+^N \times \mathfrak{R}_+^F \times \mathfrak{R}_{++}^N \times \mathfrak{R}_{++}^F \to \mathfrak{R} \text{ defined as follows:}$$
$$\vec{D}_i(x(t),I(t),y(t),K(t);g_x,g_I)$$
$$\equiv \max\left\{\beta \in \mathfrak{R}:(x(t)-\beta g_x,I(t)+\beta g_I) \in V(y(t):K(t))\right\},$$
$$\text{if}(x(t)-\beta g_x,I(t)+\beta g_I) \in V(y(t):K(t)) \text{ for some } \beta;$$
$$\vec{D}_i(x(t),I(t),y(t),K(t);g_x,g_I) = -\infty, \text{otherwise.}$$

Recall $\vec{D}_i(x(t),I(t),y(t),K(t);g_x,g_I) = \vec{D}_T(x(t),I(t),y(t),K(t);g_x,g_I,0_M)$.
The adjustment cost directional input distance function represents the maximum contraction in the variable input vector $x(t)$ in the direction of g_x and, simultaneously, the maximum expansion in the dynamic factor vector $I(t)$ in the direction of g_I. This function projects the input vector $(x(t),I(t))$, in a preassigned direction, onto the input isoquant. If $\vec{D}_i(.)\geq 0$, $(x(t),I(t)) \in V(y(t):K(t))$. If $\vec{D}_i(.)<0,(x(t),I(t)) \notin V(y(t):K(t))$.

Note that the maximization problem in definition 4.2 can be stated in terms of the other adjustment cost production sets. The directional input distance function can be defined in the production possibilities set. Alternatively, the maximization problem can be defined in the adjustment cost producible output set

$$\vec{D}_i(x(t),I(t),y(t),K(t);g_x,g_I)$$
$$= \max\left\{\beta \in \Re : y(t) \in P(x(t)-\beta g_x, I(t)+\beta g_I : K(t))\right\},$$

if $y(t) \in P(x(t)-\beta g_x, I(t)+\beta g_I : K(t))$ for some β.

Properties of $\vec{D}_i$:

DDI.1 If $V(y(t):K(t))$ is a (strict) convex set, $\forall\, y(t) \in \Re_+^M$, $\vec{D}_I(.)$ is (strict) concave in $(x(t),I(t))$.

DDI.2 $\vec{D}_i(x(t)+\alpha g_x, I(t)-\alpha g_I, y(t),K(t);g_x,g_I)= \vec{D}_i(x(t),I(t),y(t),$ $K(t);g_x,g_I)+\alpha,\ \alpha \in \Re_+$ is the translation property.

DDI.3 $(x(t),I(t)) \in V(y(t):K(t)) \Rightarrow \vec{D}_i(x(t),I(t),y(t),K(t);g_x,g_I) \geq 0$ is the sign preservation property.

DDI.4 $\vec{D}_i(x(t),I(t),y(t),K(t);\mu g_x,\mu g_I)=(1/\mu)\vec{D}_i(x(t),I(t),y(t),$ $K(t);g_x,g_I),\ \mu>0$, is the homogeneity property of degree –1 in the directional vector.

DDI.5

(a) If $y(t)' \geq y(t) \Rightarrow V(y(t)':K(t))\subset V(y(t):K(t))$, then
$$y(t)' \geq y(t) \Rightarrow \vec{D}_i(x(t),I(t),y(t)',K(t);g_x,g_I) \leq \vec{D}_i(x(t),I(t),.$$
$$y(t),K(t);g_x,g_I)$$

(b) If $V(y(t):K(t))\subset V(\lambda y(t):K(t))$, $0<\lambda<1$, then
$$\vec{D}_i(x(t),I(t),y(t),K(t);g_x,g_I) \leq \vec{D}_i(x(t),I(t),\lambda y(t),K(t);g_x,g_I).$$

DDI.6   If $K(t)' \geq K(t) \Rightarrow V(y(t):K(t)) \subset V(y(t):K(t)')$, then
$K(t)' \geq K(t) \Rightarrow \vec{D}_i(x(t),I(t),y(t),K(t);g_x,g_I) \leq \vec{D}_i(x(t),I(t),y(t),K(t)';$
$g_x,g_I)$ 0.

DDI.7   If   V.7S,   then $x'(t) \geq x(t) \Rightarrow \vec{D}_i(x\cdot(t),I(t),y(t),K(t);g_x,g_I) \geq$
$\vec{D}_i(x(t),I(t),y(t),K(t);g_x,g_I)$.

DDI.8 $I'(t) \leq I(t) \Rightarrow \vec{D}_i(x(t),I\cdot(t),y(t),K(t);g_x,g_I) \geq$
$\vec{D}_i(x(t),I(t),y(t),K(t);g_x,g_I)$.

DDI.9 $\vec{D}_i(x(t),I(t),y(t),K(t);g_x,g_I)$ is continuous with respect to $(x(t),$
$I(t))$.

The formal proof of DDI.1–DDI.9 is found in appendix 4.3.

Example 4.2: Illustration of some properties of $\vec{D}_i$
We use the data given in Table 4.1 in example 4.1 to illustrate some of the properties of the directional input distance function.

The translation property can be illustrated as follows. Recall, first, that the value of the directional distance function for firm 4 is 1.4, given the direction vector $(-1,1)$. Assume $\alpha = 1$ and translate firm 4's input bundle, $(5,3)$, in the direction $(-1,1)$. This would transpose the input bundle to the point where $(x,I) = (4,4)$. Let's calculate next the value of the directional distance function for $(x = 4, I = 4)$. Input bundle $(4,4)$ is projected onto the isoquant, in the direction $(-1,1)$, at point $4'$, whose coordinates are $(3.6,4.4)$. Hence, the value of the directional distance function for $(x = 4, I = 4)$ is 0.4, which is equal to 1.4, the value of the distance function for firm 4's input bundle $(x = 5, I = 3)$, minus 1 (the value of α in this case). The translation property implies that when x decreases by α and I increases by α, in the direction defined by (g_x,g_I), the value of the directional input distance function decreases by α.

The isoquant of the input requirement set is continuous by construction and ensures that the distance function is defined over its entire range. Homogeneity of degree -1 of the distance function in the directional vector is verified as follows. Recall again that the value of the directional distance function for firm 4 is 1.4, given the direction vector $(-1,1)$. Multiplying the directional vector by, say, 0.5 implies that the new directional vector becomes $(g_x = -0.5, g_I = 0.5)$. Project next firm 4's input bundle $(x = 5, I = 3)$, in the direction $(-0.5,0.5)$, to point $4'$, that is, $(x = 3.6, I = 4.4)$. The value of the directional distance function for $(x = 5, I = 3)$ is determined by solving one of the following equations: $5 - 0.5\beta = 3.6$ or $3 + 0.5 = 4.4$. Hence, the value of the directional distance function is 2.8; that is, the value of the directional distance function doubles.

Properties DDI.7 and DDI.8 (i.e., nondecreasing in x and nonincreasing in I) can be easily seen in Figure 4.3. Starting from the observed values for firm 4, the distance to the isoquant of the input requirement set will not decrease if firm 4 uses more of the variable input, *ceteris paribus*. Similarly, the value of the distance function will not increase if firm 4 invests more, *ceteris paribus*. Concavity is illustrated in Figure 4.3 by the dotted line connecting observations for firm 1 and firm 3. Both firms have a value of the distance function equal to zero since the firms are located on the isoquant. It can be seen that any convex combination of the input bundles of firm 1 and firm 3 is not located in the isoquant. Consequently, the value of the distance function is greater than zero.

The following lemma establishes that it is possible to recover $V(y(t):K(t))$ from the dynamic directional input distance function, $\vec{D}_i(.)$.

Lemma 4.2: If $V(y(t):K(t))$ satisfies properties V.1–V.6, V.7S, and V.8, then $\vec{D}_i(x(t), I(t), y(t), K(t); g_x, g_I) \geq 0 \Leftrightarrow (x(t), I(t)) \in V(y(t): K(t))$.

Lemma 4.2 asserts that the dynamic directional distance function defined in $V(y(t):K(t))$ describes fully the adjustment cost production technology if the input set satisfies V.7S and V.8. In other words, under those conditions, the dynamic directional input distance function and the input sets are alternative primal representations of the adjustment cost production technology. The proof of lemma 4.2 is found in Appendix 4.1.

Cases 3–7 presented in the previous section are also particular cases of the dynamic directional input distance function.

Particular cases of $\vec{D}_i(.)$:
1. If $g_x = x(t)$ and $g_I = I(t)$, then
$$\vec{D}_i(x(t), I(t), y(t), K(t); x(t), I(t))$$
$$= \max\left\{\beta \in \Re : (x(t)(1-\beta), I(t)(1+\beta)) \in V(y(t): K(t))\right\}.$$

In this case, $\vec{D}_I(.)$ represents simultaneously a maximum proportional decrease in variable inputs and a maximum proportional increase in the dynamic factors.

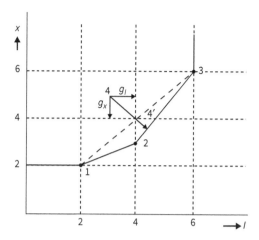

Figure 4.3. Directional projection of firm 4 in example 4.1.

2. If $g_I = 0_F$, then

$$\vec{D}_i(x(t), I(t), y(t), K(t); g_x, 0_F)$$
$$= \max\left\{\beta \in \Re : (x(t) - \beta g_x, I(t)) \in V(y(t): K(t))\right\}$$
$$= \max\left\{\beta \in \Re : (x(t) - \beta g_x) \in V(y(t): K(t), I(t))\right\}$$
$$= \vec{D}_{vi}(x(t), I(t), y(t), K(t); g_x).$$

where $\vec{D}_{vi}(x(t), I(t), y(t), K(t); g_x)$ is the directional variable input distance function.

3. If $g_I = 0_F$ and $g_x = x(t)$, then

$$\vec{D}_i(x(t), I(t), y(t), K(t); g_x, 0_F)$$
$$= \max\left\{\beta \in \Re : (x(t)(1-\beta), I(t)) \in V(y(t): K(t))\right\}$$
$$= 1 - \max_{\beta}\left\{(1-\beta) \in \Re_+ : (x(t)(1-\beta), I(t)) \in V(y(t): K(t))\right\}$$
$$= 1 - \max\left\{(1-\beta) \in \Re_+ : (x(t)(1-\beta)) \in V(y(t): K(t), I(t))\right\}$$
$$= 1 - \frac{1}{D_{vi}(x(t), I(t), y(t), K(t))}.$$

The second equality results from the fact that $x(1-\beta) \geq 0$, implying that $(1-\beta) \geq 0$. The function $D_{vi}(x(t), I(t), y(t), K(t))$ is the radial variable input distance function. This is a Shephard-type input distance function defined in the variable inputs space.

4. If $g_x = 0_N$, then

$$\vec{D}_i\left(x(t), I(t), y(t), K(t); g_I, O_N\right)$$
$$= \max\left\{\beta \in \Re : \left(x(t), I(t) + \beta g_I\right) \in V(y(t) : K(t))\right\}$$
$$= \max\left\{\beta \in \Re : \left(I(t) + \beta g_I\right) \in V(y(t) : K(t), x(t))\right\}$$
$$= \vec{D}_i\left(x(t), I(t), y(t), K(t); g_I\right),$$

where $\vec{D}_{di}(x(t), I(t), y(t), K(t); g_I)$ is the directional dynamic input distance function.

5. If $g_x = 0_N$ and $g_I = I(t)$, then

$$\vec{D}_i(x(t), I(t), y(t), K(t); g_x, O_F)$$
$$= \max\{\beta \in \Re : \left(x(t), I(t)(1 + \beta)\right) \in V(y(t) : K(t))\}$$
$$= \max\{(1 + \beta) \in \Re_+ : (x(t), I(t)(1 + \beta)) \in V(y(t) : K(t))\} - 1$$
$$= \max\{(1 + \beta) \in \Re_+ : I(t)(1 + \beta) \in V(y(t) : K(t), x(t))\} - 1$$
$$= \frac{1}{D_{di}(x(t), I(t), y(t), K(t)))} - 1,$$

where $D_{di}(x(t), I(t), y(t), K(t)) = \min_{\rho}\left\{\rho > 0 : I(t) / \rho \in V(y(t) : K(t), x(t))\right\}$ is the radial dynamic input distance function. This is a Shephard-type input distance function defined in the dynamic factors (or gross investments) space. Note that $D_{di}(x(t), I(t), y(t), K(t)) \geq 1$.

Example 4.3: Empirical illustration of $\vec{D}_i$

In this example, we consider the data presented in example 4.1 and employ data envelopment analysis (DEA) to illustrate how to determine the value of the adjustment cost directional input distance function for a particular firm. The value of the adjustment cost distance function is determined for firm 4 by running the following linear programming problem:

$$\vec{D}_i(y, k, x, I; g_x, g_I) = \max_{\beta, \gamma} \beta$$

$$s.t \quad y_4 \leq \sum_{i=1}^{4} \lambda_i y_i$$

$$k_4 \geq \sum_{i=1}^{4} \lambda_i k_i$$

$$x_4 - \beta g_x \geq \sum_{i=1}^{4} \lambda_i x_i$$

$$I_4 + \beta g_I \leq \sum_{i=1}^{4} \lambda_i I_i$$

$$\sum_{i=1}^{N} \lambda_i = 1; \quad \lambda_i \geq 0, \quad i = 1, 2, 3, 4. \tag{4.4}$$

Table 4.2 Solution to Firm 4 for Various Directions

Directional Vector (g_x, g_I)	λ_1	λ_2	λ_3	λ_4	β
$(-1, 1)$	0	0.8	0.2	0	1.4
$(-1, 0)$	0.5	0.5	0	0	2.5
$(0, 1)$	0	0.33	0.67	0	2.33
$(-0.5, 0.5)$	0	0.8	0.2	0	2.8

Inserting the values of the variable input, output, and investment presented in Table 4.1 as well as the directional vector $(-1, 1)$ yields[2]

$$\vec{D}_i(y, k, x, I; g_x, g_I) = \max_{\beta, \lambda} \beta$$
$$\begin{aligned} s.t \quad & y_4 \leq 8\lambda_1 + 8\lambda_2 + 8\lambda_3 + 8\lambda_4 \\ & k_4 \geq 10\lambda_1 + 10\lambda_2 + 10\lambda_3 + 10\lambda_4 \\ & x_4 - \beta \geq 2\lambda_1 + 3\lambda_2 + 6\lambda_3 + 5\lambda_4 \\ & I_4 + \beta \leq 2\lambda_1 + 4\lambda_2 + 6\lambda_3 + 3\lambda_4 \\ & \lambda_1 + \lambda_2 + \lambda_3 + \lambda_4 = 1 \\ & \lambda_i \geq 0, i = 1, ..., 4. \end{aligned} \quad (4.5)$$

The solution to the problem in (4.5) is $\beta = 1.4$, as already discussed in example 4.1. The solution for the maximization problem in (4.5) is presented in Table 4.2 as well as the solutions for the problem in (4.4) for other directional vectors. Now assume firm 4 is only interested in contracting variable inputs without changing the investment level and the production level. The directional vector can be defined, in this case, as $(-1, 0)$. Substituting the directional vector in problem (4.4) yields $\beta = 2.5$. This means that firm 4 can reduce the quantity of the variable input by 2.5 units, keeping the level of the output equal to 8 units and investing 3 units in the quasi-fixed factor. If firm 4 would like to expand investment in the quasi-fixed factor without changing the quantity of the variable input, the directional vector can be defined as $(0, 1)$. Using standard linear programming software, problem (4.4) using this directional vector yields $\beta = 2.33$, implying that firm 4's investment increases to 5.33 units.

---

[2] In this case, the output and the capital stock constraints can be written as $y_4 \leq 8$ and $k_4 \geq 10$, respectively, since all firms have the same capital stock and produce the same output level.

4.2.3 Directional Output Distance Function

The adjustment cost directional output distance function is defined, and its properties are presented and demonstrated. This function is shown to be a complete representation of the production technology, followed by a discussion of a particular case of the directional output distance function. The section ends by establishing a relation between the directional output distance function and the directional input distance function.

Definition 4.3: The adjustment cost directional output distance function, defined in the output sets $P(x(t), I(t) : K(t))$ in the direction g_y, is a function $\vec{D}_O : \Re_{++}^N \times \Re_{++}^F \times \Re_+^F \times \Re_+^M \times \Re_{++}^M \to \Re$ defined as

$$\vec{D}_O(x(t), I(t), y(t), K(t); g_y) \equiv \max\{\beta \in \Re : (y(t) + \beta g_y) \in P(x(t), I(t) : K(t))\},$$
if $(y(t) + \beta g_y) \in P(x(t), I(t) : K(t))$ for some β;

$$\vec{D}_O(x(t), I(t), y(t), K(t); g_y) \equiv \min\{\delta : (y(t) + \delta g_y) \in \Re_{++}^M\}, \text{ otherwise.}$$

The directional output distance function represents the maximum possible expansion of the output vector $y(t)$ in the direction of the vector g_y. If $\vec{D}_O(.) \geq 0$, $y(t) \in P(x(t), I(t) : K(t))$; if $\vec{D}_O(.) < 0$, $y(t) \notin P(x(t), I(t) : K(t))$.

Recall that $\vec{D}_O(x(t), I(t), y(t), K(t); g_y) = \vec{D}_T(x(t), I(t), y(t), K(t); 0_N, 0_F, g_y)$ (case 8 in section 4.2.1). The dynamic directional output distance function can be defined in the adjustment cost production possibilities set as in definition 4.3. Alternatively, this function can be defined in the adjustment cost input requirement set as

$$\vec{D}_O(x(t), I(t), y(t), K(t); g_y) = \max\{\beta \in \Re : (x(t), I(t)) \in V(y(t) + \beta g_y : K(t))\},$$
if $(x(t), I(t)) \in V(y(t) + \beta g_y : K(t))$.

Properties of $\vec{D}_O$:

DDO.1   If $P(x(t), I(t) : K(t))$ is a convex set, $\vec{D}_O(x(t), I(t), y(t), K(t); g_y)$ is concave in $y(t)$.

DDO.2 $\vec{D}_O(x(t), I(t), y(t) + \alpha g_y, K(t); g_y) = \vec{D}_O(x(t), I(t), y(t), K(t); g_y) - \alpha$, $\alpha \in \Re$—translation property.

DDO.3 $y \in P(x(t), I(t) : K(t)) \Rightarrow \vec{D}_O(x(t), I(t), y(t), K(t); g_y) \geq 0$ — preservation property.

DDO.4 $\vec{D}_O(x(t), I(t), y(t), K(t); \mu g_y) = (1/\mu)\vec{D}_O(x(t), I(t), y(t),$
$K(t); g_y)$, $\mu > 0$—homogeneity property in g_y.

DDO.5
(a) If $x(t)' \geq x(t) \Rightarrow P(x(t), I(t) : K(t)) \subset P(x(t)', I(t) : K(t))$, then
$x(t)' \geq x(t) \Rightarrow \vec{D}_O(x(t), I(t), y(t), K(t); g_y) \leq \vec{D}_O(x(t)', I(t), y(t), K(t); g_y)$.
(b) If $P(x(t), I(t) : K(t)) \subset P(\lambda x(t), I(t) : K(t))$, $\lambda > 1$, then
$\vec{D}_O(x(t), I(t), y(t), K(t); g_y) \leq \vec{D}_O(\lambda x(t), I(t), y(t), K(t); g_y)$.

DDO.6   If $I(t)' \geq I(t) \Rightarrow P(x(t), I(t)' : K(t)) \subset P(x(t), I(t) : K(t))$, then
$I(t)' \geq I(t) \Rightarrow \vec{D}_O(x(t), I(t)', y(t), K(t); g_y) \leq \vec{D}_O(x(t), I(t), y(t), K(t); g_y)$.

DDO.7   If $K(t)' \geq K(t) \Rightarrow P(x(t), I(t) : K(t)) \subset P(x(t), I(t) : K(t)')$, then
$K(t)' \geq K(t) \Rightarrow \vec{D}_O(x(t), I(t), y(t), K(t); g_y) \leq \vec{D}_O(x(t), I(t), y(t), K(t)'; g_y)$.

DDO.8   If $y(t) \in P(x(t), I(t) : K(t)) \Rightarrow \lambda y(t) \in P(x(t), I(t) : K(t))$, $0 < \lambda < 1$,
then $\vec{D}_O(x(t), I(t), \lambda y(t), K(t); g_y) \geq \lambda \vec{D}_O(x(t), I(t), y(t), K(t); g_y)$
$= \vec{D}_O(x(t), I(t), y(t), K(t); g_y / \lambda)$.

DDO.9 $\vec{D}_O(x(t), I(t), y(t), K(t); g_x, g_I)$ is continuous with respect to $y(t)$.

The proof of these properties is similar to the proof of properties DDI.1–DDI.9.

The next lemma shows that it is possible to recover the adjustment cost producible output set, $P(x(t), I(t) : K(t))$, from the adjustment cost directional output distance function.

Lemma 4.3: If $P(x(t), I(t) : K(t))$ satisfies properties P.1–P.5 and P.6S, then
$\vec{D}_O(x(t), I(t), y(t), K(t); g_y) \geq 0 \Leftrightarrow y(t) \in P(x(t), I(t) : K(t))$.

The proof of this lemma is similar to the proof of lemma 4.2.

Example 4.4: Empirical illustration of $\vec{D}_O$
We use the data presented in Table 4.3 and DEA to illustrate how to determine the value of the adjustment cost directional output distance function for different directional vectors.

Table 4.3 Data from Four Firms

Firm	Output 1	Output 2	Capital	Investment	Variable Input
1	2	8	10	4	2
2	4	7	10	4	2
3	5	5	10	4	2
4	3	6	10	4	2

Given a directional vector, the value of the adjustment cost directional output distance function for each firm j, $j = 1,2,3,4$, can be obtained by running the following linear programming problem:

$$\vec{D}_O(y,k,x,I;g_y)=\max_{\beta,\gamma}\beta$$

$$s.t \quad y_{mj}+\beta g_y \le \sum_{i=1}^{N}\lambda_i y_{mi}, \quad m=1,2$$

$$k_j \ge \sum_{i=1}^{N}\lambda_i k_i$$

$$x_j \ge \sum_{i=1}^{N}\lambda_i x_i$$

$$I_j \le \sum_{i=1}^{N}\lambda_i I_i$$

$$\sum_{i=1}^{N}\lambda_i =1; \quad \lambda_i \ge 0, i = 1,2,3,4., \tag{4.6}$$

where y_{mi} denotes output m for firm i. Figure 4.4 depicts the producible output set. The *Isoq P(x,I:K)* is determined by firms 1, 2, and 3, while firm 4 is in the interior of the output set. Table 4.4 reports the solution of problem (4.6) for firm 4 considering several directional vectors.

A particular case of the adjustment cost directional output distance function is case 9 presented in section 4.2.1. If $g_y = y(t)$, then

$$\vec{D}_O(x(t),I(t),y(t),K(t); y(t))$$
$$= \max\left\{\beta\in\Re: y(t)(1+\beta) \in P(x(t),I(t):K(t))\right\}$$
$$= \max\left\{(1+\beta)\in\Re_+ : y(t)(1+\beta) \in P(x(t),I(t):K(t)),\beta\in\Re\right\}-1$$
$$=\frac{1}{D_O(x(t),I(t),y(t),K(t))}-1. \tag{4.7}$$

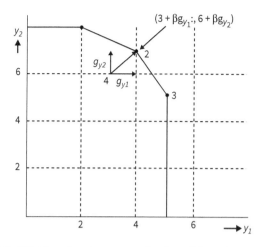

Figure 4.4. $P(x,I:K)$. Directional output projection of firm 4 in example 4.4

Table 4.4 The Value of the Output Distance Function for Firm 4

Directional Vector (g_{y1}, g_{y2})	λ_1	λ_2	λ_3	λ_4	β
(1,1)	0	1	0	0	1
(1,0)	0.5	0.5	0	0	1.5
(0,1)	0	0.5	0.5	0	1.5

The second equality results from the fact that $P(x(t), I(t) : K(t)) \subset \Re_+^M$. Thus, $y(t)(1 + \beta) \geq 0$, implying $(1 + \beta) \geq 0$. The radial output distance function is $D_O(x(t), I(t), y(t), K(t)) = \inf\{\theta : y / \theta \in P(x(t), I(t) : K(t))\}$. This is a Shephard-type output distance function defined in the output space.

A relationship between the adjustment cost directional output distance function and the directional input distance function can be established. From lemma 4.2, properties V.6S and V.7 are sufficient conditions for the following relation to hold:

$$\vec{D}_i(x(t), I(t), y(t), K(t); g_x, g_I) \geq 0 \iff (x(t), I(t)) \in V(y(t) : K(t)). \qquad (4.8)$$

From lemma 4.3, property P.5S is a sufficient condition for the following relation to hold:

$$\vec{D}_O(x(t), I(t), y(t), K(t); g_y) \geq 0 \iff y(t) \in P(x(t), I(t) : K(t)). \quad (4.9)$$

Given that $(x(t), I(t)) \in V(y(t) : K(t)) \iff y(t) \in P(x(t), I(t) : K(t))$, then

$$
\begin{aligned}
\vec{D}_O&(x(t), I(t), y(t), K(t); g_y) \\
&= \max_{\beta}\left\{\beta : (y(t) + \beta g_y) \in P(x(t), I(t) : K(t))\right\} \\
&= \max_{\beta}\left\{\beta : (x(t), I(t)) \in V(y(t) + \beta g_y : K(t))\right\} \\
&= \max_{\beta}\left\{\beta : \vec{D}_i(x(t), I(t), y(t) + \beta g_y, K(t); g_x, g_I) \geq 0\right\}, \quad (4.10)
\end{aligned}
$$

and

$$
\begin{aligned}
\vec{D}_i&(x(t), I(t), y(t), K(t); g_x, g_I) \\
&= \max_{\beta}\left\{\beta : (x(t) - \beta g_x, I(t) + \beta g_I) \in V(y(t) : K(t))\right\} \\
&= \max_{\beta}\left\{\beta : y(t) \in P(x(t) - \beta g_x, I(t) + \beta g_I : K(t))\right\} \\
&= \max_{\beta}\left\{\beta : \vec{D}_O(x(t) - \beta g_x, I(t) + \beta g_I, y(t), K(t); g_y) \geq 0\right\}. \quad (4.11)
\end{aligned}
$$

Therefore, if the adjustment cost production technology satisfies axioms V.6S, V.7, and P.5S, then

$$
\begin{aligned}
\vec{D}_O&(x(t), I(t), y(t), K(t); g_y) \\
&= \max_{\beta}\left\{\beta : \vec{D}_i(x(t), I(t), y(t) + \beta g_y, K(t); g_x, g_I) \geq 0\right\} \quad (4.12)
\end{aligned}
$$

and

$$
\begin{aligned}
\vec{D}_i&(x(t), I(t), y(t), K(t); g_x, g_I) \\
&= \max_{\beta}\left\{\beta : \vec{D}_O(x(t) - \beta g_x, I(t) + \beta g_I, y(t), K(t); g_y) \geq 0\right\}. \quad (4.13)
\end{aligned}
$$

4.3 Dynamic Duality and Measurement of Productive Efficiency

Dynamic duality is a subject matter dating back to Cooper and McLaren (1980), McLaren and Cooper (1980), and Epstein (1981). Later, Lasserre and Ouellette (1999) proposed a duality theory in discrete time for an expected cost-minimizing firm in the presence of adjustment costs. Following Epstein (1981), Caputo (2005) develops a dynamic duality theory in the context of the adjustment cost model of the firm and intertemporal profit maximization. Silva et al. (2015) establish duality between the adjustment cost directional input distance function and the current value of the optimal value function of the intertemporal cost minimization problem.

This section unfolds as follows. In section 4.3.1, we present the duality between the adjustment cost directional input distance function and the optimal value function of the intertemporal cost minimization problem. Section 4.3.2 introduces the concept of temporal cost inefficiency and its decomposition into allocative and technical inefficiency. The measurement of temporal cost inefficiency is based on the adjustment cost directional input distance function and the intertemporal duality between this function and the current value of the optimal value function. Both sections draw on Silva et al. (2015). Section 4.3.3 establishes duality between the adjustment cost directional technology distance function and the optimal value function of the intertemporal profit maximization problem and discusses temporal profit inefficiency measurement.

4.3.1 Intertemporal Cost Minimization and Duality

At any base period $t \in [0, +\infty)$, the firm is assumed to minimize the discounted flow of costs over time as presented in (3.39), which introduced the technology constraint in the form of the transformation function. Given lemma 4.2, the adjustment cost technology can be represented by the dynamic directional input distance function. Consequently, we can use the

$\vec{D}_i(y(s),K(s),x(s),I(s);g_x,g_I) \geq 0$, $s \in [t,+\infty)$ as a constraint in place of $F(y(s),x(s),K(s),I(s)) = 0$ $s \in (t,^\circ)$.

The intertemporal cost minimization problem in (3.39) can be restated as

$$W(K_t,w,c,\underline{y}) = \min_{\{x,I\}} \int_t^\infty e^{-rs}[w(s)'x(s) + c(s)'K(s)]ds \qquad (4.14)$$

$$\dot{K} = I(s) - \delta K(s),\ K(t) = K_t$$

$$\vec{D}_i(y(s),K(s),x(s),I(s);g_x,g_I) \geq 0,\ s \in [t,+\infty),$$

where $w \in \mathfrak{R}_{++}^N$ is a vector of rental prices of the variable input vector $x(s) \in \mathfrak{R}_+^N$, and $c \in \mathfrak{R}_{++}^F$ is a vector of rental prices of the capital stock vector $K(s) \in \mathfrak{R}_{++}^F$ and a gross investment vector $I(s) \in \mathfrak{R}_+^F$. The vectors w and c represent current market prices (i.e., at $s = t$) that the firm expects to persist indefinitely, that is, the static expectations hypothesis. This assumption on gross investment reflects the assumption of complete irreversibility of investment, which corresponds to an infinite adjustment cost of disinvestment. An overcapitalized firm can only shed capital at the rate of depreciation and no active disinvestment possibility is allowed.

The current value Hamilton-Jacobi-Bellman equation for any base period t is defined as

$$rW(y,K,w,c)$$
$$= \min_{x,I} \left\{ w'x + c'K + W_K(y,K,w,c)(I - \delta K) : \vec{D}(y,K,x,I;g_x,g_I) \geq 0 \right\}, (4.15)$$

assuming that $\vec{D}_i(.) \in C^{(1)}$ and $\vec{D}_{il}(.) \in C^{(1)}$, $l = y,K,x,I$ (property DDI.10).[3]

The Hamilton-Jacobi-Bellman equation in (4.15) can be rewritten as the following unconstrained minimization problem:

$$rW(y,K,w,c)$$
$$= \min_{x,I}\{w'x + c'K + W_K(y,K,w,c)(I - \delta K) + \lambda^C \vec{D}(y,K,x,I;g_x,g_I)\}. \quad (4.16)$$

The interpretation of the Lagrangian multiplier, λ^C, in (4.16) can be found by considering the following Hamilton-Jacobi-Bellman equation:

---

[3] In general, $C^{(k)}$ refers to a function that is continuous and differentiable k times.

$$rW(y,K,w,c;\alpha)$$
$$= \min_{x,I} \{w'x + c'K + W_K(y,K,w,c;\alpha)'(I - \delta K) : \vec{D}_i(y,K,x,I;g_x,g_I) \geq \alpha\},$$

(4.17)

with the associated Lagrangian problem

$$rW(k,y,w,c;\alpha) = \min_{x_t,I_t}\{w_t'x_t + c'k + W_k(k,y,w,c,;\alpha)(I - \delta k)$$
$$+ \lambda^C(\vec{D}_i(y_t,k,x,I_t;g_x,g_I) - \alpha)\}.$$

(4.18)

Once optimized, differentiating (4.18) with respect to α yields

$$r\frac{\partial W(y,K,w,c;\alpha)}{\partial \alpha} = W_{K\alpha}(.)'(I - \delta K) - \lambda^C.$$

(4.19)

Given the translation property DDI.2, (4.18) can be rewritten as

$$rW(k,y,w,c;\alpha) = \min_{x_t,I_t}\{w_t'x_t + c'k + W_k(k,y,w,c,;\alpha)(I - \delta k)$$
$$+ \lambda^C(\vec{D}_i(y_t,k,x - \alpha g_x,I_t + \alpha g_I;g_x,g_I) - 0)\},$$

(4.20)

or, equivalently,

$$rW(y,K,w,c;\alpha)$$
$$= \min_{x,I} \{w'(x - \alpha g_x) + c'K + W_k(y,K,w,c;\alpha)(I + \alpha g_I - \delta K)$$
$$+ \lambda^C(\vec{D}_i(y,K,x - \alpha g_x,I + \alpha g_I;g_x,g_I) - 0)\}$$
$$+ \alpha(w'g_x - W_k(y,K,w,c;\alpha)'g_I).$$

(4.21)

Differentiating the optimized version of (4.21) with respect to α yields

$$r\frac{\partial W(y,K,w,c;\alpha)}{\partial \alpha} = W_{K\alpha}(.)'(I - \delta K) + w'g_x - W_K(.)'g_I.$$

(4.22)

From (4.19) and (4.22), one can establish that

$$\lambda^C = W_K(\cdot)'g_I - w'g_x,$$

(4.23)

which is the firm's cost (or shadow) valuation of the directional vector.

Additional assumptions are imposed to establish the duality between $\vec{D}_i$ and the optimal value function associated with the dynamic cost minimization problem W. The following conditions are assumed to hold:

(a.1) For each (y, K_t, w, c), there exists a unique solution for problem (4.14) in the sense of convergent integrals; the policy functions $x^*(y, K_t, w, c)$ and $I^*(y, K_t, w, c)$ are $C^{(1)}$ and the current value shadow price function $\theta^*(y, K_t, w, c)$ is $C^{(2)}$.

(a.2) For each (y, K_t, x^0, I^0), there exists (y, K_t, w^0, c^0) such that (x^0, I^0) is optimal for problem (4.14) at $s = t$.

Assumption (a.1) establishes the existence of a unique and differentiable optimal solution to the dynamic cost minimization problem. Given the dynamic cost minimization problem, the only points (y, K_t, x^0, I^0) that matter are the ones satisfying condition (a.2).

Given properties DDI.1–DDI.10 of $\vec{D}_i$ and assumptions (a.1) and (a.2), by theorem 19.3 in Caputo (2005, p. 528), the current value of the optimal value function W associated with the dynamic cost minimization problem obeys the Hamilton-Jacobi-Bellman equation in (4.15). By assumption (a.2), for any (y, K, w, c), the optimal values of (x, I) for problem (4.14) are given by the values of the policy functions $x^*(y, K, w, c)$ and $I^*(y, K, w, c)$.

Theorems 4.1 and 4.2 (from Silva et al., 2015) to follow establish dynamic duality between the directional input distance function and the current value of the optimal value function.

Theorem 4.1: Let $\vec{D}_i$ satisfy properties DDI.1–DDI.10 and assume conditions (a.1) and (a.2). Define W as in (4.14). Then, W satisfies the following properties:

W.1 W is a real-valued function; $W \in C^{(2)}$ and $W_K \in C^{(2)}$.

W.2 W is increasing in y.

W.3 W is decreasing in K_t.

W.4 (a) $W_{Ky}(.)'(I^* - \delta K) - rW_y < 0^M$,

(b) $W_{KK}(.)'(I^* - \delta K) - (r + \delta)W_K(.) + c > 0^F$,

(c) $W_{Kc}(.)'(I^* - \delta K) = rW_c(.) - K$,

(d) $W_{Kw}(.)'(I^* - \delta K) = rW_w(.) - x^*$.

W.5 W is homogeneous of degree 1 in (w, c).

W.6 (a) W is increasing in w; (b) W is increasing in c.

W.7 W is concave in (w, c), given K and y.

W.8 For any (y, K, w, c), define the following problem:

$$F(y, K, x, I; g_x, g_I)$$
$$= \min_{w,c} \left\{ \frac{w'x + c'K + W_k(.)'(I - \delta K) - rW(y, K, w, c)}{w'g_x - W_k(.)'g_I} \right\}.$$

(a) For (y, K, w^0, c^0), the minimum value in the previous problem occurs at $(w, c) = (w^0, c^0)$ if $(x, I) = (x^*(y, K, w^0, c^0), I^*(y, K, w^0, c^0))$

(b) F is nonnegative and strictly concave in (x, I), given y and K.

Theorem 4.2: Let W satisfy properties W.1–W.8. Define

$$\vec{D}_i(y, K, x, I; g_x, g_I) = \min_{w,c} \left\{ \frac{w'x + c'K + W_k(.)'(I - \delta K) - rW(y, K, w, c)}{wg_x - W_k(.)'g_I} \right\}.$$

Then, over its domain of definition, $\vec{D}_i$ satisfies properties DDI.1–DDI.10.

Theorems 4.1 and 4.2 prove the existence of the following duality between the current value of the optimal value function:

$$rW(y, K, w, c) = \min_{x, I} \left\{ w'x + c'K + W_k(y, K, w, c)'(I - \delta K) \right.$$
$$\left. + (W_k(y, K, w, c)'g_I - w'g_x)\vec{D}_i(y, K, x, I; g_x, g_I) \right\}, \quad (4.24)$$

and the dynamic directional input distance function

$$\vec{D}_i(y, K, x, I; g_x, g_I) = \min_{w,c} \left\{ \frac{w'x + c'K + W_k(.)(I - \delta K) - rW(y, K, w, c)}{wg_x - W_k(.)'g_I} \right\}.$$
$$(4.25)$$

The first part of the duality result in (4.24) is illustrated in Figure 3.2, which depicts the cost minimization at any base period t, $t \in [0, +\infty)$, given a production technology. The slope of the dynamic isocost curves is $-W_k/w$ and the

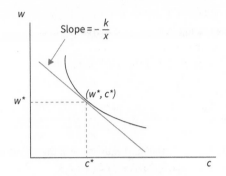

Figure 4.5. Second part of the duality result between the dynamic directional distance function and the long-term cost function.

slope of the isoquant of the input set at any point is $-\partial \vec{D}_i / \partial I \big/ \partial \vec{D}_i / \partial x$. The optimal solution is the tangency point between an isoquant and a dynamic isocost curve.

The second part of the duality result is depicted in Figure 4.5, which shows the optimization in the dual problem in (4.48). This figure illustrates that the solution (w^*, c^*) is found at the point of tangency of the long-term isocost curve (in current value terms) and a line with slope $-k/x$. Note that the expression in (4.48) is zero at the point of tangency of the two curves with optimal prices (w^*, c^*). Solving for w yields $w = \dfrac{rW - W_k(I - \delta k)}{x} - c\dfrac{k}{x}$.

4.3.2 Temporal Cost Inefficiency Measures

Using (4.24) and (4.25), the following inequality can be established:

$$rW(y,K,w,c)$$
$$\leq w'x + c'K + W_K(.)'(I - \delta K) + (W_K(.)'g_I - w'g_x)\,\vec{D}_i(y,K,x,I;g_x,g_I),$$
$$(4.26)$$

which can be rearranged as

$$OE_i = \frac{w'x + c'K + W_K(.)'(I - \delta K) - rW(y,K,w,c)}{w'g_x - W_K(.)'g_I} \geq \vec{D}_i(y,K,x,I;g_x,g_I).$$
$$(4.27)$$

The left-hand side is the measure of temporal cost inefficiency (OE_i). This measure is the normalized deviation between the shadow cost of the actual choices and the minimum shadow cost. The normalization is the shadow value of the direction vector, making the cost inefficiency a unit-free measure. The right-hand side is the adjustment cost directional input distance function measure of technical inefficiency of variable and dynamic factors.

Expression (4.27) can be modified by introducing allocative inefficiency (AE_i), rendering it as the following equality:

$$OE_i = \frac{w'x + c'K + W_K(.)'(I - \delta K) - rW(y,K,w,c)}{w'g_x - W_K(.)'g_I}$$
$$= \vec{D}_i(y,K,x,I;g_x,g_I) + AE_i, \tag{4.28}$$

with $AE_i \geq 0$.

Note that temporal cost inefficiency (and the adjustment cost directional input distance function) depends on the direction vector chosen, (g_x, g_I). As in the static context, the theoretical framework developed in the previous sections does not offer any guideline for the choice of the direction vector.

Example 4.5: Temporal cost inefficiency
The concept of temporal cost inefficiency is illustrated using the data of firms presented in Table 4.1. In addition, it is assumed that the price of the variable input (w) is 1 and the rental cost of the quasi-fixed input (c) is equal to 0.1; depreciation is assumed to be zero. For the moment, it is assumed that W_k, is the shadow value of the quasi-fixed capital stock -1. Note, however, that this value is endogenously determined in the optimization problem. In Chapter 6, we present different approaches for measuring the shadow value of the capital stock. The long-run minimum cost is found at the point where the isoquant of the adjustment cost requirement input set is tangent to an isocost line. An isocost line is written as

$$x = \frac{rW - (c - \delta W_k) \cdot k}{w} - \frac{W_k}{w} I.$$

In Figure 4.5, it can be seen that the isocost line is tangent to the isoquant at point 2. The implication is that the firms in the sample minimize their long-term costs by choosing the optimal investment level of four units and using three units of variable inputs. Hence, given the prices noted earlier, minimum long-term cost is equal to zero.

Figure 4.6 shows the projection of firm 4's input bundle, given the directional vector $(g_x = -1, g_I = 1)$ at point 4′ on the isoquant and point 4″ on the isocost line. Point 4′ is a point technically efficient with co-ordinates $(4.4, 3.6)$ and the value of the directional input distance function for firm 4 is 1.4 (already determined in example 4.3). Using (4.28), the value of the measure of temporal cost efficiency for firm 4 is $OE_4 \dfrac{5+1-3}{2} = 1.5$. In Figure 4.6, this measure is given by the distance, normalized by the value of the direction vector, between firm 4's input bundle and input bundle 4″ on the isocost line. The shadow cost of input bundle 4″ is equal to the shadow cost of input bundle 2, the cost-minimizing input vector.

The cost-minimizing vector of inputs (indicated at 4″) for this firm is at the intersection from the isocost line and the line of the directional vector (which is graphically determined as $x = 8 - I$), thus, at the point $(4.5, 3.5)$ in Figure 4.6.

Using the decomposition of temporal cost inefficiency into technical in-efficiency and allocative inefficiency in (4.28), the allocative inefficiency for firm 4 is $0.10 \, (= 1.5 - 1.4)$.

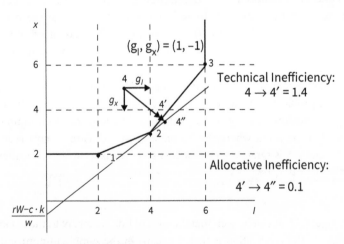

Figure 4.6 Cost Inefficiency: Example

4.3.3 Temporal Profit Inefficiency Measures

This section extends the characterization of dynamic inefficiency to the context of a long-term profit-maximizing firm. The concept of dynamic profit inefficiency is developed, and it is shown how this measure of inefficiency is decomposed into the contributions of allocative and technical inefficiency. At any base period $t \in [0,+\infty)$, the firm is assumed to maximize the discounted flow of profit over time as described in (3.49). Using $\vec{D}_T(y(s),K(s),x(s),I(s);g_y,g_x,g_I) \geq 0$, $s \in [t,+\infty)$ as a constraint in place of $F(y(s),x(s),K(s),I(s)) = 0$ $s \in (t,\infty)$, the intertemporal profit maximization problem can be defined as

$$J(p,k,w,c) = \max_{\{y,x,I\}} \int_{t_o}^{\infty} e^{-es}[p(s)y(s) - w(s)'x(s) - c(s)'K(s)]ds \quad (4.29)$$
$$\dot{K} = I - \delta K, K(t_o) = k$$
$$\vec{D}_T(y(s),K(s),x(s),I(s);g_y,g_x,g_I) \geq 0, \ s \in [t,+\infty),$$

where $p \in \mathfrak{R}_{++}^M$ is a vector of the output prices. We will now establish duality between the dynamic directional technology distance function $\vec{D}_T$ and J. Additional assumptions are imposed to use differential calculus to establish the duality between $\vec{D}_T$ and J. An additional property of $\vec{D}_T$ is assumed: DDT.9, $\vec{D}_T(.) \in C^{(1)}$ and $\vec{D}_{T_l}(.) \in C^{(1)}$, $l = y, K, x, I$.

The following conditions are assumed to hold:

(b.1) For each (p, K_t, w, c), there exists a unique solution for problem (4.29) in the sense of convergent integrals; the policy functions $y^*(p, K_t, w, c), x^*(p, K_t, w, c)$ and $I^*(p, K_t, w, c)$ are $C^{(1)}$ and the current value shadow price function $\theta^*(p, K_t, w, c)$ is $C^{(2)}$.

(b.2) For each (y^0, K_t, x^0, I^0), there exists (p^0, K_t, w^0, c^0) such that (y^0, x^0, I^0) is optimal for the problem in (4.29) at $s = t$.

Assumption DDT.9 guarantees smoothness conditions necessary to use differential calculus to establish the duality between $\vec{D}_T$ and J. Assumption (b.1) establishes the existence of a unique and differentiable J. The only points (p^0, K_t, x^0, I^0) that matter for the dynamic profit maximization problem are the ones satisfying condition (b.2).

Given properties DDT.1–DDT.9 of $\vec{D}_T$ and assumptions (b.1) and (b.2), by theorem 19.3 in Caputo (2005, p. 528), the current value of the optimal value function $J(.)$ associated with the problem in (4.29) obeys the Hamilton-Jacobi-Bellman equation:

$$rJ(p,K,w,c) = \max_{y,x,I}\{p'y - w'x - c'K + J_k(p,K,w,c)'(I - \delta K):$$
$$\vec{D}_T(y,K,x,I;g_y,g_x,g_I)\}, \qquad (4.30)$$

where K is any possible capital vector in the base period. By assumption (b.2), for any (p,K,w,c) the optimal values of (y, x, I) for the problem in (4.30) are given by the values of the policy functions $y^*(p,K,w,c)$ $x^*(p,K,w,c)$ and $I^*(p,K,w,c)$.

The Hamilton-Jacobi-Bellman equation in (4.30) can be converted to the following unconstrained problem as

$$rJ(p,K,w,c)$$
$$= \max_{y,x,I}\{p'y - w'x - c'K + J_k(p,K,w,c)'(I - \delta K) + \lambda^{\pi}\vec{D}_T(y,K,x,I;g_y,g_x,g_I)\},$$
$$(4.31)$$

where

$$\lambda^{\pi} = p'g_y + w'g_x + J_k(.)'g_I, \qquad (4.32)$$

which is the value of the directional vector and is found in an analogous way as for the intertemporal cost minimization problem in (4.14).

Theorems 4.3 and 4.4 establish dynamic duality between the adjustment cost directional technology distance function and the current value of the optimal value function.

Theorem 4.3: Let $\vec{D}_T(.)$ satisfy properties DDT.1–DDT.9 and assume conditions (b.1) and (b.2). Define $J(.)$ as in problem (4.29). Then, $J(.)$ satisfies the following properties:

J.1 $J(.)$ is a real-valued function; $J(.) \in C^{(2)}$ and $J_K(.) \in C^{(2)}$.

J.2 $J(.)$ is increasing in p.

J.3 $J(.)$ is increasing in K_t, which follows from $I(s) \in \mathfrak{R}_+^F$.

J.4 (a) $J_{KK}(.)\cdot(I^* - \delta K) - (r + \delta)J_K(.) + c < 0^F$,

   (b) $J_{Kc}(.)\cdot(I^* - \delta K) = rJ_c(.) + K$,

   (c) $J_{Kp}(.)\cdot(I^* - \delta K) = rJ_p(.) - y^*$,

   (d) $J_{Kw}(.)\cdot(I^* - \delta K) = rJ_w(.) + x^*$.

J.5 $J(.)$ is homogeneous of degree 1 in (p,w,c).

J.6 (a) $J(.)$ is increasing in p;

   (b) $J(.)$ is decreasing in (w,c).

J.7 $J(.)$ is convex in (p,w,c), given K.

J.8 For any (p,K,w,c), define the following problem:

$$F(y,K,x,I;g_y,g_x,g_I)$$
$$= \min_{p,w,c}\left\{\frac{rJ(p,K,w,c) - [py' - w'x - c'K + J_k(.)'(I - \delta K)]}{p'g_y + w'g_x + J_k(.)'g_I}\right\}.$$

   (a) For (p^0,K,w^0,c^0), the maximum value of $F(y,K,x,I;g_y,g_x,g_I)$ occurs at $(p,w,c) = (p^0,w^0,c^0)$ if $(y,x,I) = (y^*(p^0,K,w^0,c^0),x^*(p^0,K,w^0,c^0),I^*(p,K,w^0,c^0))$.

   (b) $F(.)$ is nonnegative and strictly concave in (y,x,I), given K.

Theorem 4.4: Let $J(.)$ satisfy properties J.1–J.8. Define

$$\vec{D}_T(y,K,x,I;g_y,g_x,g_I)$$
$$= \min_{p,w,c}\left\{\frac{rJ(p,K,w,c) - \left[p'y - w'x - c'K + J_k(.)'(I - \delta K)\right]}{p'g_y + w'g_x + J_k(.)'g_I}\right\}$$

Then, over its domain of definition, $\vec{D}_T(.)$ satisfies properties DDT.1–DDT.9. Using (4.31) and the definition of optimal value function, the following statement is true:

$$rJ(p,K,w,c) \geq p'y - w'x - c'K + J_K(.)'(I - \delta K)$$
$$+ (p'g_y + w'g_x + J_K(.)'g_I)\vec{D}_T(y,k,x,g_y,g_x,g_I\}. \quad (4.33)$$

This inequality can be rearranged as

$$OE_p = \frac{rJ(p,K,w,c) - [p'y - w'x - c'K + J_K(.)'(I - \delta K)]}{pg_y + w'g_x + J_K(.)'g_I}$$
$$\geq \vec{D}_T(y,K,x,I;g_y,g_x,g_I), \quad (4.34)$$

where the left-hand side becomes what we refer as to as temporal profit inefficiency (OE_p). This measure is the normalized deviation between the maximum shadow profit and the shadow profit of the actual choices. The normalization is the shadow value of the direction vector, making the temporal profit inefficiency a unit-free measure. The right-hand side is the adjustment cost directional input distance function measure of technical inefficiency of variable and dynamic factors.

Expression (4.34) can be modified by introducing allocative inefficiency (AE_p), rendering it as the following equality:

$$
\begin{aligned}
OE_p &= \frac{rJ(y,K,w,c) - [p'y - w'x - c'K + W_K(.)'(I - \delta K)]}{p'g_y + w'g_x + J_K(.)'g_I} \\
&= \vec{D}_T(y,K,x,I;g_y,g_x,g_I) + AE_p,
\end{aligned} \tag{4.35}
$$

with $AE_p \geq 0$.

4.4 Remarks

With the development of the directional distance function representation of the technology under adjustment costs, we present the fundamental dynamic programming equation for dynamic economic decision making. This serves as a point of departure for generating many concepts in production economics. In particular, we start off with the duality relationships between the technology and the value functions associated with intertemporal cost minimization and profit maximization. Taking a DEA perspective on this problem setting, we demonstrate that this dynamic problem can be solved via a sequence of two linear programming problems; that is, set up the dual and solve for the optimal shadow value of capital, and then return to the primal and solve the linear programming problem for variable and investment factors, given the shadow value of capital determined in the first stage. This can greatly simplify the prospects of solving dynamic economic problems of the framework used in this chapter.

We then go on to different concepts of productive efficiency that provide the dynamic difference measures of relative efficiency as opposed to the ratio measures found in Nemoto and Goto (2003) and hyperbolic measures in Silva and Stefanou (2007). The dynamic inefficiency measures using the directional distance technology easily disentangle the contribution of individual variable and dynamic factors of production to inefficiency. This provides a useful decision-making perspective on how each input relates to its relative contribution to inefficiency. Laying out this foundation serves as a starting point for the next chapter for developing the different measures of economics performance that we tend to measure, such as productivity, scale economies, scope economies, and capacity utilization.

Analytical tools like the adjustment cost directional distance functions have been primarily used to generate measures of productive inefficiency and total factor productivity growth. A few empirical studies employ the adjustment cost directional input distance function and the dual relation between this function and the current cost function to measure cost inefficiency. These studies include (but are not limited to) Kapelko et al. (2015b), Serra et al. (2011), Ang and Oude Lansink (2018), Tovar and Wall (2017), and Kapelko (2017). Kapelko et al. (2015b) evaluate dynamic cost inefficiency and its decomposition into technical, scale, and allocative inefficiency of the Spanish construction industry before and during the 2008 financial crisis, and Serra et al. (2011) investigate cost inefficiency and its components for the Dutch dairy farms during 1995 to 2005. Kapelko (2017) compares static versus dynamic cost inefficiency and its decomposition in the Polish meat processing industry. Tovar and Wall (2017) measure dynamic cost and technical inefficiency of Spanish ports. Setiawan and Oude Lansink (2018) employ the adjustment cost directional input distance function to investigate the relation between industrial concentration and technical inefficiency in the Indonesian food and beverages industry. Ang and Oude Lansink (2018) analyze the dynamic profit inefficiency of Belgian dairy farms under the quota system and identify the inefficiency attributable to each input and output separately.

The foundations of duality theory are established in Shephard (1953) in a static framework. For those readers who are not familiar with duality theory, please see Shephard (1953, 1970) and Färe and Primont (1995). Shephard (1953, 1970) shows that the cost and revenue functions are dual representations of the production technology. In particular, Shephard (1953, 1970) investigates duality between the cost (revenue) function and the radial input (output) distance function. Färe and Primont (1995) systematize the dual relations established by Shephard (1953, 1970).

Dynamic (or intertemporal) duality has been focused on the dual relation between the production function and the optimal value function of an intertemporal optimization problem (e.g., Epstein, 1981; Lasserre and Ouellette, 1999; Ouellette and Vigeant, 2001) as well as duality between the optimal value function and the instantaneous variable profit function (McLaren and Cooper, 1980).

4.5 Appendix: Proof of Lemmas

Proof of Lemma 4.1:

$(i)\,(x,I,y)\in T(K)\Rightarrow \vec{D}_T(x,I,y,K;g_x,g_I,g_y)\geq 0$.

Assume $(x,I,y)\in T(K)$. By definition 4.1, $(x-\vec{D}_T(.)g_x,I+\vec{D}_T(.)g_I,y+\vec{D}_T(.)g_y)\in T(K)$.

Using properties T.6S, T.7S, and T.8 yields

$$x\geq x-\vec{D}_T(x,I,y,K;g_x,g_I,g_y)g_x;$$
$$I\leq I+\vec{D}_T(x,I,y,K;g_x,g_I,g_y)g_I;$$
$$y\leq y+\vec{D}_T(x,I,y,K;g_x,g_I,g_y)g_y.$$

Since $g=(g_x,g_I,g_y)\in\Re_+^N\times\Re_+^F\times\Re_+^M$, $g\neq 0_{N+F+M}$, then $\vec{D}_T(x,I,y,K;g_x,g_I,g_y)\geq 0$.

$(ii)\,\vec{D}_T(x,I,y,K;g_x,g_I,g_y)\geq 0\Rightarrow (x,I,y)\in T(K)$.

Using definition 2.10, $(x-\vec{D}_T(.)g_x,I+\vec{D}_T(.)g_I,y+\vec{D}_T(.)g_y)\in T(K)$. By assumption, $\vec{D}_T(x,I,y,K;g_x,g_I,g_y)\geq 0$. Since $g=(g_x,g_I,g_y)\in\Re_+^N\times\Re_+^F\times\Re_+^M$, $g\neq 0_{N+F+M}$, then

$$x\geq x-\vec{D}_T(x,I,y,K;g_x,g_I,g_y)g_x;$$
$$I\leq I+\vec{D}_T(x,I,y,K;g_x,g_I,g_y)g_I;$$
$$y\leq y+\vec{D}_T(x,I,y,K;g_x,g_I,g_y)g_y.$$

Using properties T.6S, T.7S, and T.8, $(x,I,y)\in T(K)$.

Proof of Lemma 4.2:

From property DDI.3, $(x(t),I(t))\in V(y(t):K(t))\Rightarrow \vec{D}_i(x(t),I(t),y(t),K(t);g_x,g_I)\geq 0$. We only need to prove $\vec{D}_i(x(t),I(t),y(t),K(t);g_x,g_I)\geq 0$ $\Rightarrow (x(t),I(t))\in V(y(t):K(t))$ to demonstrate lemma 4.2.

Assume $\vec{D}_i(x(t), I(t), y(t), K(t); g_x, g_I) = 0$. By the definition of $\vec{D}_i(.)$,
$(x - \vec{D}_i(x, I, y, K; g_x, g_I)g_x, I + \vec{D}_i(x, I, y, K; g_x, g_I)g_I) = (x, I) \in V(y:K)$.

Now, assume $\vec{D}_i(x(t), I(t), y(t), K(t); g_x, g_I) > 0$. By the definition of $\vec{D}_i(.)$,
$(x - \vec{D}_i(x, I, y, K; g_x, g_I)g_x, I + \vec{D}_i(x, I, y, K; g_x, g_I)g_I) \in V(y:K)$.

Since $\vec{D}_i(x(t), I(t), y(t), K(t); g_x, g_I) > 0$, then

$$x \ge (x - \vec{D}_i(x, I, y, K; g_x, g_I)g_x);$$
$$I \le (I + \vec{D}_i(x, I, y, K; g_x, g_I)g_I).$$

Using properties V.7S and V.8, we conclude that $(x, I) \in V(y:K)$.

4.6 Appendix: Proof of Properties DDT.1–DDT.8

DDT.1   This property follows directly from definition 4.1.

$$\vec{D}_T(x - \alpha g_x, I + \alpha g_I, y + \alpha g_y, K; g_x, g_I, g_y)$$
$$= \max_{\beta} \left\{ \beta : (x - (\alpha + \beta)g_x, I + (\alpha + \beta)g_I, y + (\alpha + \beta)g_y) \in T(K) \right\}$$
$$= \max_{\beta} \left\{ \alpha + \beta : (x - (\alpha + \beta)g_x, I + (\alpha + \beta)g_I, y + (\alpha + \beta)g_y) \in T(K) \right\} - \alpha$$
$$= \vec{D}_T(x, I, y, K; g_x, g_I, g_y) - \alpha.$$

DDT.2   This property follows from properties T.1 and T.2.

DDT.3   This property follows from definition 4.1.

$$\vec{D}_T(x, I, y, K; \mu g_x, \mu g_I, \mu g_y)$$
$$= \max_{\beta} \left\{ \beta : (x - \beta \mu g_x, I + \beta \mu g_I, y + \beta \mu g_y) \in T(K) \right\}, \quad \mu > 0$$
$$= \frac{1}{\mu} \max_{\beta} \left\{ \beta \mu : (x - \beta \mu g_x, I + \beta \mu g_I, y + \beta \mu g_y) \in T(K) \right\}, \quad \mu > 0$$
$$= (1/\mu)\vec{D}_T(x, I, y, K; g_x, g_I, g_y), \quad \mu > 0.$$

DDT.4   Assume $y' \ge y$ and $\vec{D}_T(.) > -\infty$. Using definition 4.1 yields

$$(x - \vec{D}_T g_x, I + \vec{D}_T g_I, y + \vec{D}_T g_y) \in T(K) \text{ and } (x - \vec{D}_T' g_x, I + \vec{D}_T' g_I, y + \vec{D}_T' g_y) \in T(K),$$

where $\vec{D}_T = \vec{D}_T(x, I, y, K; g_x, g_I, g_y)$ and $\vec{D}_T' = \vec{D}_T(x, I, y', K; g_x, g_I, g_y)$.

Considering the input-output vector (x, I, y) and using definition 4.1 yields

$$x - \vec{D}_T(x, I, y, K; g_x, g_I, g_y)g_x \leq x - \vec{D}_T(x, I, y', K; g_x, g_I, g_y)g_x;$$
$$I + \vec{D}_T(x, I, y, K; g_x, g_I, g_y)g_I \geq I + \vec{D}_T(x, I, y', K; g_x, g_I, g_y)g_I;$$
$$y + \vec{D}_T(x, I, y, K; g_x, g_I, g_y)g_y \geq y + \vec{D}_T(x, I, y', K; g_x, g_I, g_y)g_y.$$

By properties T.6S, T.7S, and T.8, $(x - \vec{D}_T{}' g_x, I + \vec{D}_T{}' g_I, y + \vec{D}_T{}' g_y) \in T(K).$

Since $g = (g_x, g_I, g_y) \in \mathfrak{R}_+^N \times \mathfrak{R}_+^F \times \mathfrak{R}_+^M$, $\vec{D}_T(x, I, y', K; g_x, g_I, g_y)$
$\leq \vec{D}_T(x, I, y, K; g_x, g_I, g_y).$

If $\vec{D}_T(.) = -\infty$, then the previous relations are valid by default.

DDT.5   Proof of this property is similar to the proof of property DDT.4.

DDT.6   Proof of this property is similar to the proof of property DDT.4.

DDT.7   Let $K' \geq K$. By the definition of dynamic directional technology distance function,

$$\vec{D}_T(x, I, y, K'; g_x, g_I, g_y) = \max\left\{ \beta \in \mathfrak{R} : (x - \beta g_x, I + \beta g_I, y + \beta g_y) \in T(K') \right\}$$

By property T.9, $T(K) \subset T(K')$.
Thus, $\vec{D}_T(x, I, y, K; g_x, g_I, g_y) \leq \vec{D}_T(x, I, y, K'; g_x, g_I, g_y).$

DDT.8   Assume $T(K)$ is a convex set and $\vec{D}_T(.) > -\infty$.

$T(K)$ is a convex set if and only if $\forall (x, I, y)$ and $(x', I', y') \in T(K)$, $\forall \alpha \in [0, 1]$,

$$\left[\alpha x + (1 - \alpha)x', \alpha I + (1 - \alpha)I', \alpha y + (1 - \alpha)y' \right] \in T(K).$$

Using definition 4.1, $(x - \vec{D}_T g_x, I + \vec{D}_T g_I, y + \vec{D}_T g_y) \in T(K)$ and

$$(x' - \vec{D}_T{}' g_x, I' + \vec{D}_T{}' g_I, y' + \vec{D}_T{}' g_y) \in T(K),$$

where $\vec{D}_T = \vec{D}_T(x, I, y, K; g_x, g_I, g_y)$ and $\vec{D}_T{}' = \vec{D}_T(x', I', y', K; g_x, g_I, g_y)$.
    By the convexity property of $T(K)$, the following input-output vector is feasible:

$$\left[\alpha(x - \vec{D}_T g_x) + (1-\alpha)(x' - \vec{D}_T' g_x), \alpha(I - \vec{D}_T g_I) + (1-\alpha)(I' - \vec{D}_T' g_I), \right.$$
$$\left. \alpha(y + \vec{D}_T g_y) + (1-\alpha)(y' + \vec{D}_T' g_y) \right] \in T(K).$$

Using definition 4.1, the following input-output vector is also feasible:

$$\left[(\alpha x + (1-\alpha)x') - \vec{D}_T^C g_x, (\alpha I + (1-\alpha)I') \right.$$
$$\left. + \vec{D}_T^C g_I, (\alpha y + (1-\alpha)y') + \vec{D}_T^C g_y \right] \in T(K),$$

where $\vec{D}_T^C = \vec{D}_T(\alpha x + (1-\alpha)x', \alpha I + (1-\alpha)I', \alpha y + (1-\alpha)y', K; g_x, g_I, g_y)$.
By the definition of the distance function,

$$(\alpha x + (1-\alpha)x') - (\alpha\vec{D}_T + (1-\alpha)\vec{D}_T')g_x \geq (\alpha x + (1-\alpha)x') - \vec{D}_T^C g_x;$$
$$(\alpha I + (1-\alpha)I') + (\alpha\vec{D}_T + (1-\alpha)\vec{D}_T')g_I \leq (\alpha I + (1-\alpha)I') + \vec{D}_T^C g_I;$$
$$(\alpha y + (1-\alpha)y') + (\alpha\vec{D}_T + (1-\alpha)\vec{D}_T')g_y \leq (\alpha y + (1-\alpha)y')\vec{D}_T^C g_y$$

Thus, $\vec{D}_T^C \geq \alpha\vec{D}_T + (1-\alpha)\vec{D}_T'$.

Strict concavity of $\vec{D}_T(x, I, y, K; g_x, g_I, g_y)$ can be proved in a similar way by postulating that $T(K(t))$ is a strict convex set.

4.7 Appendix: Proof of DDI.1–DDI.9

DDI.1   Assume that $V(y: K)$ is convex and $(x^1, I^1), (x^2, I^2) \in V(y: K)$.

Case 1: Let $\vec{D}_i(x^1, I^1, y, K; g_x, g_I)$ and $\vec{D}_i(x^2, I^2, y, K; g_x, g_I)$ be finite numbers. By the definition of $\vec{D}_i(.)$,

$$\left(x^1 - \vec{D}_i(x^1, I^1, y, K; g_x, g_I)g_x, I^1 + \vec{D}_i(x^1, I^1, y, K; g_x, g_I)g_I \right) \in V(y: K) \text{ and}$$
$$\left(x^2 - \vec{D}_i(x^2, I^2, y, K; g_x, g_I)g_x, I^2 + \vec{D}_i(x^2, I^2, y, K; g_x, g_I)g_I \right) \in V(y: K).$$

Given that $V(y: K)$ is convex, $\forall \alpha[0,1]$,

$$\begin{bmatrix} \alpha(x^1 - \vec{D}_i^1)g_x + (1-\alpha)(x^2 - \vec{D}_i^2)g_x, \alpha(I^1 + \vec{D}_i^1)g_I \\ + (1-\alpha)(I^2 + \vec{D}_i^2)g_I \end{bmatrix} \in V(y:K), \quad \text{or}$$

$$\begin{bmatrix} \alpha x^1 + (1-\alpha)x^2 - (\alpha\vec{D}_i^1 + (1-\alpha)\vec{D}_i^2)g_x, \alpha I^1 \\ + (1-\alpha)I^2 + (\alpha\vec{D}_i^1 + (1-\alpha)\vec{D}_i^2)g_I \end{bmatrix} \in V(y:K),$$

where $\vec{D}_i^1 = \vec{D}_i(x^1, I^1, y, K; g_x, g_I)$ and $\vec{D}_i^2 = \vec{D}_i(x^2, I^2, y, K; g_x, g_I)$.

Since $V(y:K)$ is convex, $(\alpha x^1 + (1-\alpha)x^2, \alpha I^1 + (1-\alpha)I^2) \in V(y:K)$. By the definition of $\vec{D}_i(.)$,

$$[(\alpha x^1 + (1-\alpha)x^2) - \vec{D}_i^C g_x, (\alpha I^1 + (1-\alpha)I^2) + \vec{D}_i^C g_I] \in V(y:K),$$

where $\vec{D}_i^C = \vec{D}_i(\alpha x^1 + (1-\alpha)x^2, \alpha I^1 + (1-\alpha)I^2, y, K; g_x, g_I)$.

Using again the definition of $\vec{D}_i(.)$,

$$\vec{D}_i^C \geq \alpha\vec{D}_i(x^1, I^1, y, K; g_x, g_I) + (1-\alpha)\vec{D}_i(x^2, I^2, y, K; g_x, g_I),$$

establishing the concavity of the dynamic directional input distance function.

Strict concavity of the dynamic directional input distance function can be established in a similar way.

Case 2: If $\vec{D}_i(x^1, I^1, y, K; g_x, g_I) = -\infty$ and $\vec{D}_i(x^2, I^2, y, K; g_x, g_I) = -\infty$, then the following statement is true:

$$\vec{D}_i^C \geq \alpha\vec{D}_i(x^1, I^1, y, K; g_x, g_I) + (1-\alpha)\vec{D}_i(x^2, I^2, y, K; g_x, g_I); \text{that is, } \vec{D}_i^C \geq -\infty.$$

Thus, the concavity property holds.

DDI.2   The translation property follows from definition 4.1. For $\alpha \in \Re_+$,

$$\begin{aligned} \vec{D}_i&(x + \alpha g_x, I - \alpha g_I, y, K; g_x, g_I) \\ &= \max_\theta \left\{ \theta \in \Re : (x + \alpha g_x - \theta g_x, I - \alpha g_I + \theta g_I) \in V(y:K) \right\} \\ &= \max_\theta \left\{ \theta \in \Re : (x - (\theta - \alpha)g_x, I + (\theta - \alpha)g_I) \in V(y:K) \right\} \\ &= \alpha + \max_\theta \left\{ (\theta - \alpha) \in \Re : (x - (\theta - \alpha)g_x, I + (\theta - \alpha)g_I) \in V(y:K) \right\} \\ &= \alpha + \max_{\tilde{\theta}} \left\{ \tilde{\theta} \in \Re : (x - \tilde{\theta}g_x, I + \tilde{\theta}g_I) \in V(y:K) \right\} \\ &= \alpha + \vec{D}_i(x, I, y, K; g_x, g_I). \end{aligned}$$

DDI.3

(i) By the way of contradiction, assume $(x,I) \in V(y:K)$ and $\vec{D}_i(x,I,y,K;g_x,g_I) < 0$. By the definition of $\vec{D}_i(.)$, $(x - \vec{D}_i(x,I,y,K;g_x,g_I)g_x, I + \vec{D}_i(x,I,y,K;g_x,g_I)g_I) \in V(y:K)$.

Since $(x,I) \in V(y:K)$ and
$(x - \vec{D}_i(x,I,y,K;g_x,g_I)g_x, I + \vec{D}_i(x,I,y,K;g_x,g_I)g_I) \in V(y:K)$, then

$$x \geq (x - \vec{D}_i(x,I,y,K;g_x,g_I)g_x);$$
$$I \leq (I + \vec{D}_i(x,I,y,K;g_x,g_I)g_I).$$

Thus, $\vec{D}_i(x,I,y,K;g_x,g_I) \geq 0$. Contradiction!

(ii) Alternatively, we can prove the following:
$\vec{D}_i(x,I,y,K;g_x,g_I) < 0 \Rightarrow (x,I) \notin V(y:K)$.

Assume $\vec{D}_i(x,I,y,K;g_x,g_I) < 0$. By the definition of $\vec{D}_i(.)$,

$$(x - \vec{D}_i(x,I,y,K;g_x,g_I)g_x, I + \vec{D}_i(x,I,y,K;g_x,g_I)g_I) \in V(y:K).$$

Hence,

$$x < (x - \vec{D}_i(x,I,y,K;g_x,g_I)g_x);$$
$$I > (I + \vec{D}_i(x,I,y,K;g_x,g_I)g_I).$$

By the definition of $\vec{D}_i(.)$, $(x,I) \notin V(y:K)$.

DDI.4

$$\vec{D}_i(x,I,y,K;\mu g_x,\mu g_I) = \max_{\beta}\left\{\beta \in \mathfrak{R} : (x - \beta\mu g_x, I + \beta\mu g_I) \in V(y:K)\right\}$$
$$= \frac{1}{\mu}\max_{\beta}\left\{(\beta\mu) \in \mathfrak{R} : (x - \beta\mu g_x, I + \beta\mu g_I) \in V(y:K)\right\}$$
$$= \frac{1}{\mu}\max_{\tilde{\beta}}\left\{\tilde{\beta} \in \mathfrak{R} : (x - \tilde{\beta} g_x, I + \tilde{\beta} g_I) \in V(y:K)\right\}$$
$$= \frac{1}{\mu}\vec{D}_i(x,I,y,K;g_x,g_I).$$

DDI.5

(a) If $y' \geq y \;\Rightarrow\; V(y':K) \subset V(y:K)$, then

$$(x - \vec{D}_i(x,I,y',K;g_x,g_I)g_x, I + \vec{D}_i(x,I,y',K;g_x,g_I)g_I) \in V(y':K) \subset V(y:K).$$

Using the definition of $\vec{D}_i(.)$, $\vec{D}_i(x,I,y,K;g_x,g_I) \geq \vec{D}_i(x,I,y',K;g_x,g_I)$.

(b) If $V(y:K) \subset V(\lambda y:K)$, $0 < \lambda < 1$, then

$$(x - \vec{D}_i(x,I,y,K;g_x,g_I)g_x, I + \vec{D}_i(x,I,y,K;g_x,g_I)g_I) \in V(y:K) \subset V(\lambda y:K).$$

Hence, $(x - \vec{D}_i(x,I,y,K;g_x,g_I)g_x, I + \vec{D}_i(x,I,y,K;g_x,g_I)g_I) \in V(\lambda y:K)$.

Using definition 4.1,

$$(x - \vec{D}_i(x,I,\lambda y,K;g_x,g_I)g_x, I + \vec{D}_i(x,I,\lambda y,K;g_x,g_I)g_I) \in V(\lambda y:K)$$

and

$$\vec{D}_i(x,I,\lambda y,K;g_x,g_I) \geq \vec{D}_i(x,I,y,K;g_x,g_I).$$

DDI.6   If $K' \geq K \;\Rightarrow\; V(y:K) \subset V(y:K')$, then

$$(x - \vec{D}_i(x,I,y,K;g_x,g_I)g_x, I + \vec{D}_i(x,I,y,K;g_x,g_I)g_I) \in V(y:K) \subset V(y:K').$$

Using the definition of $\vec{D}_i(.)$, $\vec{D}_i(x,I,y,K';g_x,g_I) \geq \vec{D}_i(x,I,y,K;g_x,g_I)$.

DDI.7   Assume property V.7S holds and let $x' \geq x$. By the definition of $\vec{D}_i(.)$,

$$[x - \vec{D}_i(x,I,y,K;g_x,g_I)g_x, I + \vec{D}_i(x,I,y,K;g_x,g_I)g_I] \in V(y:K),$$
$$[x' - \vec{D}_i(x,I,y,K;g_x,g_I)g_x, I + \vec{D}_i(x,I,y,K;g_x,g_I)g_I] \in V(y:K).$$

It must be the case that

$$x' - \vec{D}_i(x',I,y,K;g_x,g_I)g_x \leq x' - \vec{D}_i(x,I,y,K;g_x,g_I)g_x.$$

Thus, $\vec{D}_i(x',I,y,K;g_x,g_I) > \vec{D}_i(x,I,y,K;g_x,g_I)$.

DDI.8   The proof is similar to the proof of DDI.7.

DDI.9   This property follows from V.1 and V.2.

5
Dynamic Structure of Production and Productivity Change

5.1 Introduction

The concept of efficiency involves measuring the current practice against the maximum potential for a given technology. We can compare efficiency across firms to the extent that they share a common technology as well as other conditioning arguments such as the current capital stock and/or output levels. In contrast, productivity begins with the measure of output per unit of input, or average product, which can reflect the maximum production potential. It is also a measure by which we can benchmark firms, industries, or national economies as we track their movement over time by employing the more general concept of productivity growth. A number of elements come into play as we observe productivity growth such as innovations (using new technologies) or efficiency gains (extracting the full potential of existing technologies). In the absence of technology changes, output changes can arise for various reasons, including applying more/fewer inputs (a scale effect), not meeting the potential (inefficiency) or momentary changes in prices impacting input allocation, and the input reallocation associated with the firm adjusting to a long-run equilibrium.

A first operational consideration is how to define "output per unit of input." Any reasonable production situation involves multiple inputs that involve variable and fixed factors producing multiple outputs. There are partial productivity measures that focus on a single input (e.g., labor productivity, land productivity), but the more common approaches embrace the notion of accounting for all factors of production. Both partial and multifactor measures of productivity have their uses. Labor productivity rates are often reported in the macroeconomic context as short-term measures of aggregate economic change, and business analysts

Dynamic Efficiency and Productivity Measurement. Elvira Silva, Spiro E. Stefanou, and Alfons Oude Lansink,
Oxford University Press (2021). © Oxford University Press. DOI: 10.1093/oso/9780190919474.001.0001

use labor productivity as one shorthand measure of comparing firm potential. But as the firm substitutes inputs as it operates optimally, the multifactor measure is better suited to measure firm adjustment beyond the short term.

Why do we care about growth? Firm-level growth is important to shareholders. While cost savings can drive earnings and shareholder value, firms that achieve productivity growth through increasing their potential have the best odds of survival in the longer term. Virtually all firms stagnate at some point in their lifetime, and their ability to rekindle growth determines their long-term prospects (Olson et al., 2008). This is often achieved through research and development (R&D) and innovation activities that include improving the average productivity or developing product-differentiating strategies such as improving the quality of products/services or even entirely new products/services. Operationally, these are embodied as changes in technology sets. At the more aggregated level of the sector and broader economy, growth is important as an indicator of competitiveness. Firms (or sectors) that are able to attract quality resources to support their production activities will be competitive and grow. At the national level, the agglomeration effects of growing sectors keep a national economy vibrant and able to contribute to economic growth across many sectors.

Assets play an important role in production potential and economic growth. Oftentimes, the discussion of growth typically revolves around thinking about the steady state. How capital inputs are adjusting in production can impact growth patterns. Clearly, there is a cost associated with being out of equilibrium, which is decomposed in sections 3.3.1 and 4.4.1. In defining dynamic measures of productivity growth, how does the current period productivity growth account for the case that the firm is not at the long-run steady-state position?

We emphasize the characterization of the production structure, which involves understanding how outputs respond to input changes, how firms can substitute inputs for given output targets, and how these responses relate to changes in productive capacity (through asset changes) and productive capabilities (through technological innovations). This chapter proceeds with the formal definitions of economies of scale and scope, capacity utilization, and productivity. This is then followed by presenting two approaches to measuring productivity growth.

5.2 Scale, Scope, and Capacity Utilization

5.2.1 Scale Elasticity

In this section, we develop and relate several measures of long-run scale economies. Using the definition of scale economies, we develop long-run primal measures of scale elasticity expressed in terms of the dynamic directional distance functions and the corresponding dual measures obtained from the dual value functions. We attempt then to relate these alternative measures of scale economies.[1]

A conventional definition of scale elasticity compares the percentage change in outputs obtained from a small percentage increase in all inputs. In the case of a single output, $y = f(x, K, I)$, the scale elasticity is traditionally computed from the adjustment cost production function as follows (Stefanou, 1989):

$$\varepsilon = \frac{\partial \ln f(\mu x, K, \mu I)}{\partial \ln \mu}\bigg|_{\mu=1} = \frac{\nabla_x f(.) \cdot x + \nabla_I f(.) \cdot I}{f(.)}. \tag{5.1}$$

This reflects that all choice inputs, (x, I), are the object of the scaling by parameter μ, while K is held fixed in the current period. The definition in (5.1) can be generalized to the multiple output case using the dynamic directional technology distance function

$$\varepsilon_T(y, K, x, I) = \frac{\partial \ln \theta}{\partial \ln \lambda}\bigg|_{\theta=\lambda=1}, \tag{5.2}$$

where

$$\vec{D}_T(\theta y, K, \mu x, \mu I; g_y, g_x, g_I) = 0. \tag{5.3}$$

Assuming that $\vec{D}_T(.)$ is differentiable and applying the implicit function rule to (5.3) yields

---

[1] Fukuyama (2003) develops a static scale elasticity measure in the context of the directional technology distance function using data envelopment analysis.

$$\sum_{n=1}^{N}\frac{\partial\vec{D}_T(.)}{\partial x_n}x_n d\mu + \sum_{f=1}^{F}\frac{\partial\vec{D}_T(.)}{\partial I_f}I_f d\mu + \sum_{m=1}^{M}\frac{\partial\vec{D}_T(.)}{\partial y_m}y_m d\theta = 0. \qquad (5.4)$$

Solving (5.4) for $d\theta/d\mu$:

$$\frac{d\theta}{d\lambda} = -\frac{\sum_{n=1}^{N}\dfrac{\partial\vec{D}_T(.)}{\partial x_n}x_n + \sum_{f=1}^{F}\dfrac{\partial\vec{D}_T(.)}{\partial I_f}I_f}{\sum_{m=1}^{M}\dfrac{\partial\vec{D}_T(.)}{\partial y_m}y_m}. \qquad (5.5)$$

Using (5.5), the long-run elasticity of scale in (5.2) can be expressed as

$$\varepsilon_T(y,K,x,I) = \frac{d\theta}{d\mu}\frac{\mu}{\theta}\bigg|_{\mu=\theta=1} = -\frac{\sum_{n=1}^{N}\dfrac{\partial\vec{D}_T(.)}{\partial x_n}x_n + \sum_{f=1}^{F}\dfrac{\partial\vec{D}_T(.)}{\partial I_f}I_f}{\sum_{m=1}^{M}\dfrac{\partial\vec{D}_T(.)}{\partial y_m}y_m}$$

$$= -\frac{\nabla_x\vec{D}_T(.)\cdot x + \nabla_I\vec{D}_T(.)\cdot I}{\nabla_y\vec{D}_T(.)\cdot y}. \qquad (5.6)$$

For an intertemporal profit-maximizing firm, the scale elasticity in (5.6) can be measured in terms of the dual value function. Consider the Hamilton-Jacobi-Bellman equation in (4.30) associated with the dynamic profit maximization problem. The optimality conditions for an interior solution yield

$$-w_n + \lambda\frac{\partial\vec{D}_T(.)}{\partial x_n} = 0, \ n = 1,...,N \qquad (5.7)$$

$$J_{K_f}(.) + \lambda\frac{\partial\vec{D}_T(.)}{\partial I_f} = 0, \ f = 1,...,F \qquad (5.8)$$

$$p_m + \lambda\frac{\partial\vec{D}_T(.)}{\partial y_m} = 0, \ m = 1,...,M. \qquad (5.9)$$

Solving (5.7)–(5.9) gives optimal solutions for variable inputs, investments, and outputs that are a function of (K,p,w,c), that is, x^*, I^*, and y^*, respectively. Using (5.7)–(5.9), the elasticity of scale in (5.6), evaluated at the optimal solution, can be rewritten as

$$\varepsilon_T(K,p,w,c) = \frac{w \cdot x^*(K,p,w,c) - J_K(.) \cdot I^*(K,p,w,c)}{p \cdot y^*(K,p,w,c)}. \qquad (5.10)$$

For an intertemporal profit-maximizing firm, the long-run scale elasticity can be computed as the ratio of the long-run variable shadow cost to the long-run total revenue.

Given that $\varepsilon_T(K,p,w,c)$ is computed using $\varepsilon_T(y,K,x,I)$, these two measures are equal at the optimal solution of the intertemporal profit maximization problem. Therefore,

$$\varepsilon_T(K,p,w,c) = \varepsilon_T(y^*,K,x^*,I^*), \qquad (5.11)$$

as long as the dynamic directional technology distance function is differentiable and satisfies properties DDT.1–DDT.7, presented in Chapter 4.

Next, consider the production technology that is characterized by the dynamic input directional distance function. The long-run scale elasticity can be defined by

$$\varepsilon_i(y,K,x,I) = \frac{\partial \ln \theta}{\partial \ln \mu}\bigg|_{\theta=\mu=1}, \qquad (5.12)$$

where

$$\vec{D}_i(\theta y, K, \mu x, \mu I; g_x, g_I) = 0. \qquad (5.13)$$

Following the same procedure as before, the elasticity of scale in (5.12) can be expressed as

$$\varepsilon_i(y,K,x,I) = \frac{d\theta}{d\mu}\frac{\mu}{\theta}\bigg|_{\mu=\theta=1} = -\frac{\sum_{n=1}^{N}\frac{\partial \vec{D}_i(.)}{\partial x_n}x_n + \sum_{f=1}^{F}\frac{\partial \vec{D}_i(.)}{\partial I_f}I_f}{\sum_{m=1}^{M}\frac{\partial \vec{D}_i(.)}{\partial y_m}y_m}$$

$$= -\frac{\nabla_x \vec{D}_i(.) \cdot x + \nabla_I \vec{D}_i(.) \cdot I}{\nabla_y \vec{D}_i(.) \cdot y}. \qquad (5.14)$$

The long-run multiple output, multiple input scale elasticity in (5.14) can be expressed in terms of the current value function of the intertemporal cost minimization problem. Consider the Hamilton-Jacobi-Bellman equation in (4.16) associated with the dynamic cost minimization problem and the following optimality conditions for an interior solution:

$$w_n + \lambda^c \frac{\partial \vec{D}_i(.)}{\partial x_n} = 0, \, n = 1,...,N, \tag{5.15a}$$

$$W_{K_f}(.) + \lambda^c \frac{\partial \vec{D}_i(.)}{\partial I_f} = 0, \, f = 1,...,F, \tag{5.15b}$$

$$\vec{D}_i(y,K,x,I;g_x,g_I) = 0, \tag{5.15c}$$

leading to $x^*(y,K,w,c)$, $I^*(y,K,w,c)$, and $\lambda^{*c}(y,K,w,c)$. Differentiating the optimized version of the Hamilton-Jacobi-Bellman equation in (4.16),

$$rW(y,K,w,c) = w'x^* + c'K + W_K(y,K,w,c)(I^* - \delta K) \\ + \lambda^{*c}\vec{D}(y,K,x^*,I^*;g_x,g_I), \tag{5.16}$$

with respect to y (and applying the envelope theorem) yields the long-run marginal cost

$$rW_y(y,K,w,c) = W_{Ky}(y,K,w,c)(I^* - \delta K) + \lambda^{c*} \frac{\partial \vec{D}_i(.)}{\partial y}. \tag{5.17}$$

Like (3.81), (5.17) represents the relationship between long-run marginal cost as equal to the instantaneous short-run marginal cost, $\lambda^{c*}\frac{\partial \vec{D}_i(.)}{\partial y}$, plus the instantaneous change in the long-run marginal cost, $W_{Ky}(y,K,w,c)(I^* - \delta K)$.

Stefanou (1989) presents an alternative construction of the intertemporal cost minimization, which follows the sequential process of first choosing the cost-minimizing variable factor level subject to a production target, yielding the restricted, time-specific cost function $C(y,K,I,w)$. The subsequent decision is to choose the optimal investment plan subject to the capital accumulation equation, $\dot{K} = I - \delta K$. The optimized Hamilton-Jacobi-Bellman equation for this construction is

$$rW(y,K,w,c) = C(y,K,I^*,w) + c'K + W_K(y,K,w,c)(I^* - \delta K),$$

where $C(y,K,I,w)$ is the short-run cost function and $C_y(y,K,I,w) = \lambda^{*c}\dfrac{\partial \vec{D}_i}{\partial y}$.

Using (5.15a), (5.15b), and (5.17), the scale elasticity in (5.14), evaluated at the optimal solution, can be expressed as

$$
\begin{aligned}
\varepsilon_i(y,K,w,c) &= \frac{w \cdot x^*(y,K,w,c) + W_K(.) \cdot I^*(y,K,w,c)}{C_y(y,K,I^*,w) \cdot y} \\
&= \frac{w \cdot x^*(y,K,w,c) + W_K(.) \cdot I^*(y,K,w,c)}{[rW_y(.) - W_{Ky}(.)(I^*(y,K,w,c) - \delta K)] \cdot y}.
\end{aligned}
\tag{5.18}
$$

The long-run elasticity of scale is the ratio of the long-run variable shadow cost to the product of the short-run marginal cost and the output vectors, which is an intertemporal version of Panzar and Willig's (1977) multiple output, multiple input measure of scale elasticity. Using the relation between the flow version of the long-run cost function and the short-run variable cost function, the scale elasticity in (5.18) can also be expressed as

$$
\varepsilon_i(y,K,w,c) = \frac{\dfrac{w \cdot x^*(y,K,w,c) + W_K(.) \cdot I^*(y,K,w,c)}{C(y,K,I^*,w)}}{C_y(y,K,I^*,w) \cdot \dfrac{y}{C(y,K,I^*,w)}},
\tag{5.19}
$$

where the numerator is equal to the ratio of the long-run variable shadow cost to the short-run variable cost and the denominator is equal to the short-run cost elasticity.

As in the case of intertemporal profit minimization, note that $\varepsilon_i(y,K,w,c)$ is computed using $\varepsilon_i(y,K,x,I)$, implying that these two measures are equal at the optimal solution of the intertemporal cost minimization problem. Therefore,

$$\varepsilon_i(y,K,w,c) = \varepsilon_i(y,K,x^*,I^*) \tag{5.20}$$

as long as the dynamic directional input distance function is differentiable and satisfies properties DDI.1–DDI.9, discussed in Chapter 4.

In general, we can establish a relation between the two pairs of measures of long-run scale elasticity, that is, the relation between $\varepsilon_T(y,K,x,I)$ and $\varepsilon_i(y,K,x,I)$ and the relation between $\varepsilon_T(K,p,w,c)$ and $\varepsilon_i(y,K,w,c)$. Notice that the scale elasticity in (5.6) must be equal to the scale elasticity in (5.14) since both measure a proportionate change in output due to a proportionate change in variable and dynamic factors:

$$\frac{d\theta}{d\mu}\frac{\mu}{\theta}\bigg|_{\mu=\theta=1} = \varepsilon_T(y,K,x,I) = \varepsilon_i(y,K,x,I). \tag{5.21}$$

We can compute $\varepsilon_T(K,p,w,c)$ using $\varepsilon_i(y,K,w,c)$ and evaluate it at the optimal solution of the intertemporal profit maximization problem. Thus,

$$\varepsilon_T(K,p,w,c) = \varepsilon_i(y^*,K,w,c) \tag{5.22}$$

as long as the dynamic directional technology distance function is differentiable and satisfies properties DDT.1–DDT.7. The relationships established in (5.11), (5.20), (5.21), and (5.22) provide four measures of long-run scale elasticity that are equivalent under certain conditions.

5.2.2 Cost Elasticities and Economics of Size

The reader will notice that the strict concept of scale elasticity involves the equiproportional change in all choice inputs. Chambers (1988, Chapter 2) notes that economic analysis focuses mostly on the impact of output changes on costs (or movements along the expansion path) rather than the equiproportional changes in all inputs, which can involve different input combinations. In the context of the static theory of production, the cost elasticity is equal to the inverse of the scale elasticity at all cost-minimizing points for homothetic technologies.[2] This relation is no longer valid within the adjustment cost model of the firm (Stefanou, 1989). We can establish a relation between the long-run cost elasticity and the long-run scale elasticity using (5.19).

The long-run cost elasticity is, by definition, given by

$$CE(y,K,w,c) = \frac{rW_y(.)\cdot y}{rW(.)}, \qquad (5.23)$$

which is the ratio of the product of long-run marginal cost and the output vector to the long-run cost. Using (3.79), the long-run cost elasticity can be expressed as

$$\begin{aligned}
CE(y,K,w,c) &= \frac{[C_y(.)+W_{Ky}(.)\cdot(I^*-\delta K)]\cdot y}{C(.)+W_K(.)\cdot(I^*-\delta K)} \\
&= \frac{C_y(.)\cdot y}{C(.)+W_K(.)\cdot(I^*-\delta K)} + \frac{W_{Ky}(.)\cdot(I^*-\delta K)\cdot y}{C(.)+W_K(.)\cdot(I^*-\delta K)}.
\end{aligned} \qquad (5.24)$$

Dividing and multiplying the first component in (5.24) by $C(.)$ yields

$$CE(y,K,w,c) = \frac{C_y(.)\cdot y}{C(.)}\frac{C(.)}{C(.)+W_K(.)\cdot(I^*-\delta K)} + \frac{W_{Ky}(.)\cdot(I^*-\delta K)\cdot y}{C(.)+W_K(.)\cdot(I^*-\delta K)}. \qquad (5.25)$$

Using (5.19) and $C(\cdot) = w'x^*$, the long-run cost elasticity is given by

$$\begin{aligned}
CE(y,K,w,c) &= \frac{w\cdot x^* + W_K(.)\cdot(I^*-\delta K)}{\varepsilon_i(y,K,w,c)C(.)}\frac{C(.)}{C(.)+W_K(.)\cdot(I^*-\delta K)} \\
&\quad + \frac{W_{Ky}(.)\cdot(I^*-\delta K)\cdot y}{C(.)+W_K(.)\cdot(I^*-\delta K)},
\end{aligned} \qquad (5.26)$$

---

[2] The analysis of the elasticity of scale involves equiproportional changes in inputs, that is, ray from the origins. The cost-based elasticity of size measure necessarily involves movement along the expansion path. See Hanoch (1975) and Chambers (1988, section 2.3b) for an extensive elaboration and demonstration.

which simplifies to

$$CE(y,K,w,c)= \frac{1}{\varepsilon_i(y,K,w,c)} + \frac{W_{Ky}(.)\cdot(I^* - \delta K)\cdot y}{C(.)+W_K(.)\cdot(I^* - \delta K)}$$
$$= \frac{1}{\varepsilon_i(y,K,w,c)} + \frac{W_{Ky}(.)\cdot(I^* - \delta K)\cdot y}{rW(.)}. \tag{5.27}$$

In contrast with static theory of production, the long-run cost elasticity is not equal to the inverse of the long-run scale elasticity. The second component in (5.27) is a disequilibrium component whose value is zero at the steady state (i.e., $I^* - \delta K = 0$).

If the long-run marginal shadow cost is less than the short-run marginal cost for all outputs, then the second component in (5.27) is negative and $CE(y,K,w,c) < 1/\varepsilon_i(y,K,w,c)$. If the long-run marginal shadow cost is greater than the short-run marginal cost for all outputs, the second component in (5.27) is greater than zero and $CE(y,K,w,c) > 1/\varepsilon_i(y,K,w,c)$.

5.2.3 Economics of Scope and Cost Concepts

Section 5.2.2 focuses on a measure of long-run shadow cost variation where output proportions remain unchanged. In this section, we focus on the interrelations among goods in production. Before analyzing these phenomena, we present some cost concepts that relate to nonproportionate changes in outputs. These cost concepts are similar to the cost notions developed by Baumol et al. (1982) but applicable to the adjustment cost model of the firm.

The concept of long-run cost elasticity relates to proportional changes in the quantities in the entire product set $P = \{1,2,...,M\}$. A firm's operations may change when there is a variation in the output of one product, holding the quantities of all the other products constant, or when there are variations involving subsets of two or more products. Following Baumol et al. (1982), we define the incremental shadow cost of a set of products as the increase in the firm's long-run total shadow cost resulting from the production of this set of products. The incremental shadow cost of a set of products $T \subseteq P$, ISC_T, at y is given by[3]

$$ISC_T(y) = rW(y) - rW(y_{P-T})$$ (5.28)

where y_{P-T}, is a vector with zero components associated with the products in T and components equal in value to those of y for products in $P\text{-}T$, and $y = y_T + y_{P-T}$. The average incremental shadow cost of $T \subseteq P$ at y, $AISC_T(y)$, is given by

$$AISC_T(y) = \frac{ISC_T(y)}{\sum_{j \in T} y_j}.$$ (5.29)

$AISC_T(y)$ is analogous to ray average cost except that the relevant ray does not go through the origin; rather, it is limited to a subspace of $\mathfrak{R}_+^M$. The $AISC_T(y)$ is decreasing (increasing) at y if $AISC_T(ty_T + y_{P-T})$ is a decreasing (increasing) function of t at $t = 1$; that is, $\left. \dfrac{dAISC_T(ty_T + y_{P-T})}{dt} \right|_{t=1} < (>) 0$.

Based on the notion of incremental shadow cost of a set of products, we can build a measure of the shadow cost elasticity specific to a product set. The cost elasticity specific to product set T at y is the elasticity of the ISC_T at y, defined as

$$e_T(y) = \left. \frac{d \ln ISC_T(ty_T + y_{P-T})}{d \ln t} \right|_{t=1} = \sum_{j \in T} \frac{\partial ISC_T(y)}{\partial y_j} \cdot \frac{y_j}{ISC_T(y)}.$$ (5.30)

Given the definition of $ISC_T(y)$. in (5.28), the elasticity in (5.30) can be rewritten as

$$e_T(y) = \sum_{j \in T} \frac{rW_{y_j}(y).y_j}{ISC_T(y)}.$$ (5.31)

---

[3] The focus here is on the products produced by a firm; thus, we suppress, for the sake of clarity of exposition, the other arguments of the cost function, that is, K, w, and c.

Similarly, the elasticity of the incremental shadow cost of the set of products P-T is equal to

$$e_{P-T}(y) = \sum_{j \in P-T} \frac{rW_{y_j}(y).y_j}{ISC_{P-T}(y)}. \tag{5.32}$$

Next, we attempt to relate the "overall" long-run cost elasticity in (5.23) to the cost elasticities specific to the product sets T and P-T. Given that $\sum_{j \in P} rW_{y_j}(y).y_j = \sum_{j \in T} rW_{y_j}(y).y_j + \sum_{j \in P-T} rW_{y_j}(y).y_j$, the long-run cost elasticity in (5.23) can be rewritten as

$$CE(y) = \frac{\sum_{j \in T} rW_{y_j}(y) \cdot y_j + \sum_{j \in P-T} rW_{y_j}(y) \cdot y_j}{rW(y)}. \tag{5.33}$$

Given that (5.31) and (5.32), $CE(y)$ can be expressed as

$$CE(y) = \frac{ISC_T(y)}{rW(y)} e_T(y) + \frac{ISC_{P-T}(y)}{rW(y)} e_{P-T}(y)$$
$$= \alpha_T(y).e_T(y) + \alpha_{P-T}(y).e_{P-T}(y). \tag{5.34}$$

The "overall" long-run cost elasticity is equal to the sum of the shadow cost elasticities of the product sets T and P-T, each one weighted, respectively, by $\alpha_T = ISC_T(y)/rW(y)$ and $\alpha_{P-T} = ISC_{P-T}(y)/rW(y)$, and suppressing the arguments (K, I, w). Note that $\alpha_T(y) + \alpha_{P-T}(y) = 1 + \dfrac{rW(y) - rW(y_{P-T}) - rW(y_T)}{rW(y)}$. When there are no production interdependencies between the product set T with those in the product set P-T, the cost of producing the entire product set P is equal to the sum of the cost of producing each product set separately, $rW(y) = rW(y_{P-T}) + rW(y_T)$ and $\alpha_T(y) + \alpha_{P-T}(y) = 1$. Thus, the "overall" long-run cost elasticity is a weighted average of $e_T(y)$ and $e_{P-T}(y)$. If $rW(y) < (>) rW(y_{P-T}) + rW(y_T)$, then $\alpha_T(y) + \alpha_{P-T}(y) < (>) 1$.

Economies of scope can be defined in the adjustment cost context in a similar fashion as in Fernandez-Cornejo et al. (1992) for the dynamic case. Let $C = \{T_1, T_2, ..., T_T\}$ denote a nontrivial partition of $S \subseteq P$, that is, $\bigcup_{i=1}^{T} T_i = S$,

$T_i \cap T_j = \varnothing$, $i \ne j$, $T_i \ne \varnothing$, for all i, and $T > 1$. There are economies (diseconomies) of scope at y_s with respect to the partition C if

$$\sum_{i=1}^{T} rW(y_{T_i}) > (<) rW(y_S).$$
(5.35)

Based on the notion in (5.35), we can build a measure of the magnitude of economies of scope. The degree of economies of scope at y relative to the product set T is measured by

$$SE_T(y) = \frac{rW(y_T) + rW(y_{P-T}) - rW(y)}{rW(y)}.$$
(5.36)

$SE_T(y)$ measures the relative difference in the current value of the long-run shadow cost resulting from partitioning the production of y into the product lines T and P-T. $SE_T(y) > (<) 0$ indicates economies (diseconomies) of scope.

Next, we relate the concept of economies of scope to the measures of cost elasticity defined previously. Consider the measure of long-run cost elasticity presented in (5.34) and the measure of economies of scope in (5.36). The long-run cost elasticity can be alternatively expressed as

$$CE(y) = \left(\frac{rW(y_T)}{rW(y)} - SE_T(y) \right).e_T(y) + \left(\frac{rW(y_{P-T})}{rW(y)} - SE_T(y) \right).e_{P-T}(y).$$
(5.37)

Equation (5.37) indicates how economies (diseconomies) of scope contract (magnify) the effects of the product set–specific cost elasticities in the determination of the "overall" long-run cost elasticity. For example, let's assume that $e_T(y) = e_{P-T}(y) = 1$ and the existence of economies of scope (i.e., $SE_T(y) > 0$). In this case, $CE(y) = 1 - SE_T(y) < 1$. This example illustrates that even if the cost elasticities specific to product sets T and P-T are unitary, the presence of scope economies leads to an "overall" long-run cost elasticity less than one.

One of the sources of economies of scope pointed out in the literature is the existence of productive inputs that are shared in the production of several different products (e.g., Willig, 1979; Baumol et al., 1982). This may result because of indivisibilities or lumpiness in capital. Consider an adjustment cost production model involving M production processes sharing capital services:[4]

$$rW(y_S,K) = \min_I \left\{ \sum_{i \in S} C^i(y_i,K_i,I) + W_K(y_S,K)(I - \delta K) + c'K \right\}, \quad (5.38)$$

where $C^i(y_i,K_i,I)$ is the variable cost function of producing y_i using K_i units of capital services, given I. Let $I^*(y_S,K) = \arg\min\left\{ \sum_{i \in S} C^i(y_i,K_i,I) + W_K(y_S,K)(I - \delta K) + c'K \right\}$. The following proposition establishes sufficient conditions for the existence of economies and diseconomies of scope in this model.

Proposition 5.1: For any nontrivial partition of P, there are economies (diseconomies) of scope if $C^i(y_i,K_i,I)$ is strictly subadditive (superadditive) in the relevant range of I and the capital shadow value function $W_K(.)$ is strictly subadditive (superadditive) in the relevant range of y.

Proof of proposition 5.1:

Let $C = \{T_1,T_2,...,T_T\}$ be a nontrivial partition of P. Define

$$
\begin{aligned}
rW(y,K) &\equiv \min_I \left\{ \sum_{i \in P} C^i(y_i,K_i,I) + W_K(y,K)(I - \delta K) + c'K \right\} \\
&= \sum_{i \in P} C^i(y_i,K_i,I^*(y,K)) + W_K(y,K)(I^*(y,K) - \delta K) + c'K \quad (P.1)
\end{aligned}
$$

where $I^*(y,K) = \arg\min\left\{ \sum_{i \in P} C^i(y_i,K_i,I) + W_K(y,K)(I - \delta K) + c'K \right\}$, By definition,

$$
\begin{aligned}
rW(y,K) &= \sum_{i \in P} C^i(y_i,K_i,I^*(y,K)) + W_K(y,K)(I^*(y,K) - \delta K) + c'K \\
&\leq \sum_{i \in P} C^i(y_i,K_i,\tilde{I}) + W_K(y,K)(\tilde{I} - \delta K) + c'K, \quad (P.2)
\end{aligned}
$$

where $\tilde{I} = \sum_{j=1}^{T} I^*(y_{T_j},K)$.

---

[4] Baumol et al. (1982) analyze this type of model in a static context. Further, for the sake of a clearer exposition, the price vectors are omitted from the value functions.

Define the following function:

$$rW(y_{T_j}, K) \equiv \min_{I} \left\{ \sum_{i \in T_j} C^i(y_i, K_i, I) + W_K(y_{T_j}, K)(I - \delta K) + c'K \right\} \tag{P.3}$$
$$= \sum_{i \in T_j} C^i(y_i, K_i, I^*(y_{T_j}, K)) + W_K(y_{T_j}, K)(I^*(y_{T_j}, K) - \delta K) + c'K$$

where $I^*(y_{T_j}, K) = \arg\min \left\{ \sum_{i \in T_j} C^i(y_i, K_i, I) + W_K(y_{T_j}, K)(I - \delta K) + c'K \right\}.$

By definition,

$$rW(y_{T_j}, K) = \sum_{i \in T_j} C^i(y_i, K_i, I^*(y_{T_j}, K)) + W_K(y_{T_j}, K)(I^*(y_{T_j}, K) - \delta K) + c'K$$
$$\leq \sum_{i \in T_j} C^i(y_i, K_i, I^*(y, K)_{T_j}) + W_K(y_{T_j}, K)(I^*(y, K)_{T_j} - \delta K) + c'K$$

$$\tag{P.4}$$

Summing (P.4) over $j, j = 1, \ldots, T$, yields

$$\sum_{j=1}^{T} rW(y_{T_j}, K)$$

$$= \sum_{j=1}^{T} \left[\sum_{i \in T_j} C^i(y_i, K_i, I^*(y_{T_j}, K)) + W_K(y_{T_j}, K)(I^*(y_{T_j}, K) - \delta K) + c'K \right] \tag{P.5}$$

$$\leq \sum_{j=1}^{T} \left[\sum_{i \in T_j} C^i(y_i, K_i, I^*(y, K)_{T_j}) + W_K(y_{T_j}, K)(I^*(y, K)_{T_j} - \delta K) + c'K \right].$$

Subtracting (P.5) from (P.2) and making use of the inequality sign in (P.2) yields

$$rW(y, K) - \sum_{j=1}^{T} rW(y_{T_j}, K)$$

$$= \sum_{i \in P} C^i(y_i, K_i, I^*(y, K)) + W_K(y, K)(I^*(y, K) - \delta K) + c'K$$

$$- \sum_{j=1}^{T} \left[\sum_{i \in T_j} C^i(y_i, K_i, I^*(y_{T_j}, K)) + W_K(y_{T_j}, K)(I^*(y_{T_j}, K) - \delta K) + c'K \right]$$

$$\leq \sum_{i \in P} C^i(y_i, K_i, \tilde{I}) + W_K(y, K)(\tilde{I} - \delta K) + c'K$$

$$- \sum_{j=1}^{T} \left[\sum_{i \in T_j} C^i(y_i, K_i, I^*(y_{T_j}, K)) + W_K(y_{T_j}, K)(I^*(y_{T_j}, K) - \delta K) + c'K \right].$$

From the previous expression, we can infer that

$$rW(y,K) - \sum_{j=1}^{T} rW(y_{T_j}, K) \le \sum_{i \in P} C^i(y_i, K_i, \tilde{I}) - \sum_{j=1}^{T} \sum_{i \in T_j} C^i(y_i, K_i, I^*(y_{T_j}, K))$$
$$+ W_K(y,K)(\tilde{I} - \delta K) - \sum_{j=1}^{T} W_K(y_{T_j}, K)(I^*(y_{T_j}, K) - \delta K). \quad \text{(P.6)}$$

Note that from (P.6) we can infer that there are economies of scope if

$$\sum_{i \in P} C^i(y_i, K_i, \tilde{I}) - \sum_{j=1}^{T} \sum_{i \in T_j} C^i(y_i, K_i, I^*(y_{T_j}, K)) < 0 \quad \text{(P.7)}$$

and

$$W_K(y,K)(\tilde{I} - \delta K) - \sum_{j=1}^{T} W_K(y_{T_j}, K)(I^*(y_{T_j}, K) - \delta K) < 0. \quad \text{(P.8)}$$

(P.7) and (P.8) are sufficient conditions for the existence of scope economies. (P.7) establishes strict subadditivity of $C^i(.)$ in I and (P.8) establishes strict subadditivity of $W_K(.)$ in y.

Subtracting again (P.5) from (P.2) and making use of the inequality sign in (P.5) yields

$$rW(y,K) - \sum_{j=1}^{T} rW(y_{T_j}, K)$$
$$= \sum_{i \in P} C^i(y_i, K_i, I^*(y, K)) + W_K(y, K)(I^*(y, K) - \delta K) + c'K$$
$$- \sum_{j=1}^{T} \left[\sum_{i \in T_j} C^i(y_i, K_i, I^*(y_{T_j}, K)) + W_K(y_{T_j}, K)(I^*(y_{T_j}, K) - \delta K) + c'K \right]$$
$$\ge \sum_{i \in P} C^i(y_i, K_i, I^*(y, K)) + W_K(y, K)(I^*(y, K) - \delta K) + c'K$$
$$- \sum_{j=1}^{T} \left[\sum_{i \in T_j} C^i(y_i, K_i, I^*(y, K)_{T_j}) + W_K(y_{T_j}, K)(I^*(y, K)_{T_j} - \delta K) + c'K \right].$$

The previous expression yields

$$rW(y,K) - \sum_{j=1}^{T} rW(y_{T_j}, K)$$

$$\geq \sum_{i \in P} C^i(y_i, K_i, I^*(y,K)) - \sum_{j=1}^{T} \sum_{i \in T_j} C^i(y_i, K_i, I^*(y,K)_{T_j})$$

$$+ W_K(y,K)(I^*(y,K) - \delta K) - \sum_{j=1}^{T} W_K(y_{T_j}, K)(I^*(y,K)_{T_j} - \delta K). \qquad \text{(P.9)}$$

Note that from (P.9) we can infer that there are diseconomies of scope if

$$\sum_{i \in P} C^i(y_i, K_i, I^*(y,K)) - \sum_{j=1}^{T} \sum_{i \in T_j} C^i(y_i, K_i, I^*(y,K)_{T_j}) > 0. \qquad \text{(P.10)}$$

and

$$W_K(y,K)(I^*(y,K) - \delta K) - \sum_{j=1}^{T} W_K(y_{T_j}, K)(I^*(y,K)_{T_j} - \delta K) > 0 \qquad \text{(P.11)}$$

(P.10) and (P.11) are the sufficient conditions for the existence of diseconomies of scope. (P.10) establishes strict superadditivity of $C^i(.)$ in I and (P.11) establishes strict superadditivity of $W_K(.)$ in y.

5.2.4 Capacity Utilization

Various notions of capacity utilization have evolved over the decades. These measures are cyclical economic indicators with longstanding use in public policy formation and analysis of business decisions. The derivation and calculation of capacity utilization rates have been historically more on data analysis, both statistical and judgmental, with more recent efforts focusing on theoretical foundations. These more rigorous efforts focus on technology-based and economic-based formulations.

Johansen (1968) presents a measure of capacity utilization that builds on a definition that plant capacity is the "the maximum amount that can be produced per unit of time with the existing plant and equipment provided that the availability of the variable factors is not restricted." This definition of plant capacity utilization is an output-oriented notion. Färe et al. (1989) develop multiple output measures of capacity utilization using the radial output distance function. Färe and Grosskopf (2000) formulate the Johansen measure of capacity utilization in terms of the directional technology distance function, allowing for the expansion of outputs and contraction of inputs.

In the context of dynamic production, the Johansen notion refined by Färe and Grosskopf (2000) amounts to allowing for the expansion of output and capacity via investment, while holding variable input use fixed along with the current capital stock.

In the dynamic context, the Johansen notion of plant capacity must now be distinguished from the way we measure capacity utilization. The dynamic directional technology distance function allows for the expansion of outputs and investment and contraction of inputs, given quasi-fixed inputs.

Following a similar procedure as Färe and Grosskopf (2000), we define a measure of capacity utilization as

$$CU = \frac{\vec{D}_T(x, I, K, y; g_x, g_I, g_y) + 1}{\vec{D}_T(x, I, K, y; g_x = 0_N, g_I, g_y) + 1} \le 1, \tag{5.39}$$

where $\vec{D}_T(x, I, K, y; g_x, g_I, g_y) = \max\{\beta : (x - \beta g_x, I + \beta g_I, y + \beta g_y) \in T(K)\}$ and $\vec{D}_T(x, I, K, y; g_x = 0_N, g_I, g_y) = \max\{\beta : (x, I + \beta g_I, y + \beta g_y) \in T(K), x \ge 0_N\}$.

A dual form is readily available using theorem 4.4, which leads to rewriting (5.39) as

$$
CU = \frac{\vec{D}_T(y, K, x, I; g_y, g_x, g_I) + 1}{\vec{D}_T(y, K, x, I; g_y, g_x = 0_N, g_I) + 1}
$$
$$
= \frac{\min\limits_{p,w,c}\left\{\dfrac{rJ(y,K,w,c) - [p'y - w'x - c'K + J_k(.)'(I - \delta K)]}{p'g_y + w'g_x + J_k(.)'g_I}\right\} + 1}{\min\limits_{p,w,c}\left\{\dfrac{rJ(y,K,w,c) - [p'y - w'x - c'K + J_k(.)'(I - \delta K)]}{p'g_y + J_k(.)'g_I}\right\} + 1}. \tag{5.40}
$$

5.3 Constructing Measures of Productivity

Productivity is essentially a ratio of output over input. In the more general case, operational units produce multiple outputs using multiple variable and quasi-fixed-factor inputs and investments. Productivity is best characterized as total factor productivity (TFP), which is essentially a ratio of aggregate outputs and aggregate (variable and quasi-fixed) inputs and investments:

$$TFP_t = \frac{Q_o(y_t)}{Q_i(x_t, I_t, K_t)}. \tag{5.41}$$

The aggregator functions for outputs and inputs are denoted by $Q_o(\cdot)$ and $Q_i(\cdot)$, respectively. TFP growth measures whether aggregate outputs grow faster over time than aggregate inputs and investments.

How to aggregate the outputs and inputs into either indexes of aggregate quantity or indexes of aggregate quantity change? One direction is a structural approach that builds on the technology directly and then embeds the behavioral restrictions of the decision maker. Ohta (1975) and Denny et al. (1981) are classic examples of this approach in a static setting.

Approaches for aggregating quantities of inputs and outputs are also categorized into those that use prices as weights (Bennet-Bowley, Fisher, and Törnqvist indexes) and those that use distance functions as aggregators (Malmquist and Luenberger indexes). The theory of aggregation is extensive, and excellent elaborations are found in Diewert (1976), Balk (2008), and, in the context of the directional distance function, Chambers (1998). Approaches for measuring TFP growth also distinguish measuring growth as a ratio versus measuring growth as a difference. Ratio approaches yield a TFP *index*, which is typically defined as a ratio of variables (notably, Malmquist index, Törnqvist index), whereas difference approaches yield a TFP *indicator*, defined in terms of the difference in variables (notably, Luenberger indicator, Bennet-Bowley indicator). In what follows we present a structural approach for measuring TFP and its decomposition, followed by an elaboration of the Luenberger indicator.

5.3.1 Structural Approach

In this section, we proceed with the structural approach, which takes its starting point from the core technology specification and offers a primal measure of productivity growth. We assume that the technology is twice differentiable with respect to outputs, variable and dynamic factor inputs, and time, which leads to differentiable value functions. These properties are developed in Chapter 4 and build on Epstein (1981). This perspective can be enhanced with the introduction of an economic objective (cost minimization or profit maximization) given a production technology.

5.3.1.1 A Primal Measure

The primal measure approach to the decomposition of TFP growth under dynamic adjustment proceeds by totally differentiating the technology with respect to time. We start with the dynamic directional technology distance function

$$\vec{D}_T(x(t), I(t), y(t), K(t), t; g_x, g_I, g_y) = \beta \geq 0, \tag{5.42}$$

which includes the argument t to represent technological progress and allowing for technical inefficiency, reflected in the scalar $\beta > 0$. Taking the natural logs of this form of the dynamic directional technology distance function and differentiating with respect to time yields

$$\nabla_y \ln \vec{D}_T \dot{y} + \nabla_x \ln \vec{D}_T \dot{x} + \nabla_I \ln \vec{D}_T \dot{I} + \nabla_K \ln \vec{D}_T \dot{K} + \frac{\partial \ln \vec{D}_T}{\partial t} = \frac{\partial \ln \beta}{\partial t}. \tag{5.43}$$

Equation (5.43) can be rewritten in terms of the proportional changes of y, x, I, and K as

$$\nabla_y \ln \vec{D}_T y \hat{y} + \nabla_x \ln \vec{D}_T x \hat{x} + \nabla_I \ln \vec{D}_T I \hat{I}$$
$$+ \nabla_K \ln \vec{D}_T K \hat{K} + \frac{\partial \ln \vec{D}_T}{\partial t} = \frac{\partial \ln \beta}{\partial t}. \tag{5.44}$$

Dividing both sides of (5.44) by $\nabla_y \ln \vec{D}_T y$ solving for the output growth component yields

$$\frac{\nabla_y \ln \vec{D}_T y \hat{y}}{\nabla_y \ln \vec{D}_T y} = -\frac{1}{\nabla_y \ln \vec{D}_T y}[\nabla_x \ln \vec{D}_T x \hat{x} + \nabla_I \ln \vec{D}_T I \hat{I}] - \frac{\nabla_K \ln \vec{D}_T K \hat{K}}{\nabla_y \ln \vec{D}_T y}$$
$$- \frac{1}{\nabla_y \ln \vec{D}_T y} \frac{\partial \ln \vec{D}_T}{\partial t} + \frac{1}{\nabla_y \ln \vec{D}_T y} \frac{\partial \ln \beta}{\partial t}. \tag{5.45}$$

This is the primal formulation of the proportional change in the dynamic directional technology distance function and can serve as the foundation for TFP growth decomposition, where the left-hand side represents the aggregate output growth.

Multiplying and dividing the first two terms on the right-hand side of (5.45) by $(\nabla_x \ln \vec{D}_T x + \nabla_I \ln \vec{D}_T I)$ yields

$$
\frac{\nabla_y \ln \vec{D}_T y \hat{y}}{\nabla_y \ln \vec{D}_T y}
$$

$$
= -\frac{\nabla_x \ln \vec{D}_T x + \nabla_I \ln \vec{D}_T I}{\nabla_y \ln \vec{D}_T y}\left[\frac{\nabla_x \ln \vec{D}_T x \hat{x}}{\nabla_x \ln \vec{D}_T x + \nabla_I \ln \vec{D}_T I} + \frac{\nabla_I \ln \vec{D}_T I \hat{I}}{\nabla_x \ln \vec{D}_T x + \nabla_I \ln \vec{D}_T I}\right]
$$

$$
- \frac{\nabla_K \ln \vec{D}_T K \check{K}}{\nabla_y \ln \vec{D}_T y} - \frac{1}{\nabla_y \ln \vec{D}_T y}\frac{\partial \ln \vec{D}_T}{\partial t} + \frac{1}{\nabla_y \ln \vec{D}_T y}\frac{\partial \ln \beta}{\partial t}
$$

or, in more extensive notation,

$$
\sum_{m=1}^{M}\frac{\partial \ln \vec{D}_T / \partial \ln y_m}{\sum_{m=1}^{M}(\partial \ln \vec{D}_T / \partial \ln y_m)}\hat{y}_m
$$

$$
= \varepsilon_T(y,K,x,I)\left[\sum_{n=1}^{N}\frac{\partial \ln \vec{D}_T / \partial \ln x_n}{\left(\sum_{n=1}^{N}\partial \ln \vec{D}_T / \partial \ln x_n + \sum_{f=1}^{F}\partial \ln \vec{D}_T / \partial \ln I_f\right)}\hat{x}_n\right.
$$

$$
\left. + \sum_{f=1}^{F}\frac{\partial \ln \vec{D}_T / \partial \ln I_f}{\left(\sum_{n=1}^{N}\partial \ln \vec{D}_T / \partial \ln x_n + \sum_{f=1}^{F}\partial \ln \vec{D}_T / \partial \ln I_f\right)}\hat{I}_f\right]
$$

$$
- \sum_{f=1}^{F}\frac{\partial \ln \vec{D}_T / \partial \ln K_f}{\sum_{m=1}^{M}(\partial \ln \vec{D}_T / \partial \ln y_m)}\hat{K}_f - \frac{1}{\sum_{m=1}^{M}(\partial \ln \vec{D}_T / \partial \ln y_m)}\frac{\partial \ln \vec{D}_T}{\partial t}
$$

$$
+ \frac{1}{\sum_{m=1}^{M}(\partial \ln \vec{D}_T / \partial \ln y_m)}\frac{\partial \ln \beta}{\partial t}.
$$

$$(5.46)$$

Equation (5.46) can be rewritten using the scale elasticity measure in (5.6) as

$$
\hat{Q}_Y = \varepsilon_T(y,K,x,I)[\hat{Q}_X + \hat{Q}_I] + \hat{Q}_K + \hat{A} + \hat{B}, \tag{5.47}
$$

where

- $\hat{Q}_Y$, represents aggregate output growth and is defined as

$$\hat{Q}_Y = \sum_{m=1}^{M} \varepsilon_m^Y \hat{y}_m \,;\, \varepsilon_m^Y = \frac{\partial \ln \vec{D}_T / \partial \ln y_m}{\sum_{m=1}^{M} (\partial \ln \vec{D}_T / \partial \ln y_m)} \,;\, \sum_{m=1}^{M} \varepsilon_m^Y = 1; \qquad (5.48.a)$$

- $\hat{Q}_X$ represents aggregate variable input growth and is defined as

$$\hat{Q}_X = \sum_{n=1}^{N} \varepsilon_n^X \hat{x}_n \,;\, \varepsilon_n^X = \frac{\partial \ln \vec{D}_T / \partial \ln x_n}{\sum_{n=1}^{N} (\partial \ln \vec{D}_T / \partial \ln x_n) + \sum_{f=1}^{F} (\partial \ln \vec{D}_T / \partial \ln I_f)} \,;$$
$$(5.48.b)$$

- $\check{Q}_I$ represents aggregate gross investment growth and is defined as

$$\hat{Q}_I = \sum_{f=1}^{F} \varepsilon_f^I \hat{I}_f \,;\, \varepsilon_f^I = \frac{\partial \ln \vec{D}_T / \partial \ln I_f}{\sum_{n=1}^{N} (\partial \ln \vec{D}_T / \partial \ln x_n) + \sum_{f=1}^{F} (\partial \ln \vec{D}_T / \partial \ln I_f)} \,; (5.48.c)$$

$$\text{and } \sum_{n=1}^{N} \varepsilon_n^X + \sum_{f=1}^{F} \varepsilon_f^I = 1;$$

- $\hat{Q}_K$ aggregate quasi-fixed-factor (capital stock) growth and is defined as

$$\hat{Q}_K = -\sum_{f=1}^{F} \frac{\partial \ln \vec{D}_T / \partial \ln K_f}{\sum_{m=1}^{M} (\partial \ln \vec{D}_T / \partial \ln y_m)} \hat{K}_f. \qquad (5.48.d)$$

The contribution of technical change is denoted as $\hat{A}$, which represents changes arising from autonomous sources and is defined as

$$\hat{A} = -\frac{1}{\sum_{m=1}^{M} (\partial \ln \vec{D}_T / \partial \ln y_m)} \frac{\partial \ln \vec{D}_T}{\partial t}. \qquad (5.49)$$

The contribution of technical inefficiency change to output growth is denoted as $\hat{B}$ and is defined as

$$\hat{B} = \frac{1}{\sum_{m=1}^{M}(\partial \ln \vec{D}_T / \partial \ln y_m)} \frac{\partial \ln \beta}{\partial t}. \qquad (5.50)$$

Defining total factor productivity growth, $\hat{TFP}$, as the difference between aggregate output growth and aggregate variable and dynamic input growth,

$$\hat{TFP} = \hat{Q}_Y - \hat{Q}_X - \hat{Q}_I = (\varepsilon_T(y,K,x,I)-1)[\hat{Q}_X + \hat{Q}_I] + \hat{Q}_K + \hat{A} + \hat{B}. \qquad (5.51)$$

This decomposition identifies four components of TFP growth: the contribution of scale economies $(\varepsilon_T -1)[\hat{Q}_X + \hat{Q}_I]$; the effect of the aggregate quasi-fixed-factor growth $\hat{Q}_K$; the contribution of technical change $\hat{A}$; and the contribution of technical inefficiency change $\hat{B}$.

5.3.1.2 A Dual Measure

The determination of the weights on $\hat{x}_n, \hat{I}_f, \hat{K}_f$ in (5.46) can also be driven by the economic objective. Intertemporal profit maximization in the context of the dynamic directional technology distance function involves augmenting the fundamental equation of optimization in (4.31) in the presence of t as an autonomous shift in the technology,[5] which leads to the current value Hamilton-Jacobi-Bellman equation

$$rJ(k,t;p,w,c) = \max_{y,x,I} \{ p'y - w'x - c'K + J_k(k,t;p,w,c)'(I-\delta K) \\ + \lambda^{\Pi}(\vec{D}_T(y,K,x,I,t;g_y,g_x,g_I)-\beta) + J_t(k,t;p,w,c)\}, \qquad (5.52)$$

where λ^{Π} is the current value Lagrangian multiplier, and $\lambda^{\Pi} = p'g_y + w'g_x + J_k(.)'g_I$, which reflects the instantaneous value of the

---

[5] Let $G(k,t;p,w,c)$ denote the present value profit from (4.45), which, converting it to the current value profit form, implies

$$G(k,t;p,w,c) = e^{-rt}W(k,t;p,w,c), \qquad (A.1)$$

leading to

$$G_k(k,t;p,w,c) = e^{-rt}J_k(k,t;p,w,c) \qquad (A.2)$$

and

$$G_t(k,t;p,w,c) = -re^{-rt}J(k,t;p,w,c) + e^{-rt}J_t(k,t;p,w,c). \qquad (A.3)$$

direction and is the profit-based analog to the cost-based value of the direction, λ^C, found in (4.44).

In fact, λ^Π and λ^C are related through the relationship that profit maximization requires cost minimization. From the relationship of intertemporal profit maximization to intertemporal cost minimization in (3.79), the optimized Hamilton-Jacobi-Bellman equation for $y = y^*$ is $rJ(p,w,c,k) = p'y - rW(w,c,k,y^*)$, which further implies that $J_k(p,w,c,k) = -W_k(w,c,k,y^*)$:

$$\lambda^\Pi = p'g_y + w'g_x + J_k(.)'g_I = p'g_y + w'g_x - W_k'g_I$$
$$= p'g_y + \lambda^C \tag{5.53}$$

Clearly, the weights on the aggregate percentage changes involve the marginal impacts of production variables on the technology. The challenge is to find alternative representations of the production technology (i.e., the derivatives of $\vec{D}_T \cdot$) that follow from the economic optimization. Incorporating the intertemporal profit-maximizing behavior presented in (5.52) leads to

$$-\frac{\partial \vec{D}_T}{\partial y_m} = \frac{p_m}{\lambda^\Pi}, \quad \frac{\partial \vec{D}_T}{\partial x_j} = \frac{w_j}{\lambda^\Pi}, \quad \text{and} \quad \frac{\partial \vec{D}_T}{\partial I_l} = -\frac{J_{K_l}}{\lambda^\Pi} \cdot$$

Since K is taken as fixed in the current decision period, the expression for $\dfrac{\partial \vec{D}_T}{\partial K_l}$ can be determined through the optimized Hamilton-Jacobi-Bellman equation in (5.52). Differentiating this optimized Hamilton-Jacobi-Bellman equation with respect to K yields the arbitrage equation

$$(r + \delta)J_k = -c + \lambda^\Pi \nabla_K \vec{D}_T + \frac{dJ_K}{dt}, \tag{5.54}$$

where $\dfrac{dJ_K}{dt} = \dot{J}_k = J_{kk}\dot{K}^* + J_{tk}$. Solving for $\nabla_K \vec{D}_T$ leads to

We can rewrite the Hamilton-Jacobi-Bellman equation associated with $G(k,t; p,w,c)$ as

$$0 = \max_{y,x,I} \{e^{-rt}[p'y - wx - c'K] + G_k(k,t; p,w,c)'(I - \delta K)$$
$$+ \mu(\vec{D}_T(y,K,x,I,t; g_y, g_x, g_I) - \beta)\} + G_t(k,t; p,w,c). \tag{A.4}$$

The current value form of the Hamilton-Jacobi equation involves using (A.2) and (A.3) in (A.4), leading to (5.52).

$$\nabla_K \vec{D}_T = \frac{\left[(r+\delta)J_k + c - \dfrac{dJ_k}{dt} \right]}{\lambda^\Pi} \tag{5.55}$$

which relates how the marginal product of the quasi-fixed factors equals the opportunity cost plus the user cost of capital of an additional unit of capital, $(r+\delta)J_k + c$, less the instantaneous capital gain (or loss) arising from one more unit of capital, $\dfrac{dJ_k}{dt}$, normalized by the value of the direction, λ^Π.

We can now use the relationship between the gradients of the dynamic directional technology distance function and intertemporal profit maximization to rewrite (5.49) as

$$\text{Outputs}: \widehat{Q}_Y = \sum_{(m=1)}^{M} \varepsilon_m^Y \, \widehat{y}_m = -\sum_{(m=1)}^{M} \frac{p_m y_m}{\sum_{(m=1)}^{M} p_m y_m} \, \widehat{y}_m, \tag{5.56}$$

where

$$\varepsilon_m^Y = \frac{\partial \ln \vec{D}_T / \partial \ln y_m}{\sum_{m=1}^{M} (\partial \ln \vec{D}_T / \partial \ln y_m)} = \frac{\partial \vec{D}_T / \partial \ln y_m}{\sum_{m=1}^{M} (\partial \vec{D}_T / \partial \ln y_m)} = \frac{p_m y_m}{\sum_{m=1}^{M} p_m y_m} \; ; \sum_{m=1}^{M} \varepsilon_m^Y = 1.$$

Technical change:

$$-\frac{1}{\sum_{m=1}^{M} \left(\overline{\partial \ln D_T} / \partial \ln y_m \right)} \frac{\partial \vec{D}_T}{\partial t} = \frac{rJ_t - J_{kt} K^* - J_{tt}}{\sum_{m=1}^{M} p_m y_m}. \tag{5.57}[6]$$

Technical inefficiency change: $\widehat{B} = \dfrac{1}{\sum_{m=1}^{M} (\partial \ln \vec{D}_T / \partial \ln y_m)} \dfrac{\partial \ln \beta}{\partial t}$

$$= -\frac{1}{\sum_{m=1}^{M} p_m y_m} \frac{\partial \ln \beta}{\partial t}. \tag{5.58}$$

[6] The right-hand side of this term emerges by totally differentiating the optimized Hamilton-Jacobi-Bellman equation in (5.52) with respect to time, leading to $rJ_t = J_{kt} \dot{K}^* + \lambda^\pi \dfrac{\partial \vec{D}_T}{\partial t} + J_{tt}$.

Variable inputs: $\hat{Q}_X = \sum_{n=1}^{N} \varepsilon_n^X \, \hat{x}_n = \sum_{n=1}^{N} \dfrac{w_n x_n^*}{\sum_{n=1}^{N} w_n x_n^* - \sum_{f=1}^{F} J_{k_f} I_f^*}$, (5.59)

where

$$\varepsilon_n^X = \dfrac{\partial \vec{D}_T / \partial \ln x_n}{\sum_{n=1}^{N} (\partial \vec{D}_T / \partial \ln x_n) + \sum_{f=1}^{F} (\partial \vec{D}_T / \partial \ln I_f)} = \dfrac{w_n x_n^*}{\sum_{n=1}^{N} w_n x_n^* - \sum_{f=1}^{F} J_{k_f} I_f^*}.$$

Investments: $\hat{Q}_I = \sum_{f=1}^{F} \varepsilon_f^I \, \hat{I}_f = -\sum_{f=1}^{F} \dfrac{J_{k_f} I_f^*}{\sum_{n=1}^{N} w_n x_n^* - \sum_{f=1}^{F} J_{k_f} I_f^*}$, (5.60)

where

$$\varepsilon_f^I = \dfrac{\partial \overline{\ln D_T} / \partial \ln I_f}{\sum_{n=1}^{N} (\partial \overline{\ln D_T} / \partial \ln x_n) + \sum_{f=1}^{F} \left(\partial \overline{\ln D_T} / \partial \ln I_f \right)}$$
$$= \dfrac{-J_{k_f} I_f^*}{\sum_{n=1}^{N} w_n x_n^* - \sum_{f=1}^{F} J_{k_f} I_f^*}.$$

Capital Stock: $\hat{Q}_K = -\sum_{f=1}^{F} \dfrac{\dfrac{\partial \overline{\ln D_T}}{\partial \overline{\ln K_f}}}{\sum_{m=1}^{M} \left(\dfrac{\partial \overline{\ln D_T}}{\partial \overline{\ln y_m}} \right)} \hat{K}_f$

$$= -\sum_{(f=1)}^{F} \dfrac{[(r+\delta) J_{(k_l)} + c_l - J_{(k_f)}] K_l]}{\sum_{(m=1)}^{M} p_m y_m} \hat{K}_f^* + \sum_{(f=1)}^{F} \dfrac{J_{(k_f)} K_l}{\sum_{(m=1)}^{M} p_m y_m} \hat{K}_f^*,$$ (5.61)

where

$$\dfrac{\partial \overline{\ln D_T} / \partial \ln K_f}{\sum_{m=1}^{M} (\partial \overline{\ln D_T} / \partial \ln y_m)} = \dfrac{\partial \vec{D}_T / \partial \ln K_f}{\sum_{m=1}^{M} (\partial \vec{D}_T / \partial \ln y_m)} = \dfrac{[(r+\delta) jk_1 + c_l - jk_f] k_1}{\sum_{m=1}^{M} p_m y_m}.$$

This last expression in (5.61) can be reorganized by considering the fth element of the last term on the right-hand side, $(\dot{J}_{k_f} K_f) \cdot \widehat{Q}_f$. Multiplying and dividing this element by J_{k_i} leads to

$$\left(\dot{J}_{k_i} K_i\right) \cdot \widehat{K}_i^* = \left(\frac{J_{K_i}}{J_{K_i}} J_{K_i} K_i\right) \cdot \frac{\dot{K}_i}{K_i} = \left(J_{k_i} \dot{K}_i^*\right) \cdot \hat{J}_{K_i} \tag{5.62}$$

so that (5.61) is now

$$\widehat{Q}_K = -\sum_{f=1}^F \frac{[(r+\delta)J_{(k_i)} + c_l - J_{(k_f)}]K_l]}{\sum_{m=1}^m p_m y_m} \widehat{K}_f^* + \sum_{f=1}^F \frac{J_{(k_f)} K_f}{\sum_{m=1}^m p_m y_m} J_{(k_f)}. \tag{5.63}$$

Separating the proportional change in output from the proportional change in inputs allows us to rewrite the proportional change in the directional distance function in (5.46) as

$$\sum_{m=1}^M \frac{p_m y_m}{\sum_{m=1}^M p_m y_m} \hat{y}_m = \sum_{n=1}^N \frac{w_n x_n}{\sum_{n=1}^N w_n x_n - \sum_{f=1}^F J_{k_f} I_f} \hat{x}_n$$

$$-\sum_{f=1}^F \frac{J_{k_f} I_f}{\sum_{n=1}^N w_n x_n - \sum_{f=1}^F J_{k_f} I_f} \hat{I}_f$$

$$-\sum_{f=1}^F \frac{[(r+\delta)J_{k_i} + c_l - \dot{J}_{k_f}]K_l}{\sum_{m=1}^M p_m y_m} \widehat{K}_f$$

$$+\sum_{f=1}^F \frac{J_{k_f} K_f}{\sum_{m=1}^M p_m y_m} \hat{J}_{k_f}$$

$$+\frac{rJ_t - J_{kt}\dot{K} - J_{tt}}{\sum_{m=1}^M p_m y_m} - \frac{1}{\sum_{m=1}^M p_m y_m} \frac{\partial \ln \beta}{\partial t}. \tag{5.64}$$

Multiplying and dividing the first two terms on the left-hand side of (5.64) by $\sum_{m=1}^M p_m y_m$ leads to

$$\sum_{m}^{M}\left(\frac{p_m y_m}{\sum_{m}^{M} p_m y_m}\right) \cdot \hat{y}_m = \frac{\sum_{j}^{N} w_j x_j - \sum_{l}^{F} J_{k_l} I_l}{\sum_{m}^{M} p_m y_m}$$

$$\times \left[\sum_{j}^{N}\left(\frac{w_j x_j}{\sum_{m}^{M} p_m y_m}\right) \cdot \hat{x}_j - \sum_{l}^{F}\left(\frac{J_{k_l} I_l}{\sum_{m}^{M} p_m y_m}\right) \cdot \hat{I}_l\right]$$

$$- \sum_{l}^{F}\left(\frac{\left[(r+\delta)J_{k_l} - c_l\right]K_l}{\sum_{m}^{M} p_m y_m}\right) \cdot \widehat{K}_l + \sum_{l}^{F}\left(\frac{J_{k_l}\dot{K}_l}{\sum_{m}^{M} p_m y_m}\right) \cdot \hat{J}_{K_l}$$

$$+ \frac{rJ_t - J_{kt}\dot{K} - J_{tt}}{\sum_{m}^{M} p_m y_m} - \frac{\dot{\beta}}{\sum_{m}^{M} p_m y_m}.$$

$$(5.65)$$

or

$$\widehat{Q}_Y = \varepsilon_T \cdot [\widehat{Q}_X + \widehat{Q}_I] + \widehat{Q}_{SS} + \widehat{Q}_{SV} + \widehat{A} + \widehat{B}, \qquad (5.66)$$

With $\widehat{Q}_Y$ representing the aggregate output growth, $\widehat{Q}_X$ representing the aggregate growth of the variable inputs, and $\widehat{Q}_I$ representing the aggregate growth of the gross physical investment demand. $\widehat{A}$ represents the technological progress arising from autonomous sources. $\widehat{B}$ represents the contribution of technical inefficiency change to output growth. The terms that diverge significantly from the static case are $\widehat{Q}_{SS}$ and $\widehat{Q}_{SV}$, which represent the disequilibrium components; that is, $\widehat{Q}_{SS}$ reflects the aggregate growth in quasi-fixed-factor levels at the long-run equilibrium where gross investment is only sufficient to cover asset depreciation. $\widehat{Q}_{SV}$ represents the aggregate change in the endogenously determined marginal (or shadow) values of capital assets, which necessarily shift as capital stocks shift. The scale effect of input growth (x, I) is scaled by the ε_T when allowing for profit maximization as denoted in (5.10).[7]

With total factor productivity growth, $T\check{F}P$, being the difference between output growth and input growth,

---

[7] When $g_x = -x, g_I = I, g_y = y$ and allowing for profit maximization implying $p_y = C_y$, the multiple output, multiple input scale elasticity in (5.19) is equal to $\varepsilon_T = \lambda^C/\lambda^R$, where λ^R is the value of the direction for intertemporal revenue maximization.

$$\hat{TFP} = \hat{Q}_Y - [\hat{Q}_X + \hat{Q}_I]$$
$$= (\varepsilon_T - 1)[\hat{Q}_X + \hat{Q}_I] + \hat{Q}_{SS} + \hat{Q}_{SV} + \hat{A} + \hat{B}. \quad (5.67)$$

This decomposition identifies the contributions of a scale effect, $(\varepsilon_T - 1)[\hat{Q}_X + \hat{Q}_I]$; technical change, $-\hat{A}$; and technical inefficiency change, $\hat{B}$, to productivity growth.

5.3.2 Luenberger Indicator

The directional distance function is a powerful approach when decomposing the contributions of various inputs to productivity changes over time. This measure has its origins in Chambers, Färe, and Grosskopf (1996), who defined a Luenberger indicator of productivity growth in the static context and draws out the difference between the ratio-based (or index) measures of productivity as in (5.43), for example, and the difference-based (or indicator) productivity measures that emerge from the directional distance function perspective. A growing literature employing this approach has emerged in recent years.[8] This indicator can be presented in both the primal form (using the directional distance function) and the dual form (using the value function) as it is extended to the dynamic setting. The primal Luenberger indicator of dynamic productivity growth is then decomposed to identify the contributions of technical change, technical inefficiency change, and scale inefficiency change. In addition to technical change, technical inefficiency change, and scale inefficiency change, the dual form also identifies the contributions of allocative inefficiency change and a disequilibrium component reflecting the change in the shadow value of capital.

5.3.2.1 Primal Setting
Focusing on the dynamic directional input distance function, the Luenberger dynamic productivity growth indicator presents the arithmetic average of productivity change measured by the technology at time $t + 1$ and

---

[8] See Chambers, Färe, and Grosskpf (1996), Chambers and Pope (1996), Boussemart et al. (2003), Färe and Primont (2003), Briec and Kerstens (2004), Färe and Grosskopf (2004), and Balk et al. (2008).

productivity change measured by the technology at time t, under the assumption of constant returns to scale. This is defined as

$$L(\cdot) = \frac{1}{2}\left\{ \begin{array}{l} [\vec{D}_i^{t+1}(x_t, I_t, k_t, y_t; g_x, g_I) - \vec{D}_i^{t+1}(x_{t+1}, I_{t+1}, k_{t+1} y_{t+1}; g_x, g_I)] \\ +[\vec{D}_i^t(x_t, I_t, k_t, y_t; g_x, g_I) - \vec{D}_i^t(x_{t+1}, I_{t+1}, k_{t+1} y_{t+1}; g_x, g_I)] \end{array} \right\}. \quad (5.68)$$

The Luenberger indicator of dynamic productivity growth is illustrated graphically in Figure 5.1. The quantities of inputs and investments at time t and time $t + 1$ are denoted as (I_t, x_t) and (I_{t+1}, x_{t+1}), respectively. The dynamic directional input distance functions measure the distance of an input bundle (I,x) to the isoquants at time t and time $t + 1$. For example, $D^{t+1}(I_t, x_t)$ is the value of the distance function for the input quantities at time t using technology at time $t + 1$.

The Luenberger indicator of dynamic productivity growth can be decomposed into the contributions of technical inefficiency change (ΔTEI) and technical change (ΔT):

$$L(\cdot) = \Delta T + \Delta TEI. \quad (5.69)$$

The decomposition of productivity growth is obtained from (5.69) by adding and subtracting the term $\vec{D}_i^{t+1}(x_{t+1}, I_{t+1}, k_{t+1}, y_{t+1}; g_x, g_I) - \vec{D}_i^t(x_t, I_t, k_t, y_t; g_x, g_I)$. Technical change is also computed in reference to (5.68) as the arithmetic average of the difference between the technology (represented by the

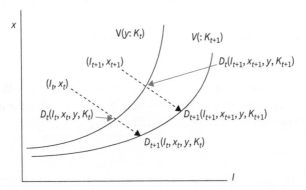

Figure 5.1. Luenberger indicator of dynamic productivity growth.

frontier) at time t and time $t + 1$, evaluated using quantities at time t (first two terms) and time $t + 1$ (last two terms), which leads to

$$\Delta T = \frac{1}{2}\left\{\begin{array}{l}[\vec{D}_i^{t+1}(x_t,I_t,k_t,y_t;g_x,g_I) - \vec{D}_i^t(x_t,I_t,k_t,y_t;g_x,g_I)] \\ +[\vec{D}_i^{t+1}(x_{t+1},I_{t+1},k_{t+1}y_{t+1};g_x,g_I) - \vec{D}_i^t(x_{t+1},I_{t+1},k_{t+1}y_{t+1};g_x,g_I)]\end{array}\right\}.$$

(5.70)

Technical change can be seen in Figure 5.1 as the average distance between the two isoquants. This entails evaluating the distance between the isoquants using quantities at time t, $\vec{D}_i^{t+1}(x_t,I_t,k_t,y_t;g_x,g_I) - \vec{D}_i^t(x_t,I_t,k_t,y_t;g_x,g_I)$ and quantities at time $t + 1$, $\vec{D}_i^{t+1}(x_{t+1},I_{t+1},k_{t+1}y_{t+1};g_x,g_I) - \vec{D}_i^t(x_{t+1},I_{t+1},k_{t+1}y_{t+1};g_x,g_I)$. Dynamic technical inefficiency change is the difference between the value of the dynamic directional input distance function at time t and time $t + 1$:

$$\Delta TEI = \vec{D}_i^t(x_t,I_t,k_ty_t;g_x,g_I) - \vec{D}_i^{t+1}(x_{t+1},I_{t+1},k_{t+1},y_{t+1};g_x,g_I).$$

(5.71)

Technical inefficiency change is easily seen from Figure 5.1 as the difference between the distance of the input bundle (I_t,x_t) to the isoquant at time t and the distance of the input bundle (I_{t+1},x_{t+1}) to the isoquant at time $t + 1$.

Example 5.1: Primal Luenberger dynamic productivity growth indicatorIn this example, we illustrate the computation of the Luenberger dynamic productivity growth indicator. Consider the data presented in Table 5.1 for a sample of four firms, in period $t = 0$ and period $t = 1$.

We can illustrate the productivity growth indicator in the two dimensions in Figure 5.2, where we assume that the directional distance vector $(g_x,g_I) = (1,-1)$ in both periods. The values of variable inputs and investments in period $t = 0$ are the same as the values used in the earlier examples. As before, it is assumed that the quantities of output and capital are the same for all firms in both periods.[9] Let firm f be denoted as f_0 and f_1 for periods 0

---

[9] To be able to illustrate the shifts in the two dimensions in Figures 5.1, 5.2, and 5.3, we need to assume that output and capital stock are the same for all firms in both periods so that we can illustrate the Luenberger productivity growth decomposition into the various components (e.g., technical inefficiency change, technical change, scale change). If the capital stock would differ between periods, then the distance between frontiers does not reflect technical change, nor can we reflect technical inefficiency change.

Table 5.1 Data of Firms in Periods $t = 0$ and $t = 1$

Firm	Output	Capital	Investment	Variable Input
$t = 0$				
1	10	10	2	2
2	10	10	4	3
3	10	10	6	6
4	10	10	3	5
$t = 1$				
1	10	10	3	2
2	10	10	6	4
3	10	10	7	6
4	10	10	5	5

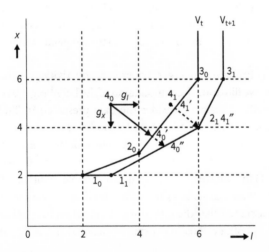

Figure 5.2. Graphical representation of the primal Luenberger dynamic productivity growth indicator.

and 1, respectively, for $f = 1, 2, 3, 4$. Firm 4 is the inefficient firm in both time periods and is located in the interior of input requirement sets at $t + 1$ and t.

The expression of the Luenberger dynamic productivity growth indicator is

$$L(\cdot) = \frac{1}{2} \left\{ \begin{array}{l} [\vec{D}_i^1(x_0, I_0, k_0, y_0; g_x = -1, g_I = 1) - \vec{D}_i^1(x_1, I_1, k_1 y_1; g_x = -1, g_I = 1)] + \\ [\vec{D}_i^0(x_0, I_0, k_0, y_0; g_x = -1, g_I = 1) - \vec{D}_i^0(x_1, I_1, k_1 y_1; g_x = -1, g_I = 1)] \end{array} \right\},$$

(5.72)

and the components of the Luenberger productivity indicator for firm 4 are computed as

$$\vec{D}_i^1(x_0, I_0, k_0, y_0; g_x = -1, g_I = 1) = 1.8$$
$$\vec{D}_i^1(x_1, I_1, k_1 y_1; g_x = -1, g_I = 1) = 1$$
$$\vec{D}_i^0(x_0, I_0, k_0, y_0; g_x = -1, g_I = 1) = 1.4$$
$$\vec{D}_i^0(x_1, I_1, k_1, y_1; g_x = -1, g_I = 1) = 0.2.$$

Inserting these computations into (5.72) yields $L(\cdot) = \frac{1}{2}\{[1.8 - 1] + [1.4 - 0.2]\} = 1$, which suggests that firm 4 has improved its productivity from period $t = 0$ to period $t = 1$ by one unit. That is, due to productivity growth, in period $t = 1$, firm 4 uses one unit less of input x and invests one unit more of the quasi-fixed factor while producing the same output level and using the same quantity of capital.

The Luenberger dynamic productivity growth indicator can be decomposed into the contributions of technical change and technical inefficiency change. Technical change is computed as

$$\Delta T = \frac{1}{2} \left\{ \begin{array}{l} [\vec{D}_i^1(x_0, I_0, k_0, y_0; g_x = -1, g_I = 1) - \vec{D}_i^0(x_0, I_0, k_0, y_0; g_x = -1, g_I = 1)] + \\ [\vec{D}_i^1(x_1, I_1, k_1, y_1; g_x = -1, g_I = 1) - \vec{D}_i^0(x_1, I_1, k_1 y_1; g_x = -1, g_I = 1)] \end{array} \right\}$$

$$= \frac{1}{2}\{[1.8 - 1.4] + [1 - 0.2]\} = 0.6,$$

and technical inefficiency change is

$$\Delta TEI = \vec{D}_i^0(x_0, I_0, k_0, y_0; g_x = -1, g_I = 1) - \vec{D}_i^1(x_1, I_1, k_1, y_1; g_x = -1, g_I = 1)$$
$$= 1.4 - 1 = 0.4$$

which implies that 60% of the productivity growth is due to technical change and 40% is due to a decrease of technical inefficiency.

We can decompose the Luenberger measure further to allow for scale and congestion effects. With the Luenberger measure historically being developed in the context of constant returns to scale and strong disposability of inputs and outputs, Epure et al. (2011) expand the decomposition of the technical inefficiency change component into a pure technical inefficiency change (ΔPEI), scale inefficiency change (ΔSEI), and congestion inefficiency change (ΔCEI). This further decomposition relaxes the technology assumptions of constant returns to scale and strong disposability to permit variable returns to scale and weak disposability.

From a primal perspective, the technical inefficiency change component in (5.71) can be decomposed as

$$\Delta PEI = \vec{D}_i^t(x_t, I_t, k_t y_t; g_x, g_I \mid VRS, WD) \\ - \vec{D}_i^{t+1}(x_{t+1}, I_{t+1}, k_{t+1}, y_{t+1}; g_x, g_I \mid VRS, WD), \quad (5.73)$$

$$\Delta SEI = \vec{D}_i^t(x_t, I_t, k_t y_t; g_x, g_I \mid CRS, SD) - \vec{D}_i^t(x_t, I_t, k_t y_t; g_x, g_I \mid VRS, SD) \\ - \left[\vec{D}_i^{t+1}(x_{t+1}, I_{t+1}, k_{t+1}, y_{t+1}; g_x, g_I \mid CRS, SD) - \vec{D}_i^{t+1}(x_{t+1}, I_{t+1}, k_{t+1}, y_{t+1}; g_x, g_I \mid VRS, SD) \right], \\ \hfill (5.74)$$

$$\Delta CEI = \vec{D}_i^t(x_t, I_t, k_t y_t; g_x, g_I \mid VRS, SD) - \vec{D}_i^t(x_t, I_t, k_t y_t; g_x, g_I \mid VRS, WD) \\ - \left[\vec{D}_i^{t+1}(x_{t+1}, I_{t+1}, k_{t+1}, y_{t+1}; g_x, g_I \mid VRS, SD) - \vec{D}_i^{t+1}(x_{t+1}, I_{t+1}, k_{t+1}, y_{t+1}; g_x, g_I \mid VRS, WD) \right], \\ \hfill (5.75)$$

where ΔPEI is pure technical inefficiency change under variable returns to scale and weak disposability of variable inputs, ΔSEI is scale inefficiency change under strong disposability, and ΔCEI is congestion inefficiency change, that is, change in productivity due to a change in variable input congestion.

5.3.2.2 Dual Setting

The dual relation between the directional input distance function and the optimal value function associated with intertemporal cost minimization is developed in theorem 4.1 and extensively exploited in section 4.3.1. The dynamic dual form of the Luenberger dynamic productivity growth indicator is formulated in terms of the differences between observed costs and minimum costs as

$$
LD(\cdot) = \frac{1}{2}
\begin{bmatrix}
\dfrac{(w_t x_t + c_t K_t + W_{kt+1,t}(I_t - \delta K_t)) - rW_{t+1}(w_t, c_t, K_t, y_t)}{w_t g_x - W_{kt+1,t} g_I} \\[2ex]
+ \dfrac{(w_t x_t + c_t K_t + W_{kt}(I_t - \delta K_t)) - rW_t(w_t, c_t, K_t, y_t)}{w_t g_x - W_{kt} g_I}
\end{bmatrix}
$$
$$
- \frac{1}{2}
\begin{bmatrix}
\dfrac{(w_{t+1} x_{t+1} + c_{t+1} K_{t+1} + W_{kt+1}(I_{t+1} - \delta K_{t+1})) - rW_{t+1}(w_{t+1}, c_{t+1}, K_{t+1}, y_{t+1})}{w_{t+1} g_x - W_{kt+1} g_I} \\[2ex]
+ \dfrac{(w_{t+1} x_{t+1} + c_{t+1} K_{t+1} + W_{kt,t+1}(I_{t+1} - \delta K_{t+1})) - rW_t(w_{t+1}, c_{t+1}, K_{t+1}, y_{t+1})}{w_{t+1} g_x - W_{kt,t+1} g_I}
\end{bmatrix},
$$

$$(5.76)$$

This indicator computes the arithmetic mean of two components, each consisting of two ratios. The first ratio in the first component measures the difference between observed shadow cost of production at time t, using the frontier in time $t + 1$ $w_t x_t + c_t K_t + W_{kt+1,t}(I_t - \delta K_t)$, and the minimum shadow costs measured by the optimal value function at time $t + 1$ using the prices in time t, that is, $rW_{t+1}(\cdot)$. The second ratio in the first component is the difference between the observed and minimum shadow costs using prices and quantities at time t and the frontier in t. The differences between the observed and minimum shadow costs in the first and second ratios are normalized by the shadow value of the directional vector, implying that the ratios are unit free. Note that the shadow price of capital ($W_{kt+1,t}$) in the first ratio is measured from the cost frontier at time $t + 1$ and prices and quantities at time t, that is, $W_{k,t+1,t} = W_{k,t+1}(w_t, c_t, K_t, y_t)$. The third and fourth ratios are similar to the first and second ratios and measure the difference between observed and minimum shadow costs using prices and quantities at time $t + 1$. The shadow price of capital ($W_{kt,+1t}$) in the fourth ratio is measured from the cost frontier at time t and prices and quantities at time $t + 1$ (i.e., $W_{k,t+1,t} = W_{k,t+1}(w_{t+1}, c_{t+1}, K_{t+1}, y_{t+1})$).

As in the primal case in section 5.3.2.1, the dual dynamic Luenberger productivity change indicator can be decomposed to identify the contributions of technical change and technical inefficiency change. But now that this measure embodies an optimization objective (intertemporal cost minimization), we can additionally address the contribution of allocative inefficiency change. A natural point of departure for the decomposition of the dual Luenberger productivity indicator is the decomposition into the contributions of technical change, overall inefficiency change, and a residual component that we name shadow value change. Technical change is computed as the arithmetic mean of the normalized distance between the optimal value frontiers, evaluated at prices and quantities in period t and period $t + 1$, respectively, as

$$\Delta TED(\cdot) = \frac{1}{2} \left[\frac{rW_t(w_t, c_t, K_t, y_t)}{w_t g_x - W_{kt} g_I} - \frac{rW_{t+1}(w_t, c_t, K_t, y_t)}{w_t g_x - W_{kt+1,t} g_I} \right]$$
$$+ \frac{1}{2} \left[\frac{rW_t(w_{t+1}, c_{t+1}, K_{t+1}, y_{t+1})}{w_{t+1} g_x - W_{kt,t+1} g_I} - \frac{rW_{t+1}(w_{t+1}, c_{t+1}, K_{t+1}, y_{t+1})}{w_{t+1} g_x - W_{kt+1} g_I} \right], \quad (5.77)$$

and overall inefficiency change is given by

$$\Delta LOEI(\cdot)$$
$$= \left[\frac{(w_t x_t + c_t K_t + W_{kt}(I_t - \delta K_t)) - rW_t(w_t, c_t, K_t, y_t)}{w_t g_x - W_{kt} g_I} - \frac{(w_{t+1} x_{t+1} + c_{t+1} K_{t+1} + W_{kt+1}(I_{t+1} - \delta K_{t+1})) - rW_{t+1}(w_{t+1}, c_{t+1}, K_{t+1}, y_{t+1})}{w_{t+1} g_x - W_{kt+1} g_I} \right].$$
$$(5.78)$$

The overall inefficiency change given in (5.78) can be further decomposed into a technical inefficiency change component and an allocative inefficiency change component, that is,

$$\Delta LOEI(\cdot) = \Delta TEI + \Delta AEID,$$

where ΔTEI can be computed using (5.71) and decomposed into ΔPEI, ΔSEI, and ΔCEI using (5.73)–(5.75); $\Delta AEID$ is by definition a residual term. The term that remains after subtracting overall inefficiency change and technical change from the Luenberger productivity indicator, that is, $LD - \Delta TED - \Delta LOEI$ [(5.76)–(5.78)], is

$$
\Delta SV(\cdot) = \frac{1}{2}\left[\frac{(w_t x_t + c_t K_t + W_{kt+1,t}(I_t - \delta K_t))}{w_t g_x - W_{kt+1,t} g_I} - \frac{(w_t x_t + c_t K_t + W_{kt}(I_t - \delta K_t))}{w_t g_x - W_{kt} g_I} \right]
$$
$$
+ \frac{1}{2}\left[\begin{array}{c} \dfrac{(w_{t+1} x_{t+1} + c_{t+1} K_{t+1} + W_{kt+1}(I_{t+1} - \delta K_{t+1}))}{w_{t+1} g_x - W_{kt+1} g_I} \\[2ex] - \dfrac{(w_{t+1} x_{t+1} + c_{t+1} K_{t+1} + W_{kt,t+1}(I_{t+1} - \delta K_{t+1}))}{w_{t+1} g_x - W_{kt,t+1} g_I} \end{array} \right],
$$

(5.79)

which is the contribution of the change in the shadow cost of production to productivity growth.

In (5.79), the component to indicate a change over time is the shadow value of capital, W_k. Note that the change in the shadow value of capital is also appearing in the TFP growth decomposition presented in section 5.3.1.2, where this term appears in (5.66). Note that W_k is contemporaneously fixed but intertemporally endogenous. Taken together, $\Delta TED + \Delta LOEI + \Delta SV$ [in (5.77)–(5.79)] equals LD in (5.76).

Example 5.2: Dual Luenberger dynamic productivity growth indicatorIn this example, we illustrate the computation of the dual Luenberger dynamic productivity growth indicator. For this example, we consider the data of four firms in period $t = 0$ and period $t = 1$ presented in Table 5.1. Additionally, we set $w_t = w_{t+1}, c_t = c_{t+1}$, and $y_t = y_{t+1} = y_O$. Further, let $I_{t+1} > I_t$, $I_{t+1} > \delta K_{t+1}$ and $I_t > \delta K_t$, implying $K_t < K_{t+1}$. This leads to $W_t(w,c,y_O,K_t) > W_{t+1}(w,c,y_O,K_{t+1})$. Furthermore, we assume that $W_{kt}(w,c,y_O,K_t) = W_{kt+1}(w,c,y_O,K_t)$ and $W_{kt}(w,c,y_O,K_{t+1}) = W_{kt+1}(w,c,y_O,K_{t+1})$, implying that the shadow value change component is zero. The latter assumption is made since the shadow value change component cannot be reflected graphically.

Figure 5.3 reflects the isoquants and the isocost lines in periods t and $t + 1$. The TFP components are given as well. The decomposition of TFP into technical inefficiency change, allocative inefficiency change, and technical change is presented in Table 5.2.

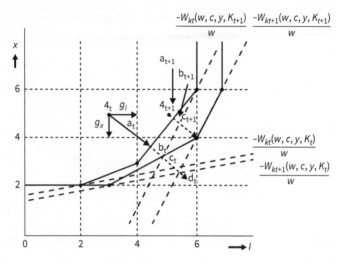

Figure 5.3. Graphical representation of the dynamic dual Luenberger productivity growth indicator.

Table 5.2 Dynamic Dual Luenberger Productivity Growth and Its Decomposition

TFP Component	Measures Indicated in Figure 5.3
ΔTEI	$a_t - (a_{t+1} + b_{t+1} + c_{t+1})$
$\Delta AEID$	$(b_t + c_t)$
ΔTED	$\frac{1}{2}(d_t + c_{t+1})$
LD	$a_t + b_t + c_t + \frac{1}{2}d_t - (a_{t+1} + b_{t+1} + \frac{1}{2}c_{t+1})$

5.4 Remarks

The measurement of productivity change for the case of multiple inputs and multiple outputs is a useful intermediate-run to long-run measure of economic performance for firms as well as sectors. By isolating the impact of technical change from the other forces that can drive change such as input growth and efficiency change, the decomposition of productivity change measures allows us to tell a more nuanced story of how firms or a sector changes. Technical change arises from new technologies that can embody new installations, equipment, or processes (or a combination of all).

The next sources of productivity change are conditioned on a given technology. The first is technical inefficiency change, which reflects the efforts of firms to extract the potential from existing technologies. These gains can typically impact productivity growth modestly. The second is allocative inefficiency change, which addresses the firm's attention to balancing the tradeoff between input bundles with a view toward choosing bundles to meet the optimization decision rule. The third is scale efficiency change, which indicates that firms can use the production potential more efficiently and succeed by moving closer to a scale of operation that is associated with constant returns to scale. The final component reflects changes arising from the disequilibrium of quasi-fixed factors, which reflect both the change in the capital stock given and how that change in the capital stock leads to the re-evaluation of the internal valuation of the capital stock. Both effects arise because the firm is not at a long-run equilibrium capital stock.

The value of identifying these different components is that different decision-making actions can impact the different components. For example, while R&D investment and policy decisions can impact technical change, the inefficiency of quasi-fixed assets may require better inventory management. Exacting scale efficiencies will require the appropriate scale operations up/down.

This outcome of such an analysis is intended to serve as a decision aid as the firm's performance is described relative to the benchmark technology defined by its peer group. The analyst offers an understanding of how markets and decision makers interact within an incentives-based paradigm and use models focusing on relative incentives to analyze the data that can capture the core economic decision-making relationships. As such, the analyst's job is to explain the themes that can catalyze the decision maker's thinking.

6
Econometric Approaches

6.1 Introduction

Econometric approaches provide another avenue to implementing the frameworks and concepts of dynamic efficiency and productivity measurement. This chapter discusses the main issues related to specifying dynamic adjustment in econometric models, selection of functional forms, data, and estimation, without having the intention to be exhaustive. In the context of econometric approaches to efficiency measurement, see Kumbhakar and Lovell (2000) and Greene (2008) for an overview of econometric approaches. In addition to the discussion of empirical issues, this chapter provides an empirical illustration using micro-level data.

The emergence of econometric approaches focuses on estimating dynamic factor demands under dynamic adjustment. Early econometric implementation of these approaches is found in Denny et al. (1981). Mahmud et al. (1987) examine the implications of functional form specification on the invariance of estimation, and Pindyck and Rotemberg (1983), Shapiro (1986), and Chirinko (1993) focus on the implicit equations approach. These approaches are a mixture of dual short-run functional specifications and primal adjustment cost function specifications. Epstein and Denny (1983) estimate the dynamic dual model for the US manufacturing sector and present a discussion of homotheticity and aggregation restrictions for the intertemporal cost minimization. Hamermesh and Pfann (1996) and Cooper (2001) provide excellent overviews of the state of modeling dynamic adjustment.

The empirical illustrations estimating dynamic efficiency presents a structural approach. This approach specifies a parametric functional form for an adjustment cost (directional) distance function that explicitly addresses the adjustment costs underlying investments in the quasi-fixed factors of production. Technical inefficiency is accounted for in a stochastic production frontier model, or distance function; similarly, cost (profit) inefficiency is

Dynamic Efficiency and Productivity Measurement. Elvira Silva, Spiro E. Stefanou, and Alfons Oude Lansink,
Oxford University Press (2021). © Oxford University Press. DOI: 10.1093/oso/9780190919474.001.0001

estimated using the current cost (profit) frontier. The estimated dynamic distance functions form the basis for the computation of total factor productivity growth in the dynamic context.

The empirical applications can be performed in many software packages allowing stochastic production frontier estimation such as STATA, LIMDEP/NLOGIT, and R. Interested readers are encouraged to explore rapidly emerging software options for econometrically estimating dynamic efficiency.

6.2 Functional Forms

Econometric approaches to estimating technical efficiency and productivity require a functional specification of the adjustment cost production technology. In line with the conceptual framework introduced in the previous chapters, this chapter introduces functional forms that are appropriate for representing a directional input distance function. The choice of functional forms for a directional input distance function is limited by the need to satisfy the properties of this function, namely, the translation property. Chambers (1998) proposes two parametric flexible functional forms for the directional input distance function: the *logarithmic transcendental* and the *quadratic*. The logarithmic transcendental form automatically satisfies the translation property as long as the directional vector is specified as a unitary vector. Parametric restrictions can be easily imposed on the quadratic form so that the translation property is satisfied.

Chambers (2002), Färe et al. (2005), and Serra et al. (2011), among others, used the quadratic specification for the directional distance function. Assuming M outputs, N variable inputs, and F quasi-fixed factors of production, the quadratic adjustment cost directional input distance function is expressed as

$$\vec{D}_i\left(y,x,I,K;g_x,g_I\right) = a_0 + \sum_{m=1}^{M} a_m^y y_m + \sum_{n=1}^{N} a_n^x x_n + \sum_{f=1}^{F} a_f^I I_f + \sum_{f}^{F} a_f^k K_f$$

$$\frac{1}{2}\sum_{m=1}^{M}\sum_{j=1}^{M} a_{mj}^{yy} y_m y_j + \frac{1}{2}\sum_{n=1}^{N}\sum_{j=1}^{N} a_{nj}^{xx} x_n x_j + \frac{1}{2}\sum_{f=1}^{F}\sum_{j=1}^{F} a_{fj}^{II} I_f I_j + \frac{1}{2}\sum_{f=1}^{F}\sum_{j=1}^{J} a_{fj}^{kk} K_f K_j +$$

$$\sum_{m=1}^{M}\sum_{n=1}^{N} a_{mn}^{yx} y_m x_n + \sum_{m=1}^{M}\sum_{f=1}^{f} a_{mf}^{yI} y_m I_f + \sum_{m=1}^{M}\sum_{f=1}^{F} a_{mf}^{yk} y_m K_f + \sum_{n=1}^{N}\sum_{f=1}^{F} a_{nf}^{xI} x_n I_f +$$

$$\sum_{n=1}^{N}\sum_{f=1}^{F} a_{nf}^{xk} x_n K_f + \sum_{f=1}^{F}\sum_{j=1}^{F} a_{fj}^{Ik} I_f K_j.$$

$$(6.1)$$

If it is assumed that $g_x = 1_N$ and $g_I = 1_P$ then the following set of parameter restrictions ensures the translation property holds:[1]

$$\sum_{f=1}^{F} a_f^I - \sum_{n=1}^{N} a_n^x = -1 \; ; \; \sum_{f=1}^{F}\sum_{j=1}^{F} a_{fj}^{Ik} - \sum_{n=1}^{N}\sum_{f=1}^{F} a_{nf}^{xk} = 0 \; ; \; \sum_{m=1}^{M}\sum_{f=1}^{F} a_{mf}^{yI} - \sum_{m=1}^{M}\sum_{n=1}^{N} a_{mn}^{yx} = 0;$$

(6.2)

$$\sum_{j=1}^{N} a_{nj}^{xx} - \sum_{f=1}^{F} a_{nf}^{xI} = 0, i = 1,...,N \quad \sum_{j=1}^{F} a_{jf}^{II} - \sum_{n=1}^{N} a_{nf}^{xI} = 0, f = 1,...,F.$$

In addition to the restrictions required by the translation property, the usual symmetry restrictions are imposed: $a_{mj}^{yy} = a_{jm}^{yy}$ $a_{fj}^{II} = a_{jf}^{II}$, $a_{nj}^{xx} = a_{jn}^{xx}$, and $a_{fj}^{kk} = a_{jf}^{kk}$.

The second functional form that is suitable for estimating an adjustment cost directional input distance function is the *logarithmic transcendental* function, which is specified as

$$\exp(\vec{D}_i (y,x,I,K,g_x,g_I))$$
$$= a_0 + \frac{1}{2}\sum_{m=1}^{M}\sum_{j=1}^{M} a_{mj}^{yy} \exp\left(\frac{-y_m}{2}\right)\exp\left(\frac{-y_j}{2}\right)$$
$$+ \frac{1}{2}\sum_{n=1}^{N}\sum_{j=1}^{N} a_{nj}^{xx} \exp\left(\frac{x_n}{2}\right)\exp\left(\frac{x_j}{2}\right) + \frac{1}{2}\sum_{f=1}^{F}\sum_{j=1}^{F} a_{fj}^{II} \exp\left(\frac{-I_f}{2}\right)\exp\left(\frac{-I_j}{2}\right)$$
$$+ \frac{1}{2}\sum_{f=1}^{F}\sum_{j=1}^{J} a_{fj}^{kk} \exp\left(\frac{K_f}{2}\right)\exp\left(\frac{K_j}{2}\right) + \sum_{m=1}^{M}\sum_{n=1}^{N} a_{mj}^{yx} \exp\left(\frac{-y_m}{2}\right)\exp\left(\frac{x_n}{2}\right)$$
$$+ \sum_{m=1}^{M}\sum_{f=1}^{f} a_{mf}^{yI} \exp\left(\frac{-y_m}{2}\right)\exp\left(\frac{-I_f}{2}\right) + \sum_{m=1}^{M}\sum_{f=1}^{F} a_{mf}^{yk} \exp\left(\frac{-y_m}{2}\right)\exp\left(\frac{K_f}{2}\right)$$
$$+ \sum_{n=1}^{N}\sum_{f=1}^{F} a_{nf}^{xI} \exp\left(\frac{x_n}{2}\right)\exp\left(\frac{I_f}{2}\right) + \sum_{n=1}^{N}\sum_{f=1}^{F} a_{nf}^{xk} \exp\left(\frac{x_n}{2}\right)\exp\left(\frac{K_f}{2}\right)$$
$$+ \sum_{f=1}^{F}\sum_{j=1}^{F} a_{fj}^{Ik} \exp\left(\frac{I_f}{2}\right)\exp\left(\frac{K_j}{2}\right).$$

(6.3)

The transcendental logarithmic specification automatically satisfies the translation property in case $g_x = 1_N$ and $g_I = 1_F$ (Hudgins and Primont,

---

[1] Hudgins and Primont (2007) also show the parametric restrictions that are required to impose the translation property in a more general specification of the direction vector.

2007). Symmetry restrictions imposed on the transcendental logarithmic are $a_{mj}^{yy} = a_{jm}^{yy}$, $a_{fj}^{II} = a_{if}^{II}$, $a_{nj}^{xx} = a_{jn}^{xx}$, and $a_{fj}^{kk} = a_{if}^{kk}$.

Estimating dynamic overall (profit or cost) inefficiency requires the estimation of a current profit or cost function. The current cost function is usually estimated along with a system of conditional input demand equations; similarly, the current profit function is estimated along with a system of input demand and output supply equations. The optimized Hamilton-Jacobi-Bellman equation developed in section 4.3.1 for a long-run cost-minimizing unit is given by

$$rW(y,K,w,c) = w'x + c'K + W_k(y,k,w,c)\dot{K}. \qquad (6.4)$$

Rewriting (6.4), taking variable costs, $w'x$, to the left-hand side, and denoting it as C provides the estimable equation

$$C = rW(y,K,w,c) - c'K - W_k(y,k,w,c)\dot{K}. \qquad .(6.5)$$

A system of variable input demand equations is derived from (6.4) using the envelope theorem as demonstrated in section 3.3.3 in (3.70):

$$x = rW_w(y,K,w,c) - W_{kw}(y,K,w,c)\dot{K}. \qquad (6.6)$$

Investment demand equations can be derived similarly by differentiating the Hamilton-Jacobi-Bellman equation (6.4) with respect to quasi-fixed-factor prices and applying the envelope theorem as demonstrated in (3.60), leading to

$$\dot{K} = W_{kc}^{-1}(rW_c + K), \qquad (6.7)$$

as long as W_{Kc} is an invertible matrix. Estimation of the system of (6.5)–(6.7) requires a functional form for the optimal value function. The quadratic form is self-dual, implying that a quadratic specification of the directional input distance function implies a quadratic specification of the dynamic cost function. The quadratic specification of the optimal value function is given by

$$W(y,w,c,K) = a_0 + \sum_{m=1}^{M} a_m^y y_m + \sum_{n=1}^{N-1} a_n^w w_n^* + \sum_{f=1}^{F} a_f^c c_f^* + \sum_{f}^{F} a_f^k K_f$$

$$\frac{1}{2}\sum_{m=1}^{M}\sum_{j=1}^{M} a_{mj}^{yy} y_m y_j + \frac{1}{2}\sum_{n=1}^{N-1}\sum_{j=1}^{N-1} a_{nj}^{ww} w_n^* w_j^* + \frac{1}{2}\sum_{f=1}^{F}\sum_{j=1}^{F} a_{fj}^{cc} c_f^* c_j^* + \frac{1}{2}\sum_{f=1}^{F}\sum_{j=1}^{J} a_{fj}^{kk} K_f K_j$$

$$\sum_{m=1}^{M}\sum_{n=1}^{N-1} a_{mn}^{yw} y_m w_n^* + \sum_{m=1}^{M}\sum_{f=1}^{f} a_{mf}^{yc} y_m c_f^* + \sum_{m=1}^{M}\sum_{f=1}^{F} a_{mf}^{yk} y_m K_f + \sum_{n=1}^{N-1}\sum_{f=1}^{F} a_{nf}^{wc} w_n^* c_f^* +$$

$$\sum_{n=1}^{N-1}\sum_{f=1}^{F} a_{nf}^{wk} w_n^* K_f + \sum_{f=1}^{F}\sum_{j=1}^{F} a_{fj}^{ck} c_f^* K_j,$$

$$(6.8)$$

where the superscript $*$ in the prices of variable and quasi-fixed inputs indicates normalized prices; that is, all prices have been normalized using the price of the Nth variable input, w_N.

6.3 Structural Parametric Approaches

6.3.1 Estimation of Dynamic Inefficiency

The quadratic adjustment cost directional input distance function can be estimated using econometric estimation techniques that are outlined in Kumbhakar and Lovell (2000) and Greene (2008). The stochastic specification of the distance function takes the following form:

$$0 = \vec{D}_i(y,x,K,I;1_N,1_F) + \varepsilon, \qquad (6.9)$$

where $\varepsilon = v - u$, $v \sim N(0,\sigma_v^2)$ is white noise and $u \sim N^+(0,\sigma_u^2)$ is the component representing technical inefficiency. Estimation of (6.9) incorporates the translation property

$$-\alpha = \vec{D}_i(y,x - \alpha,K,I + \alpha;1_N,1_F) + \varepsilon. \qquad (6.10)$$

The function $\vec{D}_i(y,x - \alpha,K,I + \alpha;1_N,1_F)$ corresponds to the quadratic form in (6.1), with α added to gross investments and subtracted from variable input quantities. By choosing α specifically for each firm, variation on the left-hand side of (6.10) is obtained. Econometric estimation can be accomplished by maximum likelihood procedures. For a sample of H observations, the logarithm of the likelihood function is defined as

$$L = \eta - H \ln \sigma_\varepsilon + \sum_{h=1}^{H} \ln \Phi \left(\frac{\varepsilon_h \tau_\varepsilon}{\sigma_\varepsilon} \right) - \frac{1}{2\sigma_\varepsilon^2} \sum_{h=1}^{H} \varepsilon_h^2, \qquad (6.11)$$

where η is a constant, $\sigma_\varepsilon = (\sigma_u^2 + \sigma_v^2)^{1/2}$, $\tau_\varepsilon = \sigma_u / \sigma_v$, and Φ is the standard normal cumulative distribution function. Estimation of dynamic technical inefficiency is accomplished by replacing u by its conditional expectation for the hth observation $E(u_h / \varepsilon_h) = \sigma^* \left[\dfrac{\phi(\varepsilon_h \tau_\varepsilon / \sigma_\varepsilon)}{1 - \Phi(\varepsilon_h \tau_\varepsilon / \sigma_\varepsilon)} - \dfrac{\varepsilon_h \tau_\varepsilon}{\sigma_\varepsilon} \right]$, where ϕ is the standard normal probability distribution function and $\sigma_*^2 = \sigma_u^2 \sigma_v^2 / \sigma_\varepsilon^2$. Estimation of the dynamic cost frontier or profit frontier is done in a similar way. Examples of the estimation of the dynamic cost frontier are found in Rungsuriyawiboon and Stefanou (2007) and Serra et al. (2011).

6.3.2 Estimation of Luenberger Total Factor Productivity Growth

The empirical application of the structural econometric approach focuses on a sample of specialized dairy farms in the Netherlands. The application decomposes dynamic cost inefficiency into technical and allocative inefficiency using the concepts presented in Chapter 4. Next, it determines the components of primal and dual Luenberger total factor productivity (TFP) growth based on the elaboration of these concepts in Chapter 5. First, a quadratic adjustment cost directional input distance function is estimated and technical inefficiency is computed. Second, a quadratic dynamic cost frontier model is estimated and dynamic cost inefficiency is computed. The estimated adjustment cost dynamic directional input distance function and the dynamic cost frontier are used to compute primal and dual Luenberger TFP growth and its components.

Farm-level data were obtained from the European Commission's Farm Accountancy Data Network (FADN) and cover the period 1995–2005. To ensure that milk output is the main farm output, those farms are selected whose milk sales represent at least 80% of total revenues from farming activities. The dataset is an unbalanced panel containing 2,614 observations on 639 farms that, on average, stay in the sample for (at least) four years. The model distinguishes one output, two variable inputs, two quasi-fixed inputs, and two fixed inputs. Output is defined as a farm's total output and includes milk, livestock products, crop products, and other output. The two variable inputs are purchased feed and variable costs other than feed expenses. Variable costs other than feed are an aggregate input that includes veterinary expenses, energy, contract work, crop-specific costs, and other variable input costs. Breeding livestock and machinery and buildings are considered as quasi-fixed inputs. Machinery and buildings are aggregated into one quasi-fixed input. Total utilized agricultural area, measured in hectares, and labor, mainly composed of family labor and measured in annual working units (AWUs), are assumed to be fixed inputs.[2] Country-level price indices are taken from Eurostat. Inputs and outputs measured in monetary values are defined as implicit quantity indices by computing the ratio of value to its corresponding Törnqvist price index. Depreciation rates considered for buildings, machinery, and breeding livestock are 3%, 10%, and 25%, respectively. The interest rate (r) is defined as the average of the annual interest rate for 10 years' maturity government bonds (Eurostat) over the period 1995–2005 and is equal to 4.97%. The rental cost price of capital is defined as $c_i = (r + \delta_i)z_i$, where δ_i is the quasi-fixed asset depreciation rate and z_i is the quasi-fixed asset price (defined as a Törnqvist price index). Table 6.1 provides descriptive statistics for the variables used in the analysis.

The presence of the fixed factors involves a modest modification of the technology specification where the input requirement set involves the choice of variable inputs and investment, (x_t, I_t), that can produce output, y_t, given the capital stock vector, K_t, and also the fixed factors of land and labor, which are now denoted as Z_t. While K_t is predetermined by the decision maker's investment choices in earlier periods, Z_t is outside the decision maker's control. As such, the input requirement set is represented as

---

[2] Many agricultural applications address land and labor as quasi-fixed factors. The case of dairy production in Holland finds that family labor and land area are unchanged over the period the farm observation participates in the data collection survey.

Table 6.1 Descriptive Statistics of the Sample

Variables	Description	Mean	Standard Deviation
y	Total output (euros)	199,665.76	115,708.47
C	Variable cost (euros)	137,006.94	75,100.78
K_1	Breeding livestock (euros)	68,747.85	39,215.14
K_2	Buildings and machinery (euros)	204,077.17	141,387.32
L_1	Land (hectares)	44.73	24.18
L_2	Labor (AWU)	1.71	0.64
x_1	Variable inputs other than feed (euros)	52,075.09	28,278.93
x_2	Feed (euros)	34,513.88	21,574.47
I_1	Gross investments in breeding livestock (euros)	17,358.42	13,565.17
I_2	Gross investments in machinery and buildings (euros)	24,754.31	53,066.53
$\dot{K}_1$	Net investments in breeding livestock (euros)	171.46	7,115.17
$\dot{K}_2$	Net investments in machinery and buildings (euros)	13,851.36	49,641.54
p	Output price (index)	0.99	0.04
w_1	Variable inputs' price (excluding feed) (index)	1.16	0.11
w_2	Feed price (index)	0.99	0.04
c_1	Breeding livestock rental price (index)	0.27	0.02
c_2	Machinery and buildings rental price (index)	0.12	0.01

Number of observations: 2,614.

$V_t(y_t : K_t, Z_t) = \{(x_t, I_t) : (x_t, I_t) \text{ can produce } y_t \text{ given } K_t, Z_t\}$. Representing this technology with fixed factors Z_t as the input-oriented dynamic directional distance function leads to the definition

$$\vec{D}_i^t(y_t, K_t, Z_t, x_t, I_t : g_x, g_I) = \max\{\beta \in \mathfrak{R} : (x_t - \beta g_x, I_t - \beta g_I) \in V_t(y_t : K_t, Z_t)\},$$

with $g_x \in \mathfrak{R}_{++}^{FN}, g_x \in \mathfrak{R}_{++}^{F}, (g_x, g_I) \neq (0^N, 0^F)$. Focusing on the primal setting presented in section 5.3.2.1, the productivity growth indicator, $LP(\cdot)$, in equation 5.68, and its components technical change, ΔT, in (5.70), and technical inefficiency change, ΔTEI, in (5.71), are easily adapted, respectively, as

$$LP(\cdot) = \frac{1}{2}\{[\vec{D}_1^{t+1}(y_t, K_t, Z_t, x_t, I_t : g_x, g_I) - \vec{D}_1^{t+1}(y_{t+1}, K_{t+1}, Z_{t+1}, x_{t+1}, I_{t+1} : $$
$$g_x, g_I)] + [\vec{D}_1^t(y_t, K_t, Z_t, x_t, I_t : g_x, g_I) - \vec{D}_1^t(y_{t+1}, K_{t+1}, Z_{t+1}, x_{t+1}, I_{t+1} : g_x, g_I)]\},$$

$$(6.12)$$

$$\Delta T = \frac{1}{2}\{[\vec{D}_1^{t+1}(y_t, K_t, Z_t, x_t, I_t : g_x, g_I) - \vec{D}_1^t(y_t, K_t, Z_t, x_t, I_t : g_x, g_I)] + $$
$$[\vec{D}_1^{t+1}(y_{t+1}, K_{t+1}, Z_{t+1}, x_{t+1}, I_{t+1} : g_x, g_I) - \vec{D}_1^t(y_{t+1}, K_{t+1}, Z_{t+1}, x_{t+1}, I_{t+1} : g_x, g_I)]\},$$

$$(6.13)$$

and,

$$\Delta TEI = \vec{D}_i^t(y_t, K_t, Z_t, x_t, I_t : g_x, g_I) - \vec{D}_i^{t+1}(y_{t+1}, K_{t+1}, Z_{t+1}, x_{t+1}, I_{t+1} : g_x, g_I).$$

$$(6.14)$$

The relationship remains additive, $LP(X) = \Delta T + \Delta TEI$.

The dual setting proceeds analogously to the presentation in section 5.3.2.2, where the value function for the intertemporal cost function, $W_t(w_t, c_t, K_t, Z_t, y_t)$, reflects the fixed factors as an argument. The dual Luenberger productivity change indicator is defined in (5.76), and its components of technical change are defined in (5.77); overall inefficiency change in (5.78), which involves both technical and allocative efficiency change; and the shadow value change in (5.79).

6.3.3 Results

Dynamic technical, allocative, and overall (cost) inefficiency estimates are presented in Table 6.2. The estimation of the adjustment cost directional input distance function is based on a unitary directional vector for variable inputs and investments. Hence, the value of the directional distance function would be interpreted as the number of units of variable inputs that can be contracted and the number of unit investments that can be expanded. To express the results on the directional distance function as a percent value, the original results have been transformed by dividing the value of the directional distance function by the quantity of variable inputs and the size of the investments and then calculating an average percentage. Technical inefficiency is, on average, 10.4%, implying that variable inputs (gross investments) can be reduced (increased) by 10.4%. Technical inefficiency is the main source of dynamic cost inefficiency. Dynamic cost inefficiency is, on average, 0.122, meaning that the actual current shadow cost exceeds the minimum current cost, and this difference represents 12.2% of the sum of the current cost of variable inputs and the shadow values of investments.

The theoretical restrictions $OEI \geq 0$ and $\vec{D} \geq 0$ are met, respectively, for 100% and 99% of the observations. The condition $OEI \geq \vec{D}$ is met for 58% of the observations. With no explicit restrictions in estimation or on parameters, the econometric estimations cannot guarantee that all properties of the estimated directions distance function hold. Consequently, the characterization of how the observations match up with the theory is a robustness check of the estimation. It is the analyst's choice whether to impose more structure to guarantee that the theoretical restrictions hold.

Table 6.3 presents the computation of the primal dynamic Luenberger TFP growth and its decomposition into the contributions of technical change

Table 6.2 Dynamic Inefficiency Ratings

Variable	Mean	1996–2000	2001–2005
OEI	0.122	0.103	0.144
TEI	0.104	0.100	0.107
AEI	0.018	0.003	0.037

Table 6.3 Primal Luenberger Dynamic Total Factor
Productivity Growth and Its Decomposition

Year	$LP(\cdot)$	ΔT	ΔTEI
1996–2000	0.021	0.012	0.009
2001–2005	0.009	0.012	−0.003
Mean	0.015	0.012	0.003
Small farms	0.012	0.013	−0.001
Large farms	0.019	0.013	0.006
KS test	0.099*	0.000	0.099*

* Significant at 5%.

(ΔT) and technical inefficiency change (ΔTEI). As in the case of the computation of cost inefficiency, the average results of the Luenberger TFP indicator and its decomposition have been translated into percentage changes relative to the sample mean to facilitate the interpretation of the results.

TFP grows, on average, 1.5% per year in the entire period 1996–2005. TFP growth is higher in the first period 1996–2000 than in the second period 2001–2005. Technical change is approximately 1.2% per year and is the major contributor, on average, to improvement of TFP. Technical improvements could have come from improvements of the genetic potential of the dairy cows, improvements in feeding, and improvements in the milking technology such as the increasing adoption of the milking robot (André et al., 2010a, 2010b). Technical inefficiency increases, on average, to make a positive contribution to productivity growth of, on average, 0.3% per year. However, the fluctuation in technical inefficiency is large and is the driver of the year-to-year changes in productivity.

Productivity growth is slightly larger for large dairy farms (1.8%) than for small[3] dairy farms (1.1%), a difference that is attributable to the higher contribution of technical inefficiency change on large dairy farms. This outcome suggests that large dairy farms better succeeded in improving the use of the current production technology than small farms. According to the

---

[3] A farm was classified as large or small depending on whether its production was above or below the median.

Kolmogorov-Smirnov (KS) test, differences between large and small farm indicators are significant, with the exception of the technical change indicator. The annual contributions of technical change and technical inefficiency change to productivity growth are displayed in Figure 6.1. The figure clearly shows that technical inefficiency change (ΔTEI) is the driver of productivity change in the period 1996–2005. Figure 6.1 also demonstrates a limitation of the parametric approach used in this application to measure the contribution of technical change to TFP, which is that it was imposed to be constant over time.

Dual TFP change of Dutch dairy farms over the period 1996–2005 and its decomposition into the contributions of technical change, technical inefficiency change, shadow value change, and allocative inefficiency change are presented in Table 6.4.

Dual TFP increases, on average, 0.1% per year, though varying between a 0.7% improvement in the period 1996–2000 and a 0.6% decline in the period 2001–2005. Both the average value and range of TFP growth are smaller than in the primal model. Technical change is around 0.5% per year and is still the major contributor, on average, to improvement of TFP. The change in the shadow value of capital has no impact on TFP growth. Technical inefficiency decreases on average by 0.3% and delivers the second largest contribution to TFP. The fluctuation in technical inefficiency is counteracted partly by reverse changes in allocative inefficiency (see also Figure 6.2). However,

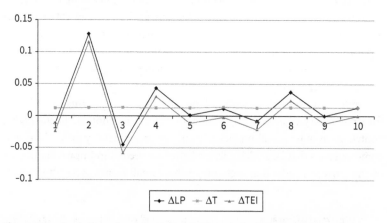

Figure 6.1. Evolution of productivity (ΔLP), technical change (ΔT), and technical inefficiency change (ΔTEI) from 1996 (= 1) to 2005 (= 10).

Table 6.4 Dual Luenberger Dynamic Total Factor Productivity (TFP) Growth and Its Decomposition*

Period	$LD(\cdot)$	ΔTD	ΔSV	ΔTEI	ΔAEI
1996–2000	0.007	0.005	0.009	0.000	−0.007
2001–2005	−0.006	0.005	−0.003	0.000	−0.008
Mean	0.001	0.005	0.003	0.000	−0.007
Small farms	*−0.002*	*0.005*	*0.000*	*−0.001*	*0.006*
Large farms	*−0.001*	*0.005*	*0.000*	*0.006*	*−0.010*

* Dual TFP growth ($LD(\cdot)$), technical change (ΔTD), shadow value change (ΔSV), technical inefficiency change (ΔTEI), and allocative inefficiency change (ΔAEI).

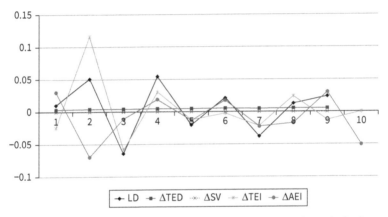

Figure 6.2. Evolution of productivity (ΔLD), technical change (ΔTED), shadow value change (ΔSV), technical inefficiency change (ΔTEI) and allocative inefficiency change (ΔAEI) from 1996 (= 1) to 2005 (= 10).

on average, allocative inefficiency change (ΔAEI) makes a negative contribution to TFP growth. This result implies that the composition of inputs and investments at prevailing prices was increasingly suboptimal over time and led to a slightly downward pressure on TFP growth. The evolution of the dual dynamic Luenberger productivity growth components is displayed in Figure 6.2 and indicates that technical inefficiency change (ΔTEI) and allocative inefficiency change are the main drivers of changes in the dual Luenberger dynamic productivity indicator in the period 1996–2005. Table 6.4 also shows that dual dynamic Luenberger productivity growth is almost equal for small and large dairy farms. Allocative inefficiency change makes a relatively large negative (−1%) contribution to dual dynamic productivity growth of large dairy farms, suggesting that large dairy farms have more problems in adjusting inputs to long-run optimal levels than small dairy farms.

6.4 Remarks

This chapter has presented structural approaches to measuring dynamic efficiency and productivity, that is, approaches that make explicit behavioral assumptions such as intertemporal cost minimization or profit maximization.

There is a deep literature on modeling dynamic adjustment technology in the context of cost minimization or profit maximization. Blackorby and Schworm (1982) and Epstein (1983) focus on aggregation in dynamic models. Paul (1999, Chapters 10 and 11) addresses data construction and estimation considerations. A number of applications are available in agriculture (Taylor and Monson, 1985; Vasavada and Chambers, 1986; Howard and Shumway, 1988; Vasavada and Ball, 1988; Luh and Stefanou, 1991; Sckokai and Moro, 2009; Serra et al., 2009; Rungsuriyawiboon and Hockmann, 2015; Yang and Shumway, 2016, in utilities (Rungsuriyawiboon and Stefanou, 2007), and in manufacturing (Bernstein and Nadiri, 1989).

While Rungsuriyawiboon and Stefanou (2007) and Serra et al. (2011) specify the dynamic dual framework in the presence of inefficiency and dynamic adjustment, the reader may wish to explore reduced-form approaches that do not require such assumptions. These approaches estimate the production technology, assuming the efficiency carries over from one period to the other as a result of the presence of costs of adjustment underlying changes in the quasi-fixed factors of production. Examples of the application of the reduced-form approach are found in Emvalomatis et al. (2011). Yet another avenue for future research is the estimation of the adjustment cost directional technology distance function and its dual, the dynamic profit frontier.

7
Nonparametric Approaches

7.1 Introduction

This chapter discusses the main issues related to the nonparametric estimation of the concepts that have been presented in Chapters 2–5, without having the intention to be exhaustive. A detailed discussion of empirical issues related to nonparametric approaches is found in the excellent examples of Greene (2008), Thanassoulis et al. (2008), and in Chapters 4 and 5 of Bogetoft and Otto (2011).

The nonparametric approach to measuring technical and cost inefficiency has been adopted in the examples in earlier chapters. Chapter 3 introduced the notions of inner-bound and outer-bound technologies. The inner-bound technology representation has dominated the nonparametric empirical applications in the literature on measuring efficiency and productivity. However, as sections 7.3 and 7.5 will show, the outer-bound representation of the technology presents a viable alternative to measuring technical and cost efficiency as well.

In addition to presenting the structural linear programming (LP) models underlying the estimation of efficiency, this chapter will also present a code for solving a number of dynamic data envelopment analysis (DEA) models. Several DEA packages have been developed that can be used to solve some of the most common DEA models. In this chapter, we focus on the *R Statistical Package*, which offers a free software environment that can be used for optimization, statistical computing, and graphics. Using *R* will offer the reader the flexibility to apply any kind of DEA model rather than only the predefined models in the more frequently used DEA software packages.

The focus is on empirical implementation of the inefficiency measures using DEA models. Within an intertemporal context, a panel data approach to the DEA framework is needed (e.g., Horta et al., 2012; Leleu et al., 2012; Chowdhury et al., 2014). Dynamic or intertemporal versions of DEA have been developed (e.g., Färe and Grosskopf, 1996; Nemoto and Goto, 1999, 2003; Silva and Stefanou, 2003, 2007; Ouellette and Yan, 2008).

A range of dynamic DEA models has been formulated. The earliest one is Färe and Grosskopf (1996), which is built on the notions of inter-mediate outputs and storable inputs that can be implemented for dynamic production by the network approach (Färe et al., 2007). The time interdependence of the production decisions result from the fact that some outputs from an earlier period are used as inputs in the next period and some inputs are storable for one period, reducing the input use in this period and increasing the input use in the next one. Nemoto and Goto (1999, 2003), Silva and Stefanou (2003, 2007), and Ouellette and Yan (2008) develop dynamic DEA models in the light of the adjustment cost theory of the firm.

An alternative approach is the dynamic DEA model found in Nemoto and Goto (1999, 2003), which is constructed on the basis of a production possibility set defined in terms of variable inputs, quasi-fixed factors, and outputs. In this approach, stocks of the quasi-fixed factors at the end of each period are treated as outputs, while the stocks of these factors at the beginning of each period are treated as inputs. The dynamic factors (i.e., the change in the level of the quasi-fixed factors) are not explicitly modeled in the firm's production technology. In the dynamic DEA models constructed in Silva and Stefanou (2003, 2007) and Ouellette and Yan (2008), the dynamic factors are explicitly incorporated in the firm's production technology. Silva and Stefanou (2007) consider that investment decisions are irreversible and develop hyperbolic dynamic efficiency measures in the long run and short run; Ouellette and Yan (2008) consider the possibility of investment and disinvestment and focus on the efficiency of variable inputs.

Kapelko et al. (2015a, 2015b) employ the adjustment cost direction distance function DEA framework to empirically estimate the Spanish construction sector's dynamic efficiency performance before and after a financial crisis. Once the dynamic inefficiency patterns are estimated, a range of empirically driven economic issues can be addressed such as the impact of investment spikes or the impact of regulation on efficiency and growth (Kapelko et al., 2015a, 2015b).

7.2 Empirical Nonparametric Construction of Dynamic Efficiency

The empirical start is the data series $\{(y^j, x^j, I^j, K^j, w^j, c^j); j = 1,...,J\}$ representing the observed behavior of each firm j and including information on w and c for each observation j. The Hamilton-Jacobi-Bellman equation representing the flow version of the minimization of the discounted flow of costs subject to the technology being feasible is presented in (3.87). Operationally, this can be generated for each observation as

$$rW(y^i, K^i, w^i, c^i) = \min_{x, I, \gamma}[w^{i\prime}x + c^{i\prime}K^i + W_K^i(I - \delta K^i)]$$

$$s.t \quad \sum_{j=1}^{J} \gamma^j y_m^j \geq y_m^i, \quad m = 1,...,M;$$

$$x_n \geq \sum_{j=1}^{J} \gamma^j x_n^j, \quad n = 1,...,N;$$

$$\sum_{j=1}^{J} \gamma^j (I_f^j - \delta_f K_f^j) \geq I_f - \delta_f K_f^i, \quad f = 1,...,F;$$

$$\gamma^j \geq 0, \, j = 1,...,J;$$

$$x_n \geq 0, \, n = 1,...,N;$$

$$I_f \geq 0, \, f = 1,...,F; \tag{7.1}$$

where $W_K^i = W_K(y^i, K^i, w^i, c^i)$ is the vector of the shadow value of capital for observation i, $i = 1, ..., J$, which is an endogenous variable in the long-run cost minimization problem. Solving the problem in (7.1) requires an estimate of the shadow value of capital. In what follows, a number of solutions for generating the shadow value of capital, W_K^i, are presented.

7.2.1 Compute Shadow Value Using the Linear Complementarity Problem

Recognize that the primal problem in (7.1) has the dual variable as part of its formulation. One approach is the linear complementarity problem (LCP), which allows for the presence of both primal and dual variables in the specification of the optimization problem in such a way as to guarantee that the dual variables are not treated as primal variables in optimization.

Interpretations of the LCP in the context of economics can be found in Paris (1979a, 1979b) and applied to the dynamic production formulation by Silva and Stefanou (2007).

Consider the Kuhn-Tucker conditions associated with the minimization problem in (7.1):

$$
\begin{aligned}
&w_l^i - \mu_l \geq 0, x_l \geq 0, x_l(w_l^i - \mu_l) = 0, \\
&W_{k_h t}^i + \mu_{I_h} \geq 0, \ I_h \geq 0, I_h(W_{k_h t}^i + \mu_{I_h}) = 0, \\
&-\mu_y y^j + \sum_l \mu_l x_l^j - \sum_h \mu_{I_h} I_h^j - \mu_\lambda \geq 0, \lambda^j \geq 0, \lambda^j[\ldots] = 0, \\
&I_h - \sum_j \lambda^j I_h^j \leq 0, \ \mu_{I_h} \geq 0, \mu_{I_h}\left(I_h - \sum_j \lambda^j I_h^j \right) = 0, \\
&\sum_j \lambda^j x_l^j - x_l \leq 0, \ \mu_l \geq 0, \mu_l\left(\sum_j \lambda^j x_l^j - x_l \right) = 0, \\
&y^i - \sum_j \lambda^j y^j \leq 0, \ \mu_y \geq 0, \ \mu_y\left(y^i - \sum_j \lambda^j y^j \right) = 0, \\
&1 - \sum_j \lambda^j = 0, \mu_\lambda \text{ free variable.}
\end{aligned}
\tag{7.2}
$$

Take specific notice of the variable $W_{k_h t}^i$, which is simply the symmetric of the current value of the Lagrangian multiplier associated with the constraint on gross investment in the quasi-fixed factor h, and the Kuhn-Tucker conditions in (7.2) becomes

$$
\begin{aligned}
&w_l^i - \mu_l \geq 0, x_l \geq 0, x_l(w_l^i - \mu_l) = 0, \\
&-\mu_y y^j + \sum_l \mu_l x_l^j - \sum_h \mu_{I_h} I_h^j - \mu_\lambda \geq 0, \lambda^j \geq 0, \lambda^j[\ldots] = 0, \\
&\sum_j \lambda^j I_h^j - \delta_h k_h^i \geq 0, \mu_{I_h} \geq 0, \mu_{I_h}\left(\sum_j \lambda^j I_h^j - \delta_h k_h^i \right) = 0, \\
&\sum_j \lambda^j x_l^j - x_l \leq 0, \mu_l \geq 0, \mu_l\left(\sum_j \lambda^j x_l^j - x_l \right) = 0, \\
&y^i - \sum_j \lambda^j y^j \leq 0, \mu_y \geq 0, \mu_y\left(y^i - \sum_j \lambda^j y^j \right) = 0, \\
&1 - \sum_j \lambda^j = 0, \mu_\lambda \text{ free variable,}
\end{aligned}
\tag{7.3}
$$

where $l = 1, \ldots, m; h = 1, \ldots, o;$ and $j = 1, \ldots, n.$

The Kuhn-Tucker conditions in (7.2) can be stated as an LCP in the following way:

$$
\begin{aligned}
s &= q + Md, \\
d &\geq 0, \\
s &\geq 0, \\
d's &= 0,
\end{aligned}
\tag{7.4}
$$

where M is a square matrix of order $(n + 2m + o + 2)$ and q is a $(n + 2m + o + 2)$ vector. The vectors s and d are the vector of slack variables and the vector of primal and dual variables, respectively. Conditions (7.4) are the Kuhn-Tucker necessary optimality conditions associated with the dynamic cost minimization problem. The LCP consists of finding vectors d and s satisfying (7.4). While there is no objective function to be optimized in an LCP, the LCP is equivalent to the problem of finding a stationary point of the following quadratic program:

$$
\min\left\{ Q(d) = q'd + \frac{1}{2}d'(M + M')d :\; q + M'd \geq 0, d \geq 0 \right\}.
\tag{7.5}
$$

The function $Q(d)$ is bounded from below on the feasible set $F = \left\{ d : q + M'd \geq 0, d \geq 0 \right\}$. If $F = \varnothing$, the LCP is not feasible. If $F \neq \varnothing$, two possible cases exist. Either $Q(d^*) = \min Q(d) = 0$, $d^* \in F$, implying d^* is the solution of the LCP, or $\min Q(d) > 0$, implying the LCP is feasible but has no solution (Al-Khayyal 1987, 1989; Cheng 1984).

The quadratic minimization problem in (7.5) is a convex quadratic program since $Q(d)$ is a convex function suggesting M is a positive semidefinite matrix. Thus, the LCP in (7.4) is the problem of finding a Kuhn-Tucker point for (7.5). By definition, if d is an optimal solution for (7.5), d must be a Kuhn-Tucker point. Consequently, (7.4) provides the necessary optimality conditions for a feasible solution d of (7.5) to be optimal. Furthermore, since (7.5) is a convex quadratic program, (7.4) provides necessary and sufficient optimality conditions (Al-Khayyal, 1987, 1989; Cheng, 1984). The solution obtained by solving (7.5) provides the optimal variable input and gross investment vectors solving the minimization problem in (7.1).

7.2.2 Compute Shadow Value from the Dual Problem

Another approach developed in Silva et al. (2015) is to exploit the dual problem associated with (7.1) as

$$w_n^i - \mu_n^x \geq 0, x_n^* \geq 0, x_n^*(w_n^i - \mu_n^x) = 0, \ n = 1,...,N;$$

$$-\sum_{m=1}^{M} \mu_m^y y_m^j + \sum_{n=1}^{N} \mu_n^x x_n^j - \sum_{f=1}^{F} \mu_f^I (I_f^j - \delta_f K_f^j) \geq 0,$$

$$\gamma^{j^*} \geq 0, \ \gamma^{j^*}[.] = 0, \ j = 1,...,J;$$

$$\sum_{j=1}^{J} \gamma^{j^*} y_m^j - y_m^i \geq 0, \mu_m^y \geq 0, \mu_m^y (\sum_{j=1}^{J} \gamma^{j^*} y_m^j - y_m^i) = 0, \ m = 1,...,M; \qquad (7.6)$$

$$x_n^* - \sum_{j=1}^{J} \gamma^{j^*} x_n^j \geq 0, \mu_n^x \geq 0, \mu_n^x (x_n^* - \sum_{j=1}^{J} \gamma^{j^*} x_n^j) = 0, \ n = 1,...,N;$$

$$W_{K_f}^i + \mu_f^I \geq 0, \ I_f^* \geq 0, \ I_f^*(W_{K_f}^i + \mu_f^I) = 0, \ f = 1,...,F;$$

$$\sum_{j=1}^{J} \gamma^{j^*}(I_f^j - \delta_f K_f^j) - (I_f - \delta_f K_f^i) \geq 0, \mu_f^I \geq 0, \mu_f^I[...] = 0, \ f = 1,...,F,$$

where the dual variables μ^Y and μ^X are the current value of the Lagrangian multipliers associated with the constraints on the m outputs and the n variable inputs, respectively. The dual variable μ^I is the current value of the Lagrangian multiplier associated with the constraint on net investment of the quasi-fixed factors. For an interior solution, the negative value of the shadow value of capital $(-W_K^i)$ is equal to μ^I. This dual variable can be interpreted as the marginal cost of adjustment for the quasi-fixed factors (Silva et al., 2015).

Computationally, the problem in (7.1) can be solved in two steps: (a) construct the dual and find the shadow value of capital $(-W_K^i)$ that is equal to μ^I, and then (b) use this shadow value of capital, μ^I, as a fixed parameter in the primal problem in (7.1), which then is a manageable LP problem.

7.2.3 Compute Shadow Value from the Directional Distance Function

It was shown using duality theory in Chapter 4 that the directional input distance function can be recovered from the current value of the optimal value function:

$$\vec{D}_i(y,K,x,I;g_x,g_I) = \min_{w,c} \left\{ \frac{w'x + c'K + W_K(.)'(I - \delta K) - rW(y,K,w,c)}{w'g_x - W_K(.)'g_I} \right\}$$

$$(7.7)$$

Applying the envelope theorem to the expression in (7.7) gives

$$\nabla_x \vec{D}_i(y,K,x,I;g) = \frac{w}{w'g_x - W_K(.)'g_I}$$

$$(7.8)$$

$$\nabla_I \vec{D}_i(y,K,x,I;g) = \frac{W_K}{w'g_x - W_K(.)'g_I}.$$

If the price of variable input j is known, then the shadow value of the capital component f can be written as

$$W_{K_f} = w_j \cdot \frac{\partial \vec{D}_i(y,K,x,I;g) \big/ \partial I_f}{\partial \vec{D}_i(y,K,x,I;g) \big/ \partial x_j}.$$

$$(7.9)$$

If the distance function is estimated parametrically as in section 6.2, then the derivatives can be obtained directly by differentiation. Serra et al. (2011) provide the derivatives of the dynamic distance function to all its arguments and discuss the extent to which the derivatives satisfy the regularity conditions for the case of Dutch dairy farms.

Alternatively, the derivatives of the dynamic directional input distance functions with respect to I_f and x_j can be obtained from the dual values of the constraints of I_f and x_j in the LP program of the adjustment cost directional input distance function in (7.1). It should be noted, though, that the dual value is not unique for observations making up the frontier. This problem can be resolved by carrying out a smooth pasting approximation for the observations that are located at the (kinks of the) frontier. For these observations, the derivative for I_f and x_j can be approximated as

$$\frac{\partial \vec{D}_i(y,K,x,I;g)}{\partial I_f} = \frac{\vec{D}_i(y,K,x,I_{-f},(I_f + \Delta I_f);g) - \vec{D}_i(y,K,x,I_{-f},(I_f - \Delta I_f);g)}{2\Delta I_f}$$

$$\frac{\partial \vec{D}_i(y,K,x,I;g)}{\partial x_j} = \frac{\vec{D}_i(y,K,x_{-j},(x_j + \Delta x_j),I;g) - \vec{D}_i(y,K,x_{-j},(x_j - \Delta x_j),I;g)}{2\Delta x_j}.$$

$$(7.10)$$

7.2.4 Compute Shadow Value from a Parametrically Estimated Value Function

The shadow value of capital is defined as the first derivative of the optimal value function with respect to capital, that is, W_K. A straightforward way for determining the shadow value of capital would be to obtain it directly from an econometrically estimated optimal value function as in (6.7) in section 6.2:

$$W_{K_f}^i(y,w,c,K) = a_f^k + \sum_{j=1}^{j} a_j^k K_j \sum_{m=1}^{M} a_{mf}^{yk} Y_m + \sum_{n=1}^{N-1} a_{nf}^{wk} w_n^* + \sum_{j=1}^{J} a_{fj}^{ck} c_j^*. \quad (7.11)$$

However, this procedure is not without risks, as an econometrically estimated optimal value function may not satisfy the regularity condition $W_K \leq 0$ for all observations. This condition can, however, be imposed during estimation. Also, note that the econometric approach to estimating the shadow value of capital implies that the shadow value is assumed to follow a parametric specification. This loss of flexibility in the specification inherent in the parametric approach is compensated, though, by a substantial increase in the variation in shadow costs of capital compared to the three nonparametric approaches discussed earlier.

7.3 Empirical Construction of the Inner-Bound and Outer-Bound Technologies

We exploit the data series $\{(y^j, x^j, I^j, K^j, w^j, c^j); j = 1,...,J\}$ representing the observed behavior of each firm j and including information on w and c for each observation j. The inner-bound technology is based on the input bundles observed for a given output bundle and is described formally in Chapter 3, section 3.4. The empirical construction of the inner bound presented in (3.83) can be accomplished using the directional distance technology by using the adjustment cost directional input distance function measure of technical inefficiency for all factors of production. For each observation i, the problem is

$$\vec{D}_i(y^i,K^i,x^i,I^i;g_x,g_I)=\max_{\beta,\gamma^i}\beta^i$$
$$s.t$$
$$y^i \le \gamma Y$$
$$\gamma X \le x^i - \beta^i g_x$$
$$I^i + \beta^i g_I - \delta K^i \le \gamma(I - \delta K)$$
$$\gamma \ge 0, \tag{7.12}$$

where γ is the $(J \times 1)$ intensity vector (J is the total number of firms in the sample). The directional vector (g_x,g_I) is to be selected by the researcher.

Chapter 3 has shown that the outer bound on the technology can be generated by using the weak axiom of dynamic cost minimization, given by (3.86) and (3.87). Assuming the outer bound on the technology, the adjustment cost directional input distance function measure of technical inefficiency for the variable inputs and investments is generated for each observation i as

$$TEI = \max \beta^i$$
$$w^{j'}(x^i - \beta^i g_x)+W_k^{j'}(I^i + \beta^i g_I) \ge w^{j'}x^j + W_k^{j'}I^{j'} \forall j \tag{7.13}$$
$$y^i \ge y^j \forall j$$
$$K^j \ge K^i \forall j.$$

Similarly, dynamic cost inefficiency can be obtained from the outer-bound technology by solving for the optimal variable input (x^{*i}) and investment (I^{*i}) of firm i in the following problem:

$$rW(w^i,c^i,y^i,K^i) = \min\{w^{i'}x^{*i} + c^{i'}k^i + W_k^{i'}(I^{*i} - \delta K^i)\}$$
$$w^{j'}(x^i - \beta^i g_x)+W_k^{j'}(I^i + \beta^i g_I) \ge w^{j'}x^j + W_k^{j'}I^{j'} \forall j \tag{7.14}$$
$$y^i \ge y^j \forall j$$
$$K^j \ge K^i \forall j$$

Like before, the solution to (7.14) gives the current value of the long-run minimum costs, which can be used to compute dynamic cost inefficiency and its components. Note that solving the problems in (7.13) and (7.14) assumes that an estimate of the endogenous shadow value of capital (W_k^j) is available for each j. This shadow value can be generated using one of the approaches outlined in section 7.2.

The empirical illustration of the two approaches focuses on panel data of Dutch dairy farms over the period 2004–2005. The application uses the inner-bound technology approach to compute overall cost inefficiency and its decomposition into technical and allocative inefficiency. Next, technical efficiency relative to the outer-bound technology approach is computed using the concepts presented in Chapter 3. The estimation of cost inefficiency and technical inefficiency relative to the outer-bound technology require shadow values of capital. The approach used here is to estimate a quadratic optimal value function as in section 7.2 with concavity in variable and quasi-fixed input prices imposed during estimation. Next, the shadow value of capital is calculated for each observation using the estimated parameters in equation (7.14).

Farm-level data were obtained from the European Commission's Farm Accountancy Data Network (FADN) and cover the period 2004–2005. Since the purpose of this section is to illustrate the nonparametric methods, we use only a subset of the data used in Chapter 6. Hence, the dataset is an unbalanced panel of 257 dairy farms covering the period 2004–2005. The definitions of the inputs and output are the same as the definitions used in Chapter 6, section 6.3. Table 7.1 presents the descriptive statistics of the variables in the sample. The directional vector of variable inputs, g_x, is the quantity of variable inputs (x); for the directional vector of investments, g_I, a different approach was followed. Investments are often zero in our panel data, and this precludes selecting the actually observed investments as the directional vector. Instead, the directional vector was set at 20% of the value of the capital stock as this percentage reflects the costs of interest, depreciation, and maintenance of the capital stock. The implication of choosing these directional vectors is that the value of the adjustment cost directional input distance function (technical inefficiency) reflects the percentage reduction of

Table 7.1 Average Estimated Shadow Values of Capital and Livestock

Period	Breeding Livestock	Buildings and Machinery
2004	−1.04	−0.13
2005	−0.84	−0.11
Mean	−0.94	−0.12

Table 7.2 Average Technical, Allocative, and Cost Inefficiency Using the Inner-Bound Technology Approach

Period	Technical Inefficiency	Allocative Inefficiency	Cost Inefficiency
2004	0.218	0.204	0.422
2005	0.227	0.253	0.480
Mean	0.223	0.228	0.451

variable inputs and the expansion of investments expressed as a fraction of 20% of the value of the capital stock.

Overall cost inefficiency relative to the inner-bound technology and its decomposition into technical and allocative inefficiency are presented in Table 7.2. Overall cost inefficiency is, on average, 0.45 in the period under investigation, that is, 45% of the sum of the market value of variable inputs and 20% of the shadow value of the capital stock. The values of the technical and allocative inefficiency are similar in both years. The mean technical inefficiency of 0.223 in period 2004–2005 implies that producers can contract variable inputs by, on average, 22.3% of the actually used quantity. Noting that the directional vector of investments is defined as 20% of the value of the capital stock, the expansion of the investments is computed as (0.2 × 0.223 × 100%) = 4.4% of the value of the capital stock. Mean allocative inefficiency in period 2004–2005 is 0.228, implying that additional savings of 22.8% of the sum of the market value of variable inputs and 20% of the shadow value of the capital stock are achieved if producers are allocatively efficient.

7.4 Remarks

This chapter demonstrated the estimation of technical, allocative, and cost inefficiency relative to the inner-bound and outer-bound technologies. The inner-bound approach is more widely applied in the literature and generally does not yield computational problems. The outer-bound approach is computationally more demanding and its technology restrictions may preclude feasible solutions, particularly when the sample is small (see, e.g., Silva and Stefanou, 2007).

More recently, bootstrapping methods were developed for directional distance functions (Simar et al., 2012) but were not yet generalized to the context of the adjustment cost technology. Development of bootstrap methods for directional distance functions in the context of adjustment cost technologies would allow for statistical inference.

Furthermore, the reader is encouraged to pursue the second-stage truncated bootstrap regression of factors explaining technical inefficiency. So-called second-stage bootstrap techniques available for the static context (Simar and Wilson, 2007) apply to the adjustment cost technology context and can be easily accessed through the package *FEAR* that runs under *R*.

7.5 Appendix: *R* Code for Estimating Dynamic Technical Inefficiency

The open source software *R* provides an excellent environment for nonparametrically generating dynamic DEA models. This appendix provides the *R* code for estimating dynamic technical inefficiency under variable returns to scale (VRS). The idea is that you start from an empty *R* script and complete the code in this script file by following steps 1 and 2.

Step 1: Developing the Linear Programming Model

A dynamic DEA model can be solved by using LP. We are going to develop an LP model in *R* of the following dynamic directional distance function:

$$\vec{D}_i(y^i, K^i, x^i, I^i; g_x, g_I) = \max_{\beta, \gamma} \beta^i$$

$$s.t.$$

$$y^i \leq \gamma^i Y$$

$$\gamma^i X \leq x^i - \beta^i g_x$$

$$I^i + \beta^i g_I - \delta K^i \leq \gamma^i (I - \delta K)$$

$$\gamma^i J1 = 1$$

$$\beta^i, \gamma^i \geq 0.$$

In *R* language, the LP model listed previously has to be rewritten into the following general format:

$$\max_{z} c \cdot z$$
$$s.t \quad Az \le b$$
$$z \ge 0,$$

where c and b are vectors of known coefficients; A is a matrix of known coefficients and z are the variables to solve for. The rewriting of the LP model in the general format is done by first rewriting the directional distance function as

$$\overrightarrow{D}_i(y^i, K^i, x^i, I^i; g_x, g_I) = \max_{\beta^i, \gamma^i} \beta^i$$

$$s.t.$$
$$-\gamma^i Y \le -y^i$$
$$\beta^i g_x + \gamma^i X \le x^i$$
$$\beta^i g_I - \gamma^i (I - \delta K) \le -(I^i - \delta K^i)$$
$$\gamma^i J1 = 1$$
$$\beta^i, \gamma^i \ge 0.$$

Note that the individual components of the general format in R are as follows:

$$c = \begin{bmatrix} 1(1 \times 1) \\ 0(J \times 1) \end{bmatrix} \quad z = \begin{bmatrix} \beta(1 \times 1) \\ \gamma(J \times 1) \end{bmatrix}$$

$$A = \begin{bmatrix} 0(M \times 1) & -Y \\ g_x & X \\ g_I & -(i - \delta K) \\ 0 & J1(1 \times J) \end{bmatrix} \quad b = \begin{bmatrix} -y^i \\ x^i \\ -(I^i - \delta K^i) \\ 1 \end{bmatrix}.$$

Other dimensions:

$Y: \rightarrow M \times J$
$X: \rightarrow N \times J$
$(I - \delta K): \rightarrow F \times J$
$y^i: \rightarrow M \times 1$
$x^i, g_x \rightarrow N \times 1$
$(I^i - \delta K^i), g_{I^i} \rightarrow F \times 1$

Note: M = number of outputs; N = number of variable inputs; F = number of quasi-fixed factors; J = number of firms.

The LP model in (A.1) is written in an R function that can be stored as R code on your working directory. Start by opening a new R script: start R, go to the File item on the menu, and click on New script. In the window that opens type the code in Box 7.1. The R function is written as

Box 7.1 R **Code of DyndirectVRS Function**

```
DynDirectVRS <- local(function(Y, X, K, I, Gx, GI, d)
{
    #===========================================================#
    # Transpose the data matrices #
    #===========================================================#
    tY <- t(Y);
    tX <- t(X);
    tK <- t(K);
    tI <- t(I);
    tGx <- t(Gx);
    tGI <- t(GI);
    #===========================================================#
    # Arrange the data for linear programming #
    #===========================================================#
    # Construct delta*K and (I-delta*K) as FxJ matrices
    tdK <- matrix(rep(0,F*J), F,J);
    for (f in 1:F)
    {
        tdK[f,] <- d[f]*tK[f,];
    }
    tIdK <- tI - tdK;
    #===========================================================#
    # Solve the problem for each firm #
    #===========================================================#
    # Matrices to store the results
    tB.opt <- matrix(rep(0,1*J), 1,J);
    tg.opt <- matrix(rep(0,J*J), J,J);
```

```
for (j in 1:J)
{
        # Objective coefficients
        cvec <- matrix(c(1, rep(0,J)), 1+J,1);

        # Construct matrix A
        Row1 <- cbind(0, -tY);
        Row2 <- cbind(tGx[,j], tX);
        Row3 <- cbind(tGl[,j], -tldK);
        Row4 <- cbind(0, matrix(rep(1,J), 1,J));
        Amat <- rbind(Row1,Row2,Row3,Row4);

        # RHS of the constraints
        bvec <- matrix(c(-tY[,j], tX[,j], -tldK[,j], 1), M+N+F+1,1);

        # Direction of the inequality constraints
        direction <- c(rep("<=",M+N+F),"==");

        # Solve the linear programming problem for the current firm
        firm.solution  <-  solveLP(cvec, bvec, Amat,direction, max-
        imum = TRUE, lpSolve = TRUE);

        # Store the results
        tB.opt[,j] <- firm.solution$solution[1];
        tg.opt[,j] <- firm.solution$solution[2:(1+J)];
}
    result <- list("B.opt" = t(tB.opt), "g.opt" = t(tg.opt));
    return(result);
}, as.environment(2))
```

Now make sure you store the script file under the name DyndirectVRS.R on your working directory (here D:\book).

Step 2: Reading Data

We have a dataset entitled "Dynam.txt" that is stored on the working directory D:\book. Start by opening a new *R* script: start *R*, go to the File item on the menu, and click on New script. In the window that opens, type the code

Box 7.2 *R* Code for Reading Data in Dynam.txt

```
# Clear everything in memory
rm(list = ls(all = TRUE));

# Set the working directory
setwd("D:\\book");
#==========================================================#
# Import the data #
#==========================================================#
dat2 <- read.table("Dynam.txt", header = TRUE);
dat2
```

Box 7.3 Output from R: Data in dat2

```
1 8 10 2 2
2 8 10 4 3
3 8 10 6 6
4 8 10 3 5
>
```

in Box 7.2 to clear the memory and set the working directory to D:\book. Next you import the data using the command "read.table".

If you have entered the code correctly, then you should see the output that appears in Box 7.3 on your *R* console.

Step 3: Running the Function DyndirectVRS

Now, you write the code in Box 7.4 in the *R* script file from step 2 to run the function DyndirectVRS. The first command calls for the package linprog that allows you to run the LP model. Next, the data needed for the function DyndirectVRS are constructed (X, K, Y, I, Gx, GI, and d). Finally, you call the function DyndirectVRS and print the outcomes, which are given by results. Dyndirect\$B.opt (inefficiency) and results.Dyndirect\$g.opt (firm weights).

Box 7.4 *R* Code for Running the DyndirectVRS Function

```
#continuation from linear program

# Install and load the linprog package
#install.packages("linprog");
require(linprog);

X <- with(dat2, cbind(x))
K <- with(dat2, cbind(k))
Y <- with(dat2, cbind(q))
I <- with(dat2, cbind(I))

M <- dim(Y)[2];      # Number of outputs
N <- dim(X)[2];      # Number of variable inputs
F <- dim(K)[2];      # Number of quasi-fixed inputs
J <- dim(Y)[1];      # Number of observations
Gx <- matrix(1,J,1)
GI <- matrix(1,J,1)
d <- matrix(rep(0,J),1,J);

# The function DyndirectVRS takes the following arguments:
# 1. Y: matrix of outputs (firms x number of outputs)
# 2. X: matrix of variable inputs (firms x number of variable inputs)
# 3. K: matrix of quasi-fixed inputs (firms x number of quasi-fixed inputs)
# 4. I: matrix of investment levels (firms x number of quasi-fixed inputs)
# 5. d: list of depreciaton rates (number of quasi-fixed inputs)

#use the DynDirectVRS function
source("DynDirectVRS.R");

# Call the DynDirectVRS function
results.Dyndirect <- DynDirectVRS(Y, X,K,I,Gx,GI, d);

# Print summary statistics of Inefficiency scores
names(results.Dyndirect);
summary(results.Dyndirect$B.opt);
results.Dyndirect$B.opt;
results.Dyndirect$g.opt;
```

Box 7.5 Output from *R*: Results from the DyndirectVRS Function

```
> summary(results.Dyndirect$B.opt);
    V1
Min.: 0.00
1st Qu.: 0.00
Median: 0.00
Mean: 0.35
3rd Qu.: 0.35
Max.: 1.40
> results.Dyndirect$B.opt;
    [,1]
[1,] 0.0
[2,] 0.0
[3,] 0.0
[4,] 1.4

> results.Dyndirect$g.opt;
    [,1] [,2] [,3] [,4]
[1,]   1 0.0 0.0   0
[2,]   0 1.0 0.0   0
[3,]   0 0.0 1.0   0
[4,]   0 0.8 0.2   0
```

If you have entered the code correctly, then the output on your *R* console should look as in Box 7.5.

The output under "results.Dyndirect$B.opt" consists of the inefficiency levels, which are 0 for observations 1, 2, and 3 and 1.4 for observation 4. "results.Dyndirect$g.opt" gives the firm weights. Observations 1, 2, and 3 are located on the frontier and hence their firm weights are 1. Observation 4 is projected on the frontier that is spanned by observations 2 and 3 with weights equal to 0.2 and 0.8. The weights add up to 1 for all observations as this is the VRS model.

References

Adams, F.G., Eguchi, H., and Meyer-zu-Schlochtern, F.J.M. (1969). *An econometric analysis of international trade.* Paris: Organization of Economic Cooperation and Development (OECD).

Afriat, S. (1972). Efficiency estimation of production functions. *International Economic Review,* 13(3), pp. 568–598.

Alchian, A. (1959). Costs and outputs. In: Abramovitz, M. (ed.), *The allocation of economic resources, essays in honor of B.F. Haley.* Stanford, CA: Stanford University Press, pp. 23–40.

Al-Khayyal, F.A. (1987). An implicit enumeration procedure for the general linear complementarity problem. *Mathematical Programming Study,* 31, pp. 1–20.

Al-Khayyal, F.A. (1989). On characterizing linear complementarity problems as linear programs. *Optimization,* 20(6), pp. 715–724.

André, G., Berentsen, P., Duinkerken, G., Engel, B., and Oude Lansink, A. (2010a). Economic potential of individual variation in milk yield response to concentrate intake of dairy cows. *Journal of Agricultural Science,* 148(3), pp. 263–276.

André, G., Berentsen, P., Engel, B., Koning, C., and Oude Lansink, A. (2010b). Increasing the revenues from automatic milking by using individual variation in milking characteristics. *Journal of Dairy Science,* 93(3), pp. 942–953.

Ang, F., and Oude Lansink, A. (2018). Decomposing dynamic profit inefficiency of Belgian dairy farms. *European Review of Agricultural Economics,* 45(1), pp. 81–99.

Aw, B.Y., Roberts, M.J., and Xu, D.Y. (2011). R&D investment, exporting, and productivity dynamics. *American Economic Review,* 101(4), pp. 1312–1344.

Balk, B.M. (2008). *Price and quantity index numbers: Models for measuring aggregate change and difference.* New York: Cambridge University Press.

Balk, B.M., Färe, R., Grosskopf, S., and Margaritis, D. (2008). Exact relations between Luenberger productivity indicators and Malmquist productivity indexes. *Economic Theory,* 35(1), pp. 187–190.

Banker, R., and Maindiratta, A. (1988). Nonparametric analysis of technical and allocative efficiencies in production. *Econometrica,* 56(6), pp. 1315–1332.

Bauer, P.W. (1990). Recent developments in the econometric estimation of frontiers. *Journal of Econometrics,* 46(1/2), pp. 39–56.

Baumol, W.J., Panzar, J.C., and Willig, R.D. (1982). *Contestable markets and the theory of industry structure.* New York: Harcourt Brace Jovanovich.

Bellman, R. (1959). *Dynamic programming.* Princeton, NJ: Princeton University Press.

Benveniste, L., and Scheinkman, J. (1979). On the differentiability of the value function in dynamic models of economics. *Econometrica,* 47(3), pp. 727–732.

Berndt, E., and Fuss, M. (1986). Productivity measurement with adjustments for variations in capacity utilization, and other forms of temporary equilibrium. *Journal of Econometrics*, 33, pp. 7–29.

Berndt, E., and Fuss, M. (1989). Economic capacity utilization and productivity measurement for multiproduct firms with multiple quasi-fixed inputs. NBER Working Paper 2932. National Bureau of Economic Research, Cambridge, MA.

Berndt, E., and Hesse, D.M. (1986). Measuring and assessing capacity utilization in the manufacturing sectors of nine OECD countries. *European Economic Review*, 30(5), pp. 961–989.

Berndt, E., and Morrison, C. (1981). Capacity utilization measures: Underlying economic theory and an alternative approach. *American Economic Review*, 71(2), pp. 48–52.

Bernstein, J.I., and Mamuneas, T.P. (2006). R&D depreciation, stocks, user costs, and productivity growth for U.S. knowledge intensive industries. *Structural Change and Economic Dynamics*, 17(1), pp. 70–99.

Bernstein, J.I., and Nadiri, M.I. (1989). Research and development and intra-industry spillovers: An empirical application of dynamic duality. *Review of Economic Studies*, 56, pp. 249–267.

Blackorby, C., and Schworm, W. (1982). Aggregate investment and consistent intertemporal technologies. *Review of Economic Studies*, 49(4), pp. 595–614.

Bogetoft, P., and Otto, L. (2011). *Benchmarking with DEA, SFA and R*. New York: Springer.

Boussemart, J., Briec, W., Kerstens, K., and Poutineau, J. (2003). Luenberger and Malmquist productivity indices: Theoretical comparisons and empirical illustration. *Bulletin of Economic Research*, 55, pp. 391–405.

Brechling, F. (1975). *Investment and employment decisions*. Manchester: Manchester University Press.

Bresnahan, T.F., and Ramey, V.A. (1994). Output fluctuations at the plant level. *Quarterly Journal of Economics*, 109(3), pp. 593–624.

Briec, W., and Kerstens, K. (2004). A Luenberger-Hicks-Moorsteen productivity indicator: Its relation to the Hicks-Moorsteen productivity index and the Luenberger productivity indicator. *Economic Theory*, 23(4), pp. 925–939.

Caballero, R. (1999). Aggregate investment. In: Taylor, J., and Woolford, M. (eds.), *Handbook of macroeconomics*, Volume 1B. Amsterdam: Elsevier, pp. 813–862.

Caballero, R., Engel, E.M.R.A., and Haltiwanger, J. (1997). Aggregate employment dynamics: Building from microeconomic evidence. *American Economic Review*, 87, pp. 115–137.

Caputo, M.R. (2005). *Foundations of dynamic economic analysis*. Cambridge: Cambridge University Press.

Carlson, S. (1939). *A study in the pure theory of production*. London: P.S. King and Sons.

Chambers, R.G. (1988). *Applied production analysis: A dual approach*. New York: Cambridge University Press.

Chambers, R.G. (1998). Input and output indicators. In: Färe, R., Grosskopf, S., and Russell, R. (eds.), *Index numbers: Essays in honour of Sten Malmquist*. Dordrecht, Netherlands: Springer.

Chambers, R.G. (2002). Exact nonradial input, output, and productivity measurement. *Economic Theory*, 20, pp. 751–765.

Chambers, R.G., Chung, Y., and Färe, R. (1996). Benefit and distance functions. *Journal of Economic Theory*, 70, pp. 407–419.

Chambers, R.G., Chung, Y., and Färe, R. (1998). Profit, directional distance functions, and Nerlovian efficiency. *Journal of Optimization Theory*, 98, pp. 351–364.

Chambers, R.G., Färe, R., and Grosskopf, S. (1996). Productivity growth in APEC countries. *Pacific Economic Review*, 1(3), pp. 181–190.

Chambers, R.G., and Pope, R. (1996). Aggregate productivity measures. *American Journal of Agricultural Economics*, 78(5), pp. 1360–1365.

Chang, C.C., and Hsu, S.H. (1990). An adjustment cost rationalization of asset fixity theory. *American Journal of Agricultural Economics*, 72(2), pp. 298–308.

Chang, C.C., and Stefanou, S.E. (1988). Specification and estimation of asymmetric adjustment rates for quasi-fixed factors of production. *Journal of Economic Dynamics and Control*, 12, pp. 145–151.

Chavas, J.-P., Aliber, M., and Cox, T.L. (1997). An analysis of the source and nature of technical change: The case of U.S. agriculture. *Review of Economics and Statistics*, 79(3), pp. 482–492.

Chenery, H. (1952). Overcapacity and the acceleration principle. *Econometrica*, 20, pp. 1–28.

Cheng, Y.C. (1984). On the gradient-projection method for solving the nonsymmetric linear complementarity problem. *Journal of Optimization Theory and Applications*, 43(4), pp. 527–541.

Chirinko, R.S. (1993). Business fixed investment spending: Modeling strategies, empirical results, and policy implications. *Journal of Economic Literature*, 31(4), pp. 1875–1911.

Chowdhury, H., Zelenyuk, V., Laporte, A., and Wodchis, W. (2014). Analysis of productivity, efficiency, and technological changes in hospital services in Ontario: How does case-mix matter? *International Journal of Production Economics*, 150, pp. 74–82.

Clark, C.W. (1976). *Mathematical bioeconomics*. New York: John Wiley and Sons.

Conrad, K., and Unger, R. (1989). Productivity gaps and capacity utilization in the manufacturing sectors of five OECD-countries, 1963–1982. *Journal of Productivity Analysis*, 1(2), pp. 101–122.

Conrad, K., and Veall, M.R. (1991). A test for strategic excess capacity. *Empirical Economics*, 16(4), pp. 433–445.

Cooper, R.J. (2001). General structural dynamic economic modeling. *Macroeconomic Dynamics*, 5(5), pp. 647–672.

Cooper, R.W., and Haltiwanger, J. (2006). On the nature of capital adjustment costs. *Review of Economic Studies*, 73(3), pp. 611–633.

Cooper, R.J., and McLaren, K. (1980). Atemporal, temporal, and intertemporal duality in consumer theory. *International Economic Review*, 21(3), pp. 599–609.

Courant, R., and Robbins, H. (1941). *What is mathematics?* Oxford: Oxford University Press.

Davidson, R., and Harris, R. (1981). Nonconvexities in continuous time investment theory. *Review of Economic Studies*, 48, pp. 235–253.

De Alessi, L. (1967). The short run revisited. *American Economic Review*, 57(3), pp. 450–461.

Debreu, G. (1959). *The theory of value: An axiomatic analysis of economic equilibrium.* New York: Wiley.

Denny, M., Fuss, M., and Waverman, L. (1981). The measurement and interpretation of total factor productivity in regulated industries with an application to Canadian telecommunications. In: Cowing, T., and Stevens, R. (eds.), *Productivity measurement in regulated industries*. New York: Academic Press, pp. 179–218.

Deprins, D., and Simar, L. (1983). On Farrell measures of technical efficiency. *Louvain Economic Review*, 49(2), pp. 123–137.

Diewert, W.E. (1976). Exact and superlative index numbers. *Journal of Econometrics*, 4(2), pp. 115–145.

Diewert, W.E., and Parkan, C. (1983). Linear programming tests of regularity conditions for production functions. In: Eichhorn, W., Henn, R., Huemann, K., and Shephard, R. (eds.), *Quantitative studies on production and prices*. Vienna: Physica-Verlag.

Doraszelski, U., and Jaumandreu, J. (2013). R&D and productivity: Estimating endogenous productivity. *Review of Economic Studies*, 80, pp. 1338–1383.

Dorfman, R. (1969). An economic interpretation of optimal control theory. *American Economic Review*, 59(5), pp. 817–831.

Eisner, R., and Strotz, R. (1963). *Determinants of business investment, research study two in impacts of monetary policy.* New York: Prentice Hall.

Emvalomatis, G., Stefanou, S.E., and Oude Lansink, A. (2011). A reduced form model for dynamic efficiency measurement: Application to dairy farms in Germany and the Netherlands. *American Journal of Agricultural Economics*, 93, pp. 161–174.

Epstein, L.G. (1981). Duality theory and functional forms for dynamic factor demands. *Review of Economic Studies*, 48, pp. 81–95.

Epstein, L.G. (1983). Aggregating quasi-fixed factors. *Scandinavian Journal of Economics*, 85(2), pp. 191–205.

Epstein, L.G., and Denny, M.G.S. (1983). The multivariate flexible accelerator model, its empirical restrictions and an application to U.S. manufacturing. *Econometrica*, 51, pp. 647–674.

Epure, M., Kerstens, K., and Prior, D. (2011). Bank productivity and performance groups: A decomposition approach based upon the Luenberger productivity indicator. *European Journal of Operational Research*, 211(3), pp. 630–641.

Färe, R., and Grosskopf, S. (1996). *Intertemporal production frontiers: With dynamic DEA*. Boston: Kluwer.

Färe, R., and Grosskopf, S. (2000). Theory and application of directional distance functions. *Journal of Productivity Analysis*, 13(2), pp. 93–103.

Färe, R., and Grosskopf, S. (2004). *New direction: Efficiency and productivity*. Norwell, MA: Kluwer.

Färe, R., Grosskopf, S., and Kokkelenberg, E. (1989). Measuring plant capacity, utilization, and technical change: A nonparametric approach. *International Economic Review*, 30, pp. 655–666.

Färe, R., Grosskopf, S., and Lovell, C.A.K. (1983). The structure of technical efficiency. *Scandinavian Journal of Economics*, 85(2), pp. 181–190.

Färe, R., Grosskopf, S., and Lovell, C.A.K. (1985). Modeling scale economics with ray-homothetic production functions. *Review of Economics and Statistics*, 67(4), pp. 624–629.

Färe, R., Grosskopf, S., and Lovell, C.A.K. (1994). *Production frontiers*. Cambridge: Cambridge University Press.

Färe, R., Grosskopf, S., Margaritis, D, and Weber, W. (2018). Dynamic efficiency and productivity. In: Grifell-Tatjé, E., Lovell, C.A.K., and Sickles, R.C. (eds.), *The Oxford handbook of productivity analysis*. Oxford: Oxford University Press, pp. 183–209.

Färe, R., Grosskopf, S., Noh, D., and Weber, W. (2005). Characterization of a polluting technology. *Journal of Econometrics*, 126(2), pp. 469–492.

Färe, R., Grosskopf, S., and Whittaker, G. (2007). Network DEA. In: Zhu, J., and Cook, W. (eds.), *Modeling data irregularities and structural complexities in data envelopment analysis*. New York: Springer, pp. 209–240.

Färe, R., and Lovell, C.A.K. (1978). Measuring the technical efficiency of production. *Journal of Economic Theory*, 19(1), pp. 150–162.

Färe, R., and Primont, D. (1995). *Multi-output and duality: Theory and application*. Boston: Kluwer.

Färe, R., and Primont, D. (2003). Luenberger productivity indicators: Aggregation across firms. *Journal of Productivity Analysis*, 20(3), pp. 425–435.

Farrell, M.J. (1957). The measurement of productive efficiency. *Journal of the Royal Statistical Society*, 120(3), pp. 253–290.

Ferguson, C.E. (1969). *Microeconomics theory*. Homewood, IL: Richard D. Irwin Press.

Fernandez-Cornejo, J., Gempesaw, C.M., Elterich, J.G., and Stefanou, S.E. (1992). Dynamic measures of scope and scale economies: An application to German agriculture. *American Journal of Agricultural Economics*, 74(2), 329–342.

Fleming, W.H., and Rishel, R.W. (1975). *Deterministic and stochastic optimal control*. New York: Springer.

Forrester, J.W. (1961). *Industrial dynamics*. Cambridge, MA: MIT Press.

Fousekis, P., and Stefanou, S.E. (1996). Capacity utilization under dynamic profit maximization. *Empirical Economics*, 21, pp. 335–359.

Fried, H., Lovell, C.A.K., and Schmidt, S. (2008). Efficiency and productivity. In: Fried, H., Lovell, C., and Schmidt, S. (eds.), *The measurement of productive efficiency and productivity change*. Oxford: Oxford University Press, pp. 3–91.

Frisch, R. (1965). *Theory of production*. Chicago: Rand McNally.

Fukuyama, H. (2003). Scale characterizations in a DEA directional technology distance function framework. *European Journal of Operational Research*, 144, pp. 108–127.

Fuss, M., and McFadden, D. (eds.). (1978). *Production economics: A dual approach to theory and application*. Amsterdam: North-Holland.

Galeotti, M. (1996). The intertemporal dimension of neoclassical production theory. *Journal of Economic Surveys*, 10, pp. 421–460.

Gardebroek, C. (2004). Capital adjustment patterns on Dutch pig farms. *European Review of Agricultural Economics*, 31(1), pp. 39–59.

Gardebroek, C., and Oude Lansink, A.G.J.M. (2005). Farm-specific adjustment costs in Dutch pig farming. *Journal of Agricultural Economics*, 55, pp. 3–24.

Gould, J.P. (1968). Adjustment costs in the theory of investment of the firm. *Review of Economic Studies*, 35, pp. 47–55.

Greene, W.H. (2008). The econometric approach to efficiency analysis. In: Fried, H., Lovell, C., and Schmidt, S. (eds.), *The measurement of productive efficiency and productivity growth*. Oxford: Oxford University Press, pp. 92–250.

Groth, C. (2008). Quantifying UK capital adjustment costs. *Economica*, 75, pp. 310–325.

Hailu, A., and Veeman, T. (2001). Non-parametric productivity analysis with undesirable outputs: An application to the Canadian pulp and paper industry. *American Journal of Agricultural Economics*, 83(3), pp. 605–616.

Hall, B. (2004). Innovation and diffusion. NBER Working Paper 10212. National Bureau of Economic Research, Cambridge, MA.

Hall, B.H., Mairesse, J., and Mohnen, P. (2010). Measuring the returns to R&D. In: Hall, B., and Rosenberg, N. (eds.), *Handbook of the economics of innovation*, Volume 2. Amsterdam: North-Holland, pp. 1033–1082.

Hamermesh, D., and Pfann, G. (1996). Adjustment costs in factor demand. *Journal of Economic Literature*, 34(3), pp. 1264–1292.

Hanoch, G. (1975). The elasticity of scale and the shape of average costs. *American Economic Review*, 65(3), pp. 492–497.

Hauver, J.H., Yee, J., and Ball, V.E. (1991). Capacity utilization and measurement of agricultural productivity. USDA-ERS Technical Bulletin 1798. United States Department of Agriculture, Economic Research Service (USDA-ERS), Washington, DC.

Hicks, J.R. (1965). *The theory of wages*, 2nd ed. London: Macmillan.

Holt, C.C., Modigliani, F., Muth, J.E., and Simon, H.A. (1960). *Planning production, inventories, and work force*. Englewood Cliffs, NJ: Prentice-Hall.

Horta, I.M., Camanho, A.S., and Moreira da Costa, J. (2012). Performance assessment of construction companies: A study of factors promoting financial soundness and innovation in the industry. *International Journal of Production Economics*, 137, pp. 84–93.

Howard, W.H., and Shumway, C.R. (1988). Dynamic adjustment in the U.S. dairy industry. *American Journal of Agricultural Economics*, 70, pp. 837–847.

Hudgins, L.B., and Primont, D. (2007). Derivative properties of directional technology distance functions. In: Färe, R., Grosskopf S., and Primont D. (eds.), *Aggregation, efficiency, and measurement: Studies in productivity and efficiency*. New York: Springer.

Hulten, C.R. (1986). Productivity change, capacity utilization, and the sources of efficiency growth. *Journal of Econometrics*, 33, pp. 31–50.

Intriligator, M.D. (1971). *Mathematical optimization and economics theory*. Englewood Cliffs, NJ: Prentice-Hall.

Johansen, L. (1968). Production functions and the concept of capacity. *Economie Mathematique et Econometrie*, 2, pp. 49–72.

Johansen, L. (1972). *Production functions*. Amsterdam: Elsevier.

Kamien, M.I., and Schwartz, N.L. (1971). Sufficient conditions in optimal control theory. *Journal of Economic Theory*, 3, pp. 207–214.

Kamien, M.I., and Schwartz, N.L. (1981). *Dynamic optimization: The calculus of variations and optimal control in economics and management*. Amsterdam: Elsevier.

Kapelko, M. (2017). Dynamic versus static inefficiency assessment of the polish meat-processing industry in the aftermath of the European Union integration and financial crisis. *Agribusiness*, 33, pp. 505–521.

Kapelko, M., Oude Lansink, A., and Stefanou, S.E. (2015a). Analyzing the impact of investment spikes on dynamic productivity growth. *Omega*, 54, pp. 116–124.

Kapelko, M., Oude Lansink, A., and Stefanou, S.E. (2015b). Effect of food regulation on the Spanish food processing industry: A dynamic productivity analysis. *PLoS ONE*, 106, e0128217.

Koopmans, T.C. (1957). *Three essays on the state of economic science*. New York: McGraw-Hill.

Kumbhakar, S.C., and Lovell, C.A.K. (2000). *Stochastic frontier analysis*. Cambridge: Cambridge University Press.

Lasserre, P., and Ouellette, P. (1999). Dynamic factor demands and technology measurement under arbitrary expectations. *Journal of Productivity Analysis*, 11(3), pp. 219–241.

Leleu, H., Moises, J., and Valdmanis, V. (2012). Optimal productive size of hospital's intensive care units. *International Journal of Production Economics*, 136(2), pp. 297–305.

Léonard, D., and Van Long, N. (1992). *Optimal control theory and static optimization in economics*. Cambridge: Cambridge University Press.

Letterie, W.A., Pfann, G.A., and Polder, J.M. (2004). Factor adjustment spikes and interrelation: An empirical investigation. *Economics Letters*, 85(2), pp. 145–150.

Lovell, C.A.K. (1993). Production frontiers and productive efficiency. In: Fried, H., and Schmidt, S. (eds.), *The measurement of productive efficiency: Technique and applications*. Oxford: Oxford University Press, pp. 3–67.

Lovell, C.A.K. (1996). Applying efficiency measurement techniques to the measurement of productivity change. *Journal of Productivity Analysis*, 7(2/3), pp. 329–340.

Lucas, R.E. (1967a). Adjustment costs and the theory of supply. *Journal of Political Economy*, 75, pp. 321–334.

Lucas, R.E. (1967b). Optimal investment policy and the flexible accelerator. *International Economic Review*, 8, pp. 78–85.

Luenberger, D.G. (1992). Benefit functions and duality. *Journal of Mathematical Economics*, 21, pp. 461–481.

Luenberger, D.G. (1995). *Microeconomic theory*. New York: McGraw-Hill.

Luh, Y.H., and Stefanou, S.E. (1991). Productivity growth in U.S. agriculture under dynamic adjustment. *American Journal of Agricultural Economics*, 73(4), pp. 1116–1125.

Luh, Y.H., and Stefanou, S.E. (1993). Learning-by-doing and the sources of productivity growth: A dynamic model with application to U.S. agriculture. *Journal of Productivity Analysis*, 4(4), pp. 353–370.

Luh, Y.H., and Stefanou, S.E. (1996), Estimating dynamic dual models under nonstatic price expectations. *American Journal of Agricultural Economics*, 78(4), pp. 991–1003.

Mahmud, S.F., Robb, A.L., and Scarth, W.M. (1987). On estimating dynamic factor demands. *Journal of Applied Econometrics*, 2, pp. 69–75.

Marshall, A. (1920). *Principles of economics*, 8th ed. London: Macmillan.

McLaren, K., and Cooper, R. (1980). Intertemporal duality: Application to the theory of the firm. *Econometrica*, 48(7), pp. 1755–1762.

Morrison, C.J. (1985a). On the economic interpretation and measurement of optimal capacity utilization with anticipatory expectations. *Review of Economic Studies*, 52, pp. 295–310.

Morrison, C.J. (1985b). Primal and dual measures of economic capacity utilization: An application to productivity measurement in the U.S. automobile industry. *Journal of Business and Economic Statistics*, 3(4), pp. 312–324.

Morrison, C.J. (1986). Productivity measurement with nonstatic expectations and varying capacity utilization: An integrated approach. *Journal of Econometrics*, 33, pp. 51–74.

Mundlak, Y. (2001). Production and supply. In: Gardner, B., and Rausser, G. (eds.), *Handbook of agricultural economics*, Volume 1A. Amsterdam: Elsevier, pp. 3–85.

Nemoto, J., and Goto, M. (1999). Dynamic data envelopment analysis: Modeling intertemporal behavior of a firm in the presence of productive inefficiencies. *Economics Letters*, 64, pp. 51–56.

Nemoto, J., and Goto, M. (2003). Measurement of dynamic efficiency in production: An application of data envelopment analysis to Japanese electric utilities. *Journal of Productivity Analysis*, 19, pp. 191–210.

Nerlove, M. (1963). Returns to scale in electricity supply. In: Christ, C. (ed.), *Measurement in economics: Studies in mathematical economics and econometrics in memory of Yehuda Grunfeld*. Stanford, CA: Stanford University Press, pp. 167–200.

Nickel, S.J. (1978). *The investment decisions of firms*. Cambridge: Cambridge University Press.

Nilsen, Ø., and Schiantarelli, F. (2003). Zeros and lumps in investment: Empirical evidence on irreversibilities and nonconvexities. *Review of Economics and Statistics*, 85(4), pp. 1021–1037.

Ohta, M. (1975). A note on the duality between production and cost functions: Rate of returns to scale and rate of technical progress. *Economic Studies Quarterly*, 24(3), pp. 63–65.

Olson, M.S., van Bever, D., and Verry, S. (2008, March). When growth stalls. *Harvard Business Review*.

Oude Lansink, A., and Stefanou, S.E. (1997). Asymmetric adjustment of dynamic factors at the firm level. *American Journal of Agricultural Economics*, 79(4), pp. 1340–1351.

Ouellette, P., Petit, P., Tessier-Parent, L-P., and Vigeant, S. (2010). Introducing regulation in the measurement of efficiency, with an application to the Canadian air carriers industry. *European Journal of Operational Research*, 200, pp. 216–226.

Ouellette, P., and Vigeant, S. (2000). A general procedure to recover the marginal products of a cost minimizing firm. *Journal of Productivity Analysis*, 14(2), pp. 143–162.

Ouellette, P., and Vigeant, S. (2001). Cost and production duality: The case of the regulated firm. *Journal of Productivity Analysis*, 16, pp. 203–224.

Ouellette, P., and Yan, L. (2008). Investment and dynamic DEA. *Journal of Productivity Analysis*, 29(3), pp. 235–247.

Palm, F.C., and Pfann, G.A. (1998). Sources of asymmetry in production factor dynamics. *Journal of Econometrics*, 82(2), pp. 361–392.

Paul, C.J.M. (1999). *Cost structure and the measurement of economic performance: Productivity, utilization, cost economies, and related performance indicators*. New York: Kluwer.

Panzar, J., and Willig, R. (1977). Economies of scale in multi-output production. *Quarterly Journal of Economics*, 91(3), pp. 481–493.

Paris, Q. (1979a). Revenue and cost uncertainty, generalized mean-variance, and the linear complementarity problem. *American Journal of Agricultural Economics*, 61, pp. 268–275.

Paris, Q. (1979b). New economic interpretations of complementarity problems. *Southern Economic Journal*, 46(2), pp. 568–579.

Peters, P., Roberts, M.J., Vuong, V.A., and Fryges, H. (2017). Estimating dynamic R&D demand: An analysis of costs and long-run benefits. *RAND Journal of Economics*, 48(2), pp. 409–437.

Peters, T.J., and Waterman, R.H., Jr. (1982). *In search of excellence*. New York: Harper and Row.

Pietola, K., and Myers, R.J. (2000). Investment under uncertainty and dynamic adjustment in the Finnish pork industry. *American Journal of Agricultural Economics*, 82(4), pp. 956–967.

Pindyck, R., and Rotemberg, J. (1983). Dynamic factor demands and the effects of energy price shocks. *American Economic Review*, 73(5), pp. 1066–1079.

Polder, M., and Verick, S. (2004). Dynamics of labour and capital adjustment: A comparison of Germany and the Netherlands. IZA Discussion Paper No. 1212, Institute of Labor Economics (IZA), Bonn, Germany.

Ramey, V. (1991). Nonconvex costs and the behavior of inventories. *Journal of Political Economy*, 91, pp. 306–334.

Rothschild, M. (1971). On the costs of adjustment. *Quarterly Journal of Economics*, 85(4), pp. 605–622.

Rungsuriyawiboon, S., and Hockmann, H. (2015). Adjustment costs and efficiency in Polish agriculture: A dynamic efficiency approach. *Journal of Productivity Analysis*, 44, pp. 51–68.

Rungsuriyawiboon, S., and Stefanou, S.E. (2007). Dynamic efficiency estimation: An application to U.S. electric utilities. *Journal of Business & Economic Statistics*, 25, pp. 226–238.

Rungsuriyawiboon, S., and Stefanou, S.E. (2008). Decomposition of total factor productivity growth in the U.S. electric utilities. *Journal of Productivity Analysis*, 30(3), pp. 177–190.

Rungsuriyawiboon, S., and Zhang, Y. (2018). Examining the economic performance of Chinese farms: A dynamic efficiency and adjustment cost approach. *Economic Analysis and Policy*, 57, pp. 74–87.

Samuelson, P. (1947). *Foundations of economic analysis*. Cambridge, MA: Harvard University Press.

Sckokai, P., and Moro, D. (2009). Modelling the impact of the CAP Single Farm Payment on farm investment and output. *European Review of Agricultural Economics*, 36, pp. 395–423.

Seierstad, A., and Sydsaeter, K. (1987). *Optimal control theory and applications*. Amsterdam: Elsevier.

Serra, T., Oude Lansink, A., and Stefanou, S.E. (2011). Measurement of dynamic efficiency: A directional distance function parametric approach. *American Journal of Agricultural Economics*, 93, pp. 756–767.

Serra, T., Stefanou, S., Gil, J.M., and Featherstone, A. (2009). Investment rigidity and policy measures. *European Review of Agricultural Economics*, 36, pp. 103–120.

Setiawan, M., and Oude Lansink, A. (2018). Dynamic technical inefficiency and industrial concentration in the Indonesian food and beverages industry. *British Food Journal*, 120, pp. 108–119.

Shapiro, M.D. (1986). The dynamic demand for capital and labor. *Quarterly Journal of Economics*, 101(3), pp. 513–542.

Shephard, R. (1953). *Cost and production functions*. Princeton, NJ: Princeton University Press.

Shephard, R. (1970). *Theory of cost and production*. Princeton, NJ: Princeton University Press.

Silva, E., Oude Lansink, A., and Stefanou, S.E. (2015). The adjustment-cost model of the firm: Duality and productive efficiency. *International Journal of Production Economics*, 168, pp. 245–256.

Silva, E., and Stefanou, S.E. (2003). Nonparametric dynamic production analysis and the theory of cost. *Journal of Productivity Analysis*, 19, pp. 5–32.

Silva, E., and Stefanou, S.E. (2007). Dynamic efficiency measurement: Theory and application. *American Journal of Agricultural Economics*, 89(2), pp. 398–419.

Simar, L., Vanhems, A., and Wilson, P. (2012). Statistical inference for DEA estimators of directional distances. *European Journal of Operational Research*, 220(3), pp. 853–864.

Simar, L., and Wilson, P. (2007). Estimation and inference in two-stage, semiparametric models of production processes. *Journal of Econometrics*, 136, pp. 31–64.

Smith, V.L. (1961). *Investment and production: A study in the theory of the capital-using enterprise*. Oxford: Oxford University Press.

Spence, M., and Starrett, D. (1975). Most rapid approach paths in accumulation problems. *International Economic Review*, 16, pp. 388–403.

Stefanou, S.E. (1989). Returns to scale in the long run: The dynamic theory of cost. *Southern Economic Journal*, 55, pp. 570–571.

Stoneman, P. (1983). *The economic analysis of technological change*. Oxford: Oxford University Press.

Takayama, A. (1985). *Mathematical economics*, 2nd ed. Cambridge: Cambridge University Press.

Tatom, J.A. (1982). Potential output and the recent productivity decline. *Federal Reserve Bank of St. Louis Review*, 1, pp. 3–16.

Taylor, T.G., and Monson, M.J. 1985. Dynamic factors demands for aggregate Southeastern United States agriculture. *Southern Journal of Agricultural Economics*, 17, pp. 1–10.

Teece, D., Pisano, G., and Shuen, A. (1997). Dynamic capabilities and strategic management. *Strategic Management Journal*, 18(7), pp. 509–533.

Thanassoulis, E., Portela, M., and Despić, O. (2008). Data envelope analysis: The mathematical programming approach to efficiency analysis. In: Fried, H., Lovell, C., and Schmidt, S. (eds.), *The measurement of productive efficiency and productivity growth*. Oxford: Oxford University Press.

Tovar, B., and Wall, A. (2017). Specialisation, diversification, size, and technical efficiency in ports: An empirical analysis using frontier techniques. *European Journal of Transport and Infrastructure*, 17(2), pp. 279–303.

Treadway, A.B. (1969). On rational entrepreneurial behavior and the demand for investment. *Review of Economic Studies*, 36, pp. 227–240.

Treadway, A.B. (1970). Adjustment costs and variable inputs in the theory of the competitive firm. *Journal of Economic Theory*, 2, pp. 329–347.

Tsionas, E.G. (2006). Inference in dynamic stochastic frontier models. *Journal of Applied Econometrics*, 21(5), pp. 669–676.

Vaneman, W.K., and Triantis, K. (2003). The dynamic production axioms and system dynamics behaviors: The foundation for future integration. *Journal of Productivity Analysis*, 19, pp. 93–113.

Varian, H.R. (1984). The nonparametric approach to production analysis. *Econometrica*, 52(3), pp. 579–597.

Vasavada, U., and Ball, V.E. (1988). A dynamic adjustment model for U.S. agriculture, 1948–79. *Agricultural Economics*, 2(2), pp. 123–137.

Vasavada, U., and Chambers, R.G. (1986). Investment in U.S. agriculture. *American Journal of Agricultural Economics*, 68, pp. 950–960.

Viner, J. (1931). Cost curves and supply curves. *Zeitschrift für Nationalökonomie*, 3, pp. 23–46.

Wibe, S. (2008). Efficiency: A dynamic approach. *International Journal of Production Economics*, 115, pp. 86–91.

Williamson, O. (1985). *The economic institutions of capitalism*. New York: Free Press.

Willig, R. (1979). Multiproduct technology and market structure. *American Economic Review*, 69(2), pp. 346–351.

Yang, S., and Shumway, C.R. (2016). Dynamic adjustment in US agriculture under climate change. *American Journal of Agricultural Economics*, 98, pp. 910–924.

Zieschang, K. (1984). An extended Farrell technical efficiency measure. *Journal of Economic Theory*, 33(2), pp. 387–396.

Index